D1445890

THE FORMATION OF
A MODERN LABOR FORCE

THE FORMATION OF
A MODERN LABOR FORCE

UPPER SILESIA, 1865-1914

by Lawrence Schofer

UNIVERSITY OF CALIFORNIA PRESS

BERKELEY   LOS ANGELES   LONDON

University of California Press
Berkeley and Los Angeles, California

University of California Press, Ltd.
London, England

Copyright © 1975, by
The Regents of the University of California

ISBN 0-520-02651-9
Library of Congress Catalog Card Number: 73-90658
Printed in the United States of America

For Jane

Contents

Tables

Figures

Abbreviations

BIKH	Berginspektion Königshütte
DZA	Deutsches Zentralarchiv
JRGB	*Jahresberichte der königlichen Regierungs- und Gewerberäte und Bergbehörden*
OBB	Oberbergamt zu Breslau
OBHV	Oberschlesischer Berg- und Hüttenmännischer Verein
OT	Oddzial terenowy (provincial archive branch)
PAP	Powiatowe archiwum państwowe (county archive)
RO	Rejencja opolska (Regierungsberzirk Oppeln)
WAP	Wojewódzkie archiwum państwowe (provincial archive)
ZBHS	*Zeitschrift für das Berg-, Hütten-, und Salinenwesen*
ZOBH	*Zeitschrift des oberschlesischen Berg- und Hüttenmännischen Vereins*

Note On Sources

Materials from archives in Poland are designated by type of archive, city, collection, volume number, and page number (if not paginated, by date whenever possible).

Bibliographic Note

In the footnotes I have given the full bibliographic reference for each citation the first time it appears in the book; authors' names or short titles are used thereafter. Complete bibliographic information appears in the bibliography at the end of the book. Printing problems prevented use of the complete Polish orthography.

Preface

Labor historians in the United States and Great Britain in the last decade or so have exhibited enormous ingenuity in finding new avenues for understanding the experiences of workers in industrial society. Many of these approaches have turned to leisure time activities, from political discussion groups to music halls to sex life. Yet much remains to be said about the workplace itself. In order to understand worker content or dissatisfaction, to grasp the aristocracy of labor and "blue-collar blues," to probe managerial power and its abuse we need once again to pose questions to labor and management as they functioned in the mines and mills.

None of these things are feasible without historical perspective, and in this study I write about German and Polish history in the late nineteenth century as well as about labor force development. Imperial Germany continues to provoke great interest among historians in the United States, England, and Poland as well as among Germans themselves. However, Silesia and other eastern provinces have on the whole been omitted from the considerations of all but the Polish scholars. In part this situation derives from the patterns of nationality conflict in the twentieth century and in part from the difficulty in obtaining source materials, but it also stems from the perception that one studies industry in the West and agriculture in the East. This book points in another direction, to the continuous interaction between the populations employed in these sectors.

Part of this research was financed by a grant from the American Philosophical Society (Penrose Fund). The editor of the *Journal of Social History* has granted permission for me to use parts of my article published in volume 5 (summer 1972).

My vision of history and history writing owes a great deal to Hans Rosenberg, an outstanding teacher and scholar. Not only did he help me develop my doctoral dissertation, a distant relation to this book, but in his teaching and writing he has set the highest standards for aspiring historians. He saved me from many pitfalls and would have saved me from others had I let him.

Other people kindly read and discussed parts of this manuscript with me and offered very useful advice: Michael Zuckerman, Alfred Rieber, Charles Tilly, Edward Shorter, Jerry Feldman, Jack Reece, Vartan Gregorian, George Alter, and members of the University of Pennsylvania workshops in economic history and European history. In Poland I received much needed advice and encouragement from Professors Adam Galos and Karol Jonca in Wroclaw and Waclaw Dlugoborski in Katowice; my thanks also to Marek Czapliński for numerous services and to Józef Pucilowski, librarian and friend.

And finally to my wife.

1

Introduction

"Upper Silesia"—the name conjures up visions of German versus Pole and the League of Nations plebiscite of 1921, or perhaps of the territories beyond the Oder-Neisse line after 1945. But Upper Silesia as an important industrial center before World War I, as the site of intense social conflict similar to that experienced in other industrializing areas, as a test case for suppositions about the social problems inherent in the formation of a modern industrial labor force—such notions rarely appear in historical literature.[1] Before 1945 the reigning Germans looked to politics and administration for the subjects of their academic treatises; the Poles, current proprietors of the area, have spawned a whole generation of historians of Silesia who normally concentrate on extremely limited topics and who shy away from broad-ranging probes, while their sociologists and economists keep their distance from historically oriented studies. It is time to bring the synthetic view of the outsider to the social problems of nineteenth and early twentieth century industrializing central Europe; for too long we in the West have missed the opportunity to pose new questions about the area and have been fixated on small nation nationalism practically to the exclusion of everything else.

The switch from an agricultural to an industrial society is often understood in terms of the difficulties involved in breaking one's ties to the land and shifting to novel occupations and life styles. In fact, the treatment of the formation of a modern industrial labor force can roughly be dichotomized into works by scholars who emphasize all such fascinating elements which interrupt the emergence of a freely competitive market for labor and goods, and the works of those who minimize these intervening developments and lay greatest emphasis on the workings of the market. Workers, from the first point of view, are often considered irrational (that is, not cognizant of their own long-run interests); they seem to behave in ways that disrupt production, such as by insubordination and by high rates of turnover and absenteeism. Even when workers are accepted on their own terms without being judged as irrational, this approach emphasizes that their variant notions of time and discipline bring them to act in a way that can disrupt a rudimentary factory system.[2] Of course other

1

approaches, less consciously ideological, can also be used to elucidate
the novel quality of the life experiences of early industrial workers—for
instance, Rudolf Braun has used an anthropological microscope to
investigate the life style and mores of the employees of a single factory
over a given period of time.[3] Nonetheless, all such treatments retain
the quality of underlining the non-economic sources of human
behavior.

This emphasis on nonmarket factors results in seeing "conditions
of the workers" and the consequent trade unions and socialist parties
as the central element of working-class life. Because information on
such trends is often readily available, the picture of the labor force
becomes predominantly one of union organization or class consciousness, a picture reinforced by the implicit preferences of historians. One of the most widely discussed books of recent years, E. P.
Thompson's *The Making of the English Working Class*, is so imba-
lanced by the author's fervent search for any trace of worker organization that the structure of the book outweighs some of the very
interesting materials displayed there.[4]

Upper Silesia is no exception to the working-class-labor-unions-
conditions-of-the-workers structure. When Karol Jonca followed this
tack in his survey of Upper Silesian workers from 1889 to 1914, one
typical reviewer implicitly emphasized the validity of this conceptualization by suggesting that Jonca should have begun his study with
the 1860s, not 1889, because ". . . the end of the sixties and the
beginning of the seventies signifies the beginnings of the organized
labor movement in Upper Silesia and the first contact with the worker
organizations of the other provinces of Prussia."[5] There are certainly
many gaps in Jonca's book, not the least being its periodization, but
the timing error is hardly corrected by pointing to some insignificant
precursors of a perennially weak trade-union movement.

Economic historians, new and old, turn to the market and assume
that men act in accordance with their economic interests, especially
as determined by the supply of and demand for goods and labor.
The individual functions as "economic man," one who calculates his
opportunities in a kind of informal cost-benefit analysis and responds
relatively rapidly to shifts in the demand for labor. In its extreme
position, this view holds that "tastes"—for example, ties to agriculture,
ethnic identification, class consciousness, and all those items intervening between the individual and the market—play a residual role
in understanding the course of worker action; shifts can be induced
by changes in the market.[6]

I propose to deal here with the emerging free market for labor,
but I do not wish blithely to eliminate those intervening sociological
variables which have been emphasized for so long by historians and
sociologists. This does not mean simply that the truth lies somewhere

between the sociologists and the economists, but that in the early years of industrial buildup, preferences for agricultural or open-air occupations and older notions of time and work-discipline strongly influenced the course of production and labor-management relations in Upper Silesia. However, over the course of a generation (say twenty to thirty years), the new employees shed their older predilections and acculturated into a new kind of work system. Some of their so-called anti-industrial behavior remained, especially high rates of turnover and absenteeism, but it is my contention that these modes of action came to perform essential bargaining tasks for otherwise powerless workers. Eric Hobsbawm has gone so far as to label this kind of activity "collective bargaining by riot," but he restricts himself to early nineteenth-century England, primarily to agricultural and textile hand workers. I go even further along this line and carry the analysis into the period of high industrialization in Germany.[7]

Management usually lies in the background or is treated as an independent entity, often enough being regarded as a group quite in tune with industrial realities.[8] Even when managers are discussed critically as an economic resource and as a system of authority,[9] they ordinarily do not figure as one of those sociological elements impeding the full emergence of a modern labor force. Yet my closer observations in Upper Silesia and those of scholars in other areas illustrate that too little attention has been paid to the effects of management action on labor activity.[10] One must ask what entrepreneurs learned about their employees from the changing market. After all, these top decision makers cannot be taken as infallible arbiters of all workplace conflicts; industrial records must be read with an eye to determining what labor and management learned from their mutual experiences and how each group applied the lessons learned.

I will flesh out these notions in the body of the book with particular emphasis on disputes over authority in the mines and steel mills. Much of this information is new for an English-speaking public often ignorant of central European affairs, but my analysis pushes beyond the universe of historians of Germany and Poland. I wish to suggest to labor historians and historical sociologists new ways of understanding the conflicts that have arisen and are still arising in areas undergoing the transition to an economy and society dominated by mechanized industrial production.

2

The Economic Setting:
The Upper Silesian Labor Market

The Upper Silesian mineral basin is unquestionably a geological unity, but geology was until 1945 outweighed by political geography. During the nineteenth century the area was divided among Russia, Austria, and Prussia, the last named holding the largest part of the land and natural resources of the area. This political partition, established in the eighteenth century as the result of the Seven Years' War and the partitions of Poland, determined that the histories of the three parts of the basin would be quite divergent. The demarcation of a frontier running between Myslowitz in Prussia and Sosnowiec in Russian Poland and continuing south of the counties of Pless and Rybnik was of crucial importance for the development of the labor force in the Prussian area. (See Figures 1 and 2 for maps of the area.)

For this study of the labor force, chronological limits are not to be found in the "big spurt" of German and Prussian industry—generally dated from the 1830s to 1873—because I focus on the behavior of workers and managers rather than on the growth of total output. The main story begins in 1865, when the Prussian state completely withdrew from its formerly key position of hiring and firing all mining workers and some smelting workers. The hitherto merely formal title to ownership now changed into a patent for powerful owners; as output grew these men were supported by an expanding body of top managers and by the managers of the swiftly rising metallurgical industry. Starting with the outbreak of the war in 1914, the labor market situation changed drastically—skilled workers drafted, war prisoners in the mines, no-strike pledges, overt government support of big industrialists—and the experience of the labor force entered a new phase, one marked by struggles of a sort better left to another study.

People seek jobs in a labor market, "the area, defined occupationally, industrially, and geographically, within which workers are willing to move and do move comparatively freely from one job to another."[1] In a rapidly changing economy, such an area must include the agricultural hinterland directly tributary to the manufacturing and trading center being discussed.[2] In other words, political boundaries can play a crucial role in determining the extent of the labor market

4

Figure 1. Eastern Prussia and neighboring states, 1914. The areas named were Prussian regencies (*Regierungsbezirke*). The province of Silesia consisted of the regencies of Liegnitz, Breslau, and Oppeln. Oppeln comprised administrative Upper Silesia.

by interposing barriers to free movement between "natural" economic units and by encouraging new patterns of migration within a state.

As a result of the location of the eastern frontier of Silesia, the local labor market lost a logical and prolific source of supply, the agricultural areas to the east and southeast. With advancing technology and sharply increased output, the Upper Silesian mining and smelting industries were hard put to staff their plants, and the whole process of recruitment and motivation of the local labor force was affected by their various attempts to improve their situation.

The market for industrial labor in Upper Silesia was not highly

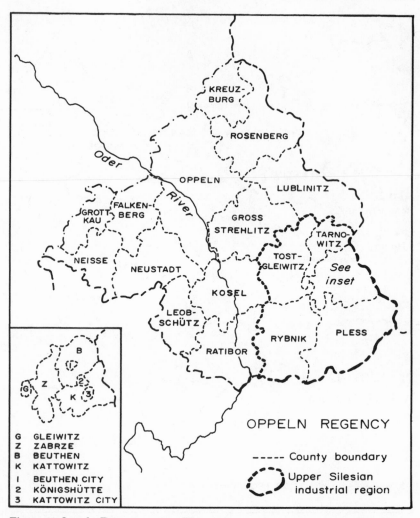

Figure 2. Oppeln Regency, 1914. The areas named were counties. The Upper Silesian industrial region consisted of the southeastern counties outlined on the map.

diversified. Coal mining stood out among the non-agricultural industries in the area; together with the mining of other minerals and the allied smelting industries, it employed most of the industrial workers in the region. This area, within which workers could and did move freely from one mining or smelting job to another, or more generally from agriculture to heavy industry, was defined geographically on two sides by Russia to the east and Austria to the east and south. On the west, the area of the potential local labor supply reached more or less to the Oder River; to the north, industry could draw directly on those counties adjacent to the industrial area. In sum, the string of mines and smelters clustered around the line from Gleiwitz to Myslowitz formed a manufacturing center, with an agricultural hinterland existing in the surrounding counties. In addition, smaller mining and smelting installations were scattered through this agricultural hinterland, particularly in Pless and Rybnik. All of these firms could draw on this Upper Silesian area as a labor market.

Administratively, the area consisted of these counties (*Kreise* as noted in the census of 1910): Gleiwitz, Tost-Gleiwitz, Tarnowitz, Beuthen city, Beuthen, Kattowitz city, Kattowitz, Königshütte, and Zabrze, plus the feeder areas of Pless and Rybnik. (In Polish: Gliwice, Toszek-Gliwice, Tarnowskie Góry, Bytom, Katowice, Królewska Huta [Chorzów], Zabrze; Pszczyna and Rybnik.) Some mining and smelting industry was established in Ratibor (Racibórz) in the last few years before the war. It was this small area in south-eastern Upper Silesia that formed the basic labor market for the Upper Silesian mining and smelting complex.

The frontiers with Austria and Russia limited what otherwise might be considered a "natural" supply of labor. Both western Galicia and Russian Poland were apparently overpopulated from the 1870s on, and large numbers of agricultural laborers sought any kind of work. In the 1870s transit across these borders was relatively free, but demand for labor in Upper Silesia had not yet triggered a flood of migrants. In 1885 the Prussian government closed the border and began to expel all non-Prussian Poles. This policy of exclusion meant that as industrial production climbed and the need for workers grew from the late 1880s on, the Upper Silesian employers could not ordinarily draw on the under-employed masses to the east; in the main, workers had to be drawn from Germany itself.

Germany, or even Prussia alone, by no means constituted a single labor market. Even modern countries with far more sophisticated transportation and employment exchange systems have not been able to overcome sheer physical separation to bring workers perfectly together with available jobs. Still, the remarkable population shift in nineteenth-century Germany, whatever its cause, allowed many German industrial employers to attract workers from distant provinces. This migration of population and the conditions of rapid natural increase, both so important to the shaping of German industrial society, were also crucial for the formation of the Upper Silesian industrial work force.

Production, Technology, and the Labor Force

Upper Silesian coal was of poor quality, often unsuitable for coking; even its coking coal was inferior to that of the Ruhr, resulting in smaller blast furnaces and consequently in lower output.[3] Moreover, supplies of iron ore gave out in the 1880s; even though the blast furnaces of the Ruhr also subsisted on imported ore, the need to import ore into Upper Silesia eliminated an advantage which might have compensated for the poor quality of local coal, a situation which in turn led to higher costs of semi-finished steel goods. Zinc mines escaped the fate of iron by applying new technology, but competition from western Germany, Belgium, and the United States ended the predominance which Upper Silesian zinc had once known in European and even in world markets.

The geographic position of Upper Silesia was similarly disadvantageous. Its major foreign markets for coal included Russian Poland and the various sections of the Austro-Hungarian Empire, primarily the area around Vienna but also including Galicia, Hungary, and Bohemia. Most sales took place within Germany, the major customer being Upper Silesia itself, followed by Breslau, the rest of Lower Silesia and Posen; then came the Berlin-Brandenburg area and the German Baltic provinces. Sales were sometimes hampered by foreign actions against German products, such as the Russian protective tariff established in 1877; on the home market the competition of Ruhr and British coal became noticeable in Berlin and in the Baltic coast cities.[4]

This problem of domestic markets was very much connected with the question of transportation facilities within Germany. Bulk products like coal can be moved quite cheaply by water, a fact exploited by the Ruhr Valley and British producers. Upper Silesia, on the other hand, had only the Oder, a river not navigated easily by coal barges. Besides, the river itself was about thirty miles away from the actual area of production, and the eighteenth-century Klodnitz Canal (from Zabrze to Cosel on the Oder), even though somewhat modernized, proved highly unsatisfactory. Despite the enlargement of facilities at Cosel in 1897 and 1905 and the improvement of the Upper Oder, movement of coal on the Oder amounted to only 3 percent of production in 1903 and 6.6 percent in 1912; by way of contrast, 27 percent of Ruhr coal moved along the Rhine in 1903 and 17 percent in 1912.[5] No wonder then that Upper Silesian industrialists were firm allies of the Junker rye producers in the fight against the east-west *Mittelland* canal, which would carry cheap coal as well as cheap grain. Besides the Oder, there was only the Przemsa, a tributary of the Vistula; it was of negligible commercial use.

The major method of shipping coal was by rail, and the pages of the journal of the employers' association, *Zeitschrift des Oberschle-*

sischen Berg- und Hüttenmännischen Vereins, indicate a passionate interest in railway tariffs and the shortage of railway cars. Every reduction in transportation costs could mean greater markets, and the Prussian coal basins vied for special privileges on the railroads. The Ruhr had special rates to North Sea ports; Upper Silesia, to Baltic ports. With the growth of production, Upper Silesia and the Ruhr became the only national producers, together producing 54 percent of the nation's coal in 1860 and nearly 80 percent in 1900. Consequently, ". . . the line, drawn from north to south across central Germany, where the delivered price of Ruhr coal was equal, quality for quality, to that of Upper Silesian coal, became of crucial importance." In addition to Ruhr competition in Berlin, English coal in the twentieth century was invading not only eastern Germany but also Berlin itself via the Stettin-Berlin canal.[6]

The question of railway carriages, to become so strategically crucial during World War I, bothered the German coal industry all through the period of rapid industrialization. From the 1870s on the annual report of the chairman of the Upper Silesian Mine and Smelter Owner Association generally complained about inadequate means of transport; even the shortage of labor paled in the light of the shortage of railway carriages. As production increased, the crisis worsened, so much so that in 1912 at least one mine (the Hohenzollern) limited production to two days per week because of the impossibility of moving coal out on other days.[7]

The metallurgical industries, less dependent on water transportation and not so tied to seasonal production, did not face such basic problems. Much of the iron, steel, and zinc production was purchased by local producers or by factories in nearby provinces (Breslau, to a lesser extent Posen, Berlin, and the Saxon machine-industry centers). This time, geographical proximity somewhat compensated for the disadvantage of poor coking coal. Moreover, marketing was not a major problem for the smelting industries because of their relatively small place in the German market; from 15 percent of German pig-iron production in 1871, Upper Silesia dropped to 10 percent in 1891, and 6 percent in 1912. Despite a declining relative position, however, output continued to expand and could still absorb over 20 percent of the local coal production on the eve of the First World War.[8] Coal was indeed king; Silesian metallurgy was of only local importance.

To understand the problems of the labor force, one must keep in mind not only transportation but also technological change. Whereas the first half of the nineteenth century witnessed a decided decline in the productivity of coal mines due to technical difficulties, after 1850 new modes of transport and of working the deposits and the deepening of mines all contributed to a decided increase in productivity per miner (till the 1880s) and in total production.[9] New and larger steam engines came into use; electric motors appeared at the end of the century; more efficient explosive materials were introduced; lighter and more precise mining tools were used, an improvement possible only with the high quality steels produced by the recently invented Bessemer and Siemens-Martin methods of steelmaking. These new methods probably constituted the most significant technological advances of the time. The Bessemer blast of air into iron, the Siemens-Martin open-hearth process, the Thomas-Gilchrist furnace for high-phosphorous iron ore had by the 1890s left ironmaking by the laborious hand process of puddling moribund in Upper Silesia. The day of the puddler as the aristocrat of labor had lasted longer in Upper Silesia than in the Ruhr and other areas farther west, but now in his place stood large numbers of newly recruited and freshly trained metalworkers. All these advances permitted an appreciably higher output, and the labor force, of course, grew along with production.

The mining and manufacture of zinc was also quite important in Upper Silesia. The area had been a leading world supplier of zinc in the first part of the nineteenth century, having supplied some 25 percent of the world production in the 1820s. By the end of the century deposits in other areas had assumed greater importance, but local zinc mining was still of consequence on the continental scene. Zinc technology did not develop on the scale of coal and steel, but the industry was saved by the successful switch to blende ore from declining reserves of calamine in the 1880s. Zinc production and manufacture on the whole expanded steadily from 1870 to 1914, but Upper Silesia lost its dominant place in European production to western European competitors. The mining and smelting of lead also expanded, but total production was so small in relation to other mineral works that it is not worth exploring in detail.

Iron, the last of the major local minerals, profited little from new technology because Silesian deposits were giving out. Production peaked about 1890; thereafter, the local steel industry was increasingly dependent on ores imported from Sweden, Hungary, and the Ukraine.

Advances in coal mining supplied fuel to the steel foundries; the steel foundries in turn supplied better tools to all the mines, encouraging greater output. Mining and metallurgy moved forward to fantastic levels as Germany overtook England in steel production at the end of the century. It is true that the Ruhr Valley led in this expansion, but the contribution of Upper Silesia was not insignificant. Production of coal in Upper Silesia, for example, increased from 3,800,000 metric tons in 1870 to 12,700,000 metric tons in 1885, 18,000,000 tons in 1895, 27,000,000 tons in 1905, and to 43,900,000 tons in 1913.[10]

How was the labor force affected by these changes? Most obviously, it grew at an enormous rate to unprecedented size. Somehow, from an essentially agrarian, peasant-oriented society, a work force of tens of thousands of men had to be recruited, trained, housed, and ushered into the routine of industiral life. These tasks were not simple, and some of their ramifications will be discussed in later chapters. It is, however, worthwhile to pause for a moment over certain other implications of the new technology for the work force, because from here one can glean important bits of information concerning the quantity and quality of the growing work force in mining and smelting.

The technical advances that helped Germany to a successful industrial revolution were abundant in coal mining; in particular, expansion into deep-shaft mines would never have been successful without the adaptation of the steam engine and later of the electric motor. Interestingly enough, although production per mine soared from the 1850s to 1914, productivity per miner rose only until the 1880s; it then leveled off and actually fell somewhat in the early twentieth century. The average annual production per worker at the royal König mine, the leading coal producer in Upper Silesia, was 238 tons in the 1850–1859 decade, 368 tons in the 1880-1889 decade, and 340 tons in the 1901-1910 decade. Upper Silesian coal mines as a whole presented a similar pattern, although at a level of production below that of the König mine: from 1880 to 1913, the work force grew almost 3.8 times while coal production increased almost 4.4 times, not an astounding rise in productivity per worker in an age when economies of scale were appearing everywhere in industry. Difficult geological formations prevented significantly increased productivity until the advent of advanced boring machines, which supplemented the traditional hand mining. This breakthrough was slow to spread, however, even though introduced at the König in 1878. In 1909 there were only 1,300 machines in all of Silesia (with over 100,000 miners!), and only in the last few years before the war were they adopted in large numbers.[11] In these years the use of mechanical borers, together with a more rational application of manpower, began to pay dividends. For example, the Higher Mining Office reported a decline of the work force by 1,330 men while maintaining production in the third quarter of 1911; in the first quarter of 1912, production rose six times while the number employed rose only 153 percent.[12] Both of these reports note the newly arranged allocation of manpower as essential to improvements, in addition to new boring machines.

However, mining in both Upper Silesia and in the more productive Ruhr Valley remained essentially hand work until the loading machine of the 1920s was introduced. Only then could the need for haulers be satisfied; only then was there a drastic change from the traditional mining pattern, in which each room in the mines in some

ways resembled a "cottage" in cottage industry.[13] So, despite dyna-
mite, deep shafts, electric motors, and other improvements, in almost
the entire period under consideration increased coal output was
attained mainly by hiring proportionally more workers, a condition
that had important results for the social development of the industrial
working force of Upper Silesia.

Steel production was quite another story. From the 1860s on foreign
ore supplemented declining reserves of local iron ore, and the foundries
came to form a basic segment of the economy of the region. The
location of the great steel works of the world, for example, the Ruhr
and Bethlehem Steel at Baltimore, indicates that local supplies of
iron ore are not always of crucial importance. A more important
factor has been the supply of coal. Despite the drawbacks of Upper
Silesian coal, it did provide sufficient coke to feed the local ovens.
Transportation facilities are also to be considered, and here Upper
Silesia paid premium railway tariffs to move its products in and out,
as opposed to the Ruhr where a large percentage of production could
be cheaply moved by water. This disadvantage, however, was in part
counterbalanced by previous capital investment, for in the late
eighteenth and early nineteenth century Upper Silesia had been the
pacesetter in Prussian metallurgy and until the 1860s continued to
profit from that head start. The first steam engine on the continent
was set up at Tarnowitz in 1786-1789, and the first continental blast
furnace based on coke was built in Gleiwitz in 1796. In contrast,
the Ruhr Valley steelmakers used no coke for smelting until 1849.
By the 1850s there was a large amount of capital already invested
in Upper Silesia, then the iron and steel center of Germany. The
Ruhr moved out in front in the 1860s and 1870s, the era of the great
steelmaking advances. The Bessemer converter was the first major
advance, but the Siemens-Martin open-hearth process was more
important for Upper Silesia after its introduction there in 1884. In
1912, the area housed 52 open-hearth furnaces, 5 Thomas furnaces,
and, a symptom of the slowness of change, 97 puddling furnaces.[14]

One may maintain that technological change is the crucial variable
in the industrializing process, but that contention should not prevent
the student of social change from taking technology as a given and
from looking more closely at the human beings involved in the process
of growth.

The Growth of the Labor Force

Upper Silesian mining and smelting grew rapidly in the second half
of the nineteenth century, thanks to railroads, advances in metallurgical technology, and increased demands for home-heating fuel.
Despite a declining share in total German production, Upper Silesian

coal output increased 750 percent from 1870 to 1913; production of pig iron increased over 400 percent; and the amount of smelted zinc by almost 500 percent. Labor-saving technological improvements were instituted during these years, but increases in production of such magnitude required significantly larger work forces. Coal mining increased employment by almost 400 percent; pig iron production, almost 150 percent; smelted zinc production, over 200 percent.[15] The large-scale metalworking industry, nonexistent in the late 1860s, grew to employ a quite formidable labor force by the eve of the First World War.

Based on the size of the work force as well as on total production, coal mining grew ever more dominant. The Prussian Minister Heinitz had estimated that 11,366 workers were engaged in Upper Silesian mining and smelting in 1786, and the work force in 1806 had been estimated at 20,000. All the mineral industries underwent swift growth in the 1850s and 1860s, but coal rapidly outstripped the others.[16] In 1870, there were over 23,000 coal miners, as opposed to some 3,000 iron miners and 6,800 zinc miners (the latter two figures include most of the lead and silver miners). This disparity grew rapidly. In 1885, when non-Prussian Poles were expelled, coal had 40,000 workers to 3,800 in iron and 10,100 in zinc; in 1890, when the first seasonal workers arrived, coal miners numbered almost 50,000 while the other two extractive groups had grown only slightly. From then on, coal increasingly eclipsed the others. As iron mining declined to about 1,000 workers in 1913 and zinc leveled off to between 10,000 and 13,000, coal miners crossed the 100,000 mark in 1906 and reached 123,000 in 1913. (See Table 1.) It is obvious then that coal mines should be the focus of any discussion of miners, although the others should not be omitted. After all, the various kinds of mining were not so different as to require radically different skills of workers. One might even assume that the kind of job taken by a worker depended in large measure on the geographical location of a mine or on some other nontechnical consideration, not on the kind of ore to be mined.

The Upper Silesian smelting and metal-finishing industries, despite being secondary to mining, employed more than negligible work forces. Although some metalworkers are hard to trace because many of the finished metal products came out of small workshops and not large plants, most employees can be categorized into one of the following areas: blast furnaces for production of raw iron and steel, foundries for iron and steel, rolling mills for iron and steel, zinc smelters and roasting ovens, and workshops producing pipe, nails, and chains. This last was a catchall which included machine-tool workshops, hammering mills, and other specialized shops for finished metal products.[17]

The number of iron miners approached the vanishing point, but

TABLE 1

Number of Employees in Upper Silesian Mining and Smelting, 1852-1913

Year	Coal mining	Iron mining	Zinc mining (incl. lead and silver)	Blast furnaces (iron and steel)	Zinc smelting	Iron and steel foundries	Iron and steel rolling mills	Pipes, nails, chains, etc.	Lead smelting	Total
1852	7,418	2,615	3,992	1,913	2,720				59	18,717
1865	17,955	3,441	7,130	3,881	3,679				220	36,306
1885	40,214	3,868	10,194	3,736	5,945	1,111	10,315	1,496	585	77,464
1900	69,147	3,044	10,873	4,675	7,682	3,281	19,540	3,591	707	122,540
1913	123,649	1,011	11,198	5,483	11,369[a]	3,623	19,646	16,894	777	193,560

SOURCES: 1852 and 1865: ZBHS, compiled by Kazimierz Popiolek, *Górnosląski przemysl górniczo-hutniczy w drugiej polowie XIX wieku* [The Upper Silesian mining and smelting industry in the second half of the nineteenth century] (Katowice, 1965) pp. 205-219. 1885, 1900, 1913: ZOBH, annual volumes. Lead smelting cited from Popiolek, pp. 218-219.

[a]For 1913 including 2,875 listed separately under zinc roasting smelters.

the importing of iron ore enabled iron smelting and steelmaking to continue growing. About 5,000 men were engaged in making pig iron in 1913, and the number of zinc smelting workers increased at an even quicker pace, from about 3,600 in 1865 to almost 12,000 in 1913 (Table 1). Metalworking figures are more difficult to distribute according to industry, but by 1913 there were about 45,000 employed in the various firms. Besides the 5,000 at the iron and steel blast furnaces, there were 4,000 in the foundries, 20,000 in the rolling mills, and 16,000 in the workshops for pipes, nails, and chains. The total number thus agrees with another estimate of 50,000 to 60,000 metalworkers in 1913;[18] in addition, there were probably another 15,000 to 20,000 in small workshops.

In sum, mining as an employer overshadowed the smelting industry in Upper Silesia, but the latter was not insignificant. Around 1910, miners comprised about 68 percent of the mining and smelting workers (coal mining alone, 61 percent); lead, zinc, and silver working, 7 percent of the workers; iron and steel, about 23 percent.[19] The absolute figures are given in Table 1.

To place these figures into the perspective of total German development, one should observe that Ruhr coal mining alone employed a much larger work force than all of Upper Silesian heavy industry. (See Table 2.) Obviously, the Ruhr was a giant even in comparison to Upper Silesia. Still, Upper Silesia was extremely important for pre-World War I Germany, and this area has such distinctive problems as to warrant a separate study.

TABLE 2

Number of Miners Employed in Ruhr Coal Mining, 1851–1913

1851	14,299
1870	51,391
1885	101,829
1890	154,702
1900	226,902
1905	267,798
1913	382,951

SOURCE: Gerhard Adelmann, *Quellensammlung zur Geschichte der sozialen Betriebsverfassung,* 1 (Bonn: Peter Hanstein, 1960), p. 144. Based on ZBHS 40 (1892), and Gottlieb Vowinckel, *Das Oberbergamt zu Dortmund und der Westfälisch-Niederrheinische Bergbau 1792–1942* (Dortmund, 1942, typescript).

The Shortage of Workers

Upper Silesian mining and smelting employers persistently complained more about the shortage of workers than about any other single bottleneck in their factors of production (except perhaps for the shortage of railway cars),[20] particularly from the late 1880s on when deeper mines, increasing output, and expulsion of non-Prussian Poles forced greater efforts in recruiting workers. For example, the number of coal miners grew by about 9,000 in the 1870-1879 decade, by 17,000 in 1880-1889, by 20,000 in 1890-1899, and by 48,000 in 1900-1910.[21] The metal industries followed a similar pattern of numerical growth of the labor force though on a lower absolute level, starting with the introduction of open-hearth furnaces in 1884.

Despite such increases, the employers' association and individual employers continued to complain of shortages. In 1906, a quite prosperous year, the board of directors of the OBHV reported that the local work force had been increased by 5.2 percent but that another 15 to 20 percent could have been used: "Thus the chronic shortage of workers was present in Upper Silesia, despite the fact that appreciably higher wages had been paid. . . ."[22] Without determining here the justice of the complaint or the reasons for the configuration of the local labor market, one may note that this lament was not unique. The board of directors made the same comment in 1908,[23] and individual mines also complained, an example being the repeated notes on this subject to government authorities by the giant Cleophas mine. The Rybnik coal fields, developed after 1900, felt the shortage very acutely in their few years of mining before 1914.[24]

Earlier years, when production was lower, were also plagued by this problem. It was noted by the official mining authorities in 1900, and by the government-sponsored ZBHS in 1899; the Donnersmarck mining and smelting complex spoke of higher wages caused by a shortage of labor in 1899, and of a general lack of workers in 1897.[25]

The demand for workers apparently was not insatiable before 1890. Complaints about scarcity of labor are difficult to discover for this early period,[26] and local supply seems to have been sufficient for current needs. However, increasing production and diversification of heavy industry starting in the 1880s made the problem acute. Pressures built up to import foreign workers on at least a seasonal basis, and after 1890 such alien contract labor became an integral part of the Upper Silesian scene. Note, however, that the decisive pressure for importing workers came from the large capitalist farmers of the east; the Upper Silesians alone exerted no such influence in Prussian government circles.[27]

When dealing with the shortage of labor, one must differentiate between the mining and smelting industries. Steel and zinc foundries were staffed by a large variety of skilled workers, in addition to the supporting unskilled and semi-skilled workmen. Mining, on the other hand, employed a mass of unskilled and semi-skilled workers and only one large group of skilled workers, the hewers (*Hauer, Häuer, hajer*) of coal underground. The major shortage seemed to be in haulers (*Schlepper, szleper*) who assisted the hewers underground. At the Cleophas mine, for example, many hewers in 1907 were required to work all year as haulers (at lower pay and with a considerable loss in prestige) because of the labor shortage.[28]

In general, this shortage of labor and the effects of changing mining technology seem to have had a very depressing effect on the status of the skilled hewers. Other examples pointing to the need for haulers in particular come to mind. At Cleophas in 1906 some 800 haulers and other underground workers were needed, and hewers were forced to do this lower paid work;[29] and at the Hohenlohe mines in 1895 ten men were refused promotion from hewer to hauler (a move that normally took place after less than ten years in the mines): "For at the Neu-Helene mine there are haulers who have been working at these jobs since 1879 [16 years] and whose claim to being hewers must be considered first." The phenomenon of down-grading of hewers was so widespread that some of them even took their complaints to governmental authorities.[30] This shortage of relatively unskilled workers created a situation whereby it was possible to utilize a largely unskilled group of foreign contract laborers to help operate the mines.

Haulers definitely seem to have been unskilled workers.[31] Although in the second half of the nineteenth century they worked with hewers to form a mining team, the haulers performed the physically unskilled labor of aiding the hewers get the coal ready to take out of the mine. Because becoming a hewer required experience as a hauler, the haulers stood second to the hewers in the hierarchy of miners, but the essentially unskilled nature of their work is evidenced by the ability of foreign contract laborers fresh from the countryside to perform this work. Thus in 1905, forty-four Ruthenians, the most unreliable of the foreign workers, performed hauler work in the Charlotte mine near Rybnik.[32]

It is something of a mystery that unskilled workers should be in short supply, for even in the pre-industrial period complaints about shortage of labor were ordinarily confined to the lack of skilled labor only. In Ruhr mining in the 1870-1914 period, the industry and region most comparable to Upper Silesia, the shortage of workers was one of skilled workers.[33] The most that can be said at this point is that perhaps haulers should be classified as semi-skilled, given the context of early industrialization and the difficulty of settling people of rural background into such positions. Still, the example of the Ruthenians in 1905 indicates that the problem may have lain in an absolute shortage of people presenting themselves for industrial employment of any kind.

It is not so easy to find out about availability of labor for the metallurgical industries. On labor questions the employers' *Zeitschrift des oberschlesischen Berg- und Hüttenmännischen Vereins* and the government *Zeitschrift für das Berg-, Hütten, und Salinenwesen* both tended to emphasize mining almost to the exclusion of smelting, as did the leading Upper Silesian industrialists, who often had holdings in both the mining and smelting industries.[34] All one can say is that complaints similar to those of the mine owners did not occur on a regular basis, and it will be shown later that the bulk of the Slavic contract laborers in Upper Silesia worked in mining, not in smelting. This is not to say that there was no labor shortage in the metallurgical industries, but merely that most publicity on this subject went to mining, which in turn employed the majority of the workers.

One would hardly expect a demand for unskilled workers to go unfilled in a highly industrialized society not suffering any great shortage of population; even industrializing societies like Germany in the late nineteenth century are ordinarily supposed to be capable of furnishing an ample number of raw recruits to industrial enterprises. As a matter of fact, one would tend to think of nineteenth-century Germany, and Prussia in particular, as a land of surplus population, a situation pointed up by the mass emigrations and rural-urban movement of the nineteenth century.

It is sometimes assumed that "... an unlimited supply of labor may be said to exist in those countries where population is so large relatively to capital and capital resources, that there are large sectors of the economy where the marginal productivity of labor is negligible, zero, or even negative."[35] It is not necessary to attempt to calculate the marginal productivity of labor in nineteenth-century German agriculture, for we do know that the process of industrialization in Germany was accompanied by a tremendous flight from the land and by a decided increase in the productivity of agriculture,[36] conditions that indicate a redundant agricultural population. Similar conditions in early nineteenth-century England provided evidence for Marx's concept of the "reserve army of the unemployed." Silesia may well have exhibited possibilities for "unlimited supplies of labor," but for various social reasons entrepreneurs had difficulty in effectively mobilizing these reserves in Upper Silesia. In fact, Upper Silesia may prove to be a case where certain assumptions about economic development based on classical economics turn out to be in need of revision from a sociological point of view[37]—after all, there was a shortage of labor in Upper Silesia despite conditions that would lead one to expect an unlimited supply—and one of my purposes here is to illustrate some of those social problems involved in dealing with economic development of the western European variety. In a way, one object of this study is to show why it is difficult to recognize where unlimited supplies of labor exist and why in this particular historical situation W. Arthur Lewis's theory (and Marx's) cannot be applied in full.

Population Movement

The "demographic transition" did not bypass Prussia. Indeed, one can perceive rapid population growth even before industrialization set in during the 1830s: the Prussian crude death rate in 1816-1819 was 29.4 per 1,000, while the crude birth rate in this same period was 44.3 per 1,000;[38] both of these rates are now considered to be within the range of "underdeveloped" countries. Deaths remained relatively constant until the late 1870s, when a steady decline set in; the rates per 1,000 were 29.1 in 1872-1875, 22.2 in 1896-1900, and 15.8 in 1913. Birth rates in this century declined steadily: per 1,000 population, the rates were 40.9 in 1876-1880, 36.0 in 1896-1900, and 29.0 in 1913.[39] The high birth and death rates and their decline fit clearly into the pattern observed in England, then in other European countries, and now in other parts of the world. Even though about 25 percent of the total German increase before 1890 emigrated abroad,[40] the whole state experienced very rapid growth down to World War I. Within post-1870 Prussia, the most prolific contributors to population increase were the eastern areas (the provinces of East Prussia, West Prussia, Posen and Upper Silesia [Oppeln regency]), and the industrial west (regencies of Arnsberg, Düsseldorf, and Cologne).[41] Here, certainly, was a population and a rate of increase which might lead one to expect "unlimited supplies of labor."

Even though rates of growth were highest in the east (including Silesia), the internal rate of migration from east to west in Prussia was very great—this was the so-called "flight from the countryside" (*Landflucht*) or "flight from the East" (*Ostflucht*). There has been much historical controversy over the nature of this flight, in many ways reminiscent of the controversy over the effects of the enclosures in Britain. Was this flight correlated with the existence of the great entailed estates? Or was it the more general western European phenomenon of leaving agricultural occupations and entering industrial ones, for which there were few opportunities in the east?[42]

Some incidental light may be thrown on this controversy by looking more closely at the Upper Silesian industrial region, one of the major industrial complexes of east Elbia and located in the midst of a largely agricultural area. However, the center of interest here is not the flight from the east in itself, but rather the labor market conditions in the area as affected by the migratory trends and the characteristics of the rural economy of Upper Silesia which affected these trends.

Rural overpopulation—understood as a condition when the law of diminishing marginal returns to agriculture has set in, that is when an increased number of workers produces less than a proportional increase in output—was nothing new to Silesia. At least a century before Prussia began to industrialize, land had been scarce in this province, and a landless rural proletariat had come into being.[43] This condition clearly antedated the emancipation of the peasants and indicated gross rural poverty, and one might venture to guess that only the absorptive capacity of industry saved the area from a disastrous Malthusian-type positive check in the second half of the nineteenth century. As a matter of fact, the handloom weavers in the Sudeten highlands of Silesia (in Liegnitz regency), made immortal by Gerhart Hauptmann, did suffer acute deprivation in the 1830s and 1840s; the 1840s also ushered in widespread hunger typhus, the result of an inability to maintain a minimal standard of living.

The German (and European) phenomenon of population pressure on food supply was met at first by out-migration, mainly to other sections of the country but also abroad.[44] The inhabitants of the east started leaving toward the middle of the century; interestingly enough, the first Poles to settle in America came from Upper Silesia in 1854. Emigration abroad fluctuated with the business cycle, but after a great surge in the 1880s it slowed to negligible proportions after 1893.[45]

Not so the east-west migration—it swelled in the second half of the nineteenth century and did not stop until the war in 1914 placed restrictions on movement. East Prussia, to name the most obvious case, sent out about 560,000 people in the period 1871-1910, and from Silesia almost 600,000 people emigrated in this same period. In general, the only eastern counties to show a surplus of immigrants over emigrants during 1871-1910 were the counties with large cities, and the only concentration of such counties in the east lay (outside of Berlin) in the Upper Silesian industrial region.[46]

In an earlier period, the huge but sparsely populated Silesia had been the recipient of migrants, especially under the colonization policies of Frederick the Great. In the late eighteenth and early nineteenth centuries it had received many migrants from other territories in Prussia and from other states; from about 1810 until the 1860s it grew by natural increase without significant immigration; and only from the 1870s on did it become a population exporter.[47]

Of the three regencies in the province, that of Oppeln (Upper Silesia) came after 1870 to have the greatest population movement, probably attributable to this region's having the highest rate of natural increase in Silesia. (See Figures 1 and 2.) After advancing from some 368,000 inhabitants in 1816 to 900,000 in 1871, the local population grew to 1,300,000 on the eve of the war. All the counties (except for two) within this one regency gained in population during 1871-1905, but the majority lost a good percentage of their natural gains (births minus deaths) via emigration. The only rural counties to lose only a small percentage of their natural growth were Tost-Gleiwitz and Tarnowitz, which actually were partially industrialized; the agricultural counties all lost a large part of their increase. Those counties showing large gains were Bytom, Zabrze, and Kattowitz, the only completely industrialized counties. Rybnik and Pless, the other two counties directly contiguous to the industrial area, showed large emigration losses, with Pless losing more people than any other county in the regency. Rybnik was essentially an agricultural county with little industry until the opening of a new branch of the Silesian coal field in the early twentieth century; it had no metal industry. In the 1905-1910 period, with developing industry, it showed a gain of 20,000 inhabitants.[48] Pless, on the other hand, had a number of scattered mines antedating the industrial revolution (but no metal industry), all employing few men; one must regard this county not only as a mixed agricultural-industrial area (like Tarnowitz and Tost-Gleiwitz) but also as a rural feeder to industries located in adjacent counties. Note that these figures refer to a loss of natural increase, not to a decline in resident population.

Johannes Ziekursch over fifty years ago explored the peasant problems of Silesia under Frederick the Great and in the first half of the nineteenth century. This work has been supplemented and extended down to 1914 by Seweryn Wyslouch, a scholar who pioneered in taking post-World War II Polish studies of Silesia out of the realm of nationalistic propaganda, although he too had to don an oversized ideological jacket.[49] Wyslouch contends that landowning patterns in most of Silesia in the second half of the nineteenth century show the growing dominance of large farm enterprises and the decline of medium-size peasant holdings. His work, based primarily on official Prussian statistical publications, points to the southeastern counties of Silesia (those surrounding the industrial region and those comprising that region) as constituting an area of small and economically nonviable farms. This area of nonfertile soil on the right bank of the Oder had the lowest average income (per measure of land) in Silesia. While other regions of the province had a large rural proletariat, these right-bank counties had few "real" proletarians and a large quasi-proletariat of cottars, that is, farmers working dwarf holdings and subsisting by performing agricultural day labor.[50] Thus the setting of the flight from the east differed from that in other areas, where landless laborers predominated in the rural population and where there was no industry to employ such workers.

Precisely in those counties where developing industry was inclined to make its first call for labor the rural population base was still attached to the land. On the other hand, most of the natural increase of the area could find little local agricultural employment because the big farms lay farther north. The alternatives to starving at home were working in Upper Silesian industry, becoming agricultural day laborers in the central regions of Silesia, or leaving the province altogether in search of work.

The first possibility forms one of the major topics of this study and will be dealt with at a later point. As for migrating northward, the suspicion exists that this was a regular route for agricultural laborers, at least toward the end of the nineteenth century. According to the census of 1900, 104,266 Upper Silesians lived in Lower Silesia, whereas only about 58,000 Lower Silesians lived in Upper Silesia.[51] Of course, many of these came from counties outside the industrial area, but it is safe to say that this trek was also made by many from the deep south of Silesia.

Leaving the province completely was also a viable aternative. The "*Sachsengänger*"—those traveling to Saxony for seasonal and permanent work—were familiar figures in contemporary literature. Other popular destinations were the Berlin-Brandenburg area and, less often, the Rhenish-Westphalian industrial region. In 1900, 138,000 Silesians lived in Berlin (population 1,750,000), and 73,000 lived in the provinces of Rhineland and Westphalia.[52] More will be said later as to how many of these came from the industrial region itself because emigration from there ties in with the whole problem of recruiting and molding a modern labor force.

Finally, immigration of German citizens into Silesia was light. In 1907 there were not many more than 200,000 of these outsiders in the entire province, and only 75,000 of these worked in mining and industry (again in the entire province, not just in the industrial area).[53]

In sum, it is clear that both *Landflucht* and *Ostflucht* were real phenomena in Silesia although in the latter case the industrial region was not so deeply affected as were the more fertile counties in the center of the province. In this Lower Silesian area, the aggrandizement of the large estates and the growth of the numbers of rural landless laborers developed rapidly after 1850, and the area also sent large numbers of people to other parts of Germany.[54] In the industrial region of Upper Silesia and in the surrounding counties the rural population tended more to remain in the area because they had their own piece of land and because the nearby industries, in a stage of accelerated development after the 1860s, provided employment.

Foreign Workers

Surplus population on the land, however, did not suffice to man the mines and smelters of Upper Silesia. Because the local labor market would not under existing circumstances furnish sufficient labor to industry, the industrialists resorted to unusual sources of labor—to foreign workers imported from all over Europe and to women and children, both of which forms are usually associated with early stages of industrial activity.

Those non-Prussian aliens in Upper Silesia were in the main migrants from Congress Poland (Russia) and Galicia (Austria), and their sojourn in Prussia during this period can be easily subdivided into three periods: the latter 1860s to 1885, 1885 to 1890, and 1890 to 1914.[55]

In the early years, when mining and metallurgy were first beginning to expand in Upper Silesia, there were few aliens in the area. The number of foreigners, those born in Russia and Austria-Hungary and living in all of Upper Silesia, has been estimated to be about 16,000 in 1880, of whom 8,000 were resident in the industrial counties, where the total population numbered 500,000.[56] Since the number of foreigners includes whole families, not just wage earners, it seems safe to say that on the whole they did not form a significant portion of the industrial labor force except perhaps in firms lying close to the border and employing daily commuters from Russia or Austria.

In 1885, the Prussian government, reacting in part to Russian Pan-Slavism and Balkan unrest, in part following a wave of nationalistic xenophobia at home, and in part continuing its policy of trying to create a uni-national German state, ordered the expulsion of all alien Poles resident in Prussia.[57] It is apparent, however, that industrial employers as a group were not bothered by this ruling because for the moment the needs of local industry were small enough to be served by the local population. There were only some 37,000 miners in 1871 and only 45,000 in 1881; the smelting industries were still run mainly by puddling and in consequence employed only about 7,000 people in 1871 and 8,800 in 1881;[58] the metal-finishing industries were still too small to employ large numbers of workers. Local workers, who had staffed the expanding mines of the 1870s, were still forthcoming in the next two decades, although mines near the border filled out their crews with daily commuters from across the border. This border traffic, both daily and weekly, involved almost 8,000 people before 1885, and it continued to involve thousands of daily migrants down to 1914.[59]

The numerical results of the expulsions in Upper Silesia were not great—fewer than 7,000 left—but the policy was disturbing to Upper Silesian employment patterns in that it shut off a great employment hinterland—a concept often mentioned at that time—just at a time when demand for workers was increasing rapidly.[60]

The expulsions which started in 1885 came at precisely the wrong time for east German employers, both agricultural and industrial. Agricultural needs were growing swiftly because of the spread of the sugar beet, a labor-intensive crop. This new demand coincided with that massive flight from the land already mentioned. It has been estimated that at the turn of the twentieth century the Prussian rural population was expanding by 345,000 per year, but 200,000 people were simultaneously leaving the countryside. However, agriculture could afford to give up only 125,000.[61] From this situation arose the demand for foreign workers on the large farms. Industrial needs in Upper Silesia were also growing more pressing as the mining and smelting industries started a period of rapid and almost uninter-rupted rise in all phases of production, a rise stopped only by the war in 1914.

Finally, in 1890 the government agreed to admit a number of foreign contract laborers. These were subject to rigid restraints: application for each individual group of imported workers,[62] and the requirement (starting in 1895) that they all leave for a specified waiting period each year (the *Karenzzeit*). This period was originally different for agricultural and industrial workers, but the administrative cumber-someness of two different periods caused the government in 1901 to decree a single waiting period. Significantly enough, in a Prussia dominated by agricultural interest groups this pause fell in the winter, when agricultural demands were low but industrial demands high—from November 15 to April 15, later shortened to December 1 to March 1, and later to December 20 to February 1.[63] This whole program of importing Slavic laborers obviously was intended primari-ly to benefit agricultural, not industrial, employers. Rural predomi-nance appears not only in the timing of the waiting period, but also in the constant friction between Upper Silesian industrialists and the group hiring agricultural workers (*Deutsche Feldarbeiterzentra-le*).[64]

The program also conflicted with the official Germanization policy, which was otherwise expressed in the expulsions of the 1880s and the land colonization laws of the three decades before the First World War. The Poles were considered to be the major enemy of the state in the east, and for this reason many stratagems were devised to reduce the number of even these temporary workers. The misgivings of the government about the whole program of bringing non-Germans into the "racially" divided east are vividly illustrated by the relent-lessness of the effort to expel a solitary Galician worker in 1896-1897.[65] Attempts to limit the Poles also lay behind the proposals made at various times to bring in Swedes, Lithuanians, Estonians, Finns, White Russians, Ukrainians, Germans from Hungary, Italians, even Chinese.[66] Some of these proposals were acted on, and the Caritas charity organization noted that the more than one million foreign workers in Germany in 1912 came from more than twelve different countries. Occasionally one might find such groups as the sixty Italian stonecutters employed at the Heinitz mine for a while,[67] but non-Slavs were few.

In the 1890s, almost all the foreign contract workers were Poles from Russia and Austria, but in 1905 Ruthenians were introduced in order to offset Polish nationalist agitation and the Polish presence in general. They soon came to outnumber the foreign Poles working in Upper Silesian industry (the Poles remained in the majority in Germany as a whole).[68] Furthermore, the Ruthenians were not subject to the annual waiting period. Still, those firms utilizing foreign labor continued to demand Poles. One mine administrator pleaded in 1910: "Despite the greatest efforts we have not succeeded in covering our need for workers with local and Ruthenian workers."[69]

On one point the authorities were adamant—no Jews. This restriction was repeated a number of times, but need was so great that the employers, presumably no less fearful of the "injurious" effects of the Jewish "character," kept asking for and even hiring such workers, even to the point of discussing the establishment of a Jewish labor office for importing Polish Jewish miners.[70] These measures of the employers indicate how desperately they felt the shortage of workers.

In the 1890s, when the native industrial force in Upper Silesia began to increase very rapidly, not too many workers were imported. After an initial upsurge of 5,000 in 1891, the annual figure hovered between 1,000 and 2,000, despite ringing complaints of the employers about a shortage of haulers. From 1900 to 1906, the total labor force grew swiftly, and the numbers of foreign workers increased to an average of 3,000 annually. Then, in the last few years before the war, the number multiplied to an annual figure of between 13,000 and 20,000. The majority of the migrants, some 80 percent, worked in coal mining; most of the others found jobs in basic iron and steel production.[71] The totals are given in Table 3.

Within each industry, the foreign workers were concentrated in certain firms. The Cleophas mine in Zaleze (near Kattowitz), for example, employed a large number of such workers; seven other mines at one point had work forces composed of about 20 percent or more foreign workers.[72] Or, in the metal industry, several works had groups of foreign workers, and the zinc industry was known as a large user of such labor. Others had few or no workers of this type.[73]

In sum, although there was much talk about the foreign workers from the late 1880s on, they were not numerically important in Upper Silesian mining and smelting until after 1900; but by 1913 they comprised some 10 percent of the local mining force and formed a noticeable group among the metalworkers.

Women and Minors

To secure labor for factory work ... the factory agents ... were confronted by the fact that to bid labor away from existing farm work, they must needs offer a margin large enough to overcome not merely the normal elements of labor immobility, but, in addition, the fearful vision of factory work. The agents and proprietors, however, rejected any contest bidding up rates. Instead, changing their hiring preference function, they turned primarily to the use of two relatively non-competing groups in the labor market—children and women.[74]

This phenomenon has been encountered in most industrializing countries, and Upper Silesian mining and smelting employers in like fashion changed their hiring preference function: rather than bid up wages, they employed not only easily handled foreign workers but

TABLE 3

Foreign Contract Laborers in Upper Silesian Mining

Year	Total mining force	Total foreign workers	Poles[b]	Ukrainians
1891	54,476	5,267		
1892	54,819	912		
1893	53,697	219		
1894	53,018	504		
1895	53,167	227		
1896	56,032	1,103		
1897	57,870	1,743		
1898	59,416	1,731		
1899	63,115	2,213		
1900	69,147	2,839		
1902	80,038	3,125		
1903	82,327	3,987		
1904	83,049	3,813		
1906 (spring)[a]	90,074	?	?	1,900
1907 (spring)	95,932	9,466	6,344	3,122
1908 (spring)	106,575	16,396	5,121	7,268
1909 (15 Feb.)	116,593	20,056	8,579	6,078
1910 (15 Apr.)	117,977	14,472	5,786	7,623
1911 (31 Mar.)	117,791	15,890	6,504	8,221
1912 (30 Mar.)	120,638	14,642	6,730	6,738
1913 (15 Mar.)	123,349	15,792	7,232	7,172
1913 (28 Oct.)		19,366	7,648	10,627

SOURCES: Foreign workers: Andrzej Brozek, *Robotnicy spoza zaboru pruskiego w przemyśle na Górnym Śląsku (1870–1914)* [Workers from beyond the Prussian partition area in Upper Silesian industry, 1870–1914] (Wroclaw, 1966), pp. 55–57. 1891–1900 based on DZA Merseburg, Rep. 77, Tit. 1135, nr. 1, Adh. 1, vols. 1–3, passim. 1902–1904 based on DZA Merseburg, Rep. 87B, 210:147–148. 1906–1913 based on WAP Wroclaw, RO I 12355:55ff.; RO I 12356:158; ZOBH 1910:606; 1912:41; 1913:227,485. Total mining force: Kazimierz Popiolek, *Górnośląski przemysl górniczohutniczy w drugiej polowie XIX wieku* [The Upper Silesian mining and smelting industry in the second half of the nineteenth century] (Katowice, 1965), pp. 205–206, based on ZOBH.
[a]Monthly dates (1906–1913) refer to foreign workers only, not to the total mining force.
[b]All foreign contract laborers were Poles before 1905.

also women and children in their enterprises. These noncompeting groups must be included as part of the potential unlimited supplies of labor.

The purpose of employing these groups obviously is to avoid raising wages while simultaneously satisfying a demand for labor. Traditionally, women and minors are more docile and less mobile than adult male workers; employers in Upper Silesia used them extensively in the same way that they used foreign workers, that is, to staff their crews without completely depending on recruiting in a free competitive market.

According to official sources, Upper Silesian mining and smelting employed about 6,800 women in 1875, 8,400 in 1880, and 12,000 in 1889. From then on until the First World War, the figure hovered around the 10,000 mark; even though the total employed declined relative to the size of the work force, women still comprised over 5 percent of the total Silesian (Upper and Lower) mining force in 1912.[75] Of these women, the largest group was active in coal mining, but zinc mining and smelting also employed very large numbers of them (30 to 40 percent of the total), though female employment in zinc smelting fluctuated considerably.[76]

Although the number of women employed leveled off after 1889, the number of minors continued to rise, despite the statistical lowering around 1900 of "adult" age from eighteen to sixteen by which many "youthful workers" (jugendliche Arbeiter) miraculously were transformed into adults. As the demand for labor rose, employers increasingly turned not only to foreign workers but also to minors to fill out their work forces. In 1907, for example, new state regulations about clearing coal dust out of mines forced a significant increase in the number of workers; minors formed the major part of these new employees. In 1912 the workers aged sixteen and below comprised 4.3 percent of the total number of miners in all of Silesia. Like the women, they were divided among the various types of activity: in 1902, over 40 percent of the minors worked in coal mining and over 40 percent in smelting.[77]

To get some notion of absolute and relative figures, one might glance at the composition of the mining force in 1912.[78] Of 117,585 coal miners in Upper Silesia, 5,835 were under age sixteen and 5,711 were women (almost all over age sixteen)— a considerable percentage. To these must be added about 2,800 female workers in ore mining. In comparison, of 363,879 coal miners under the jurisdiction of the Dortmund mining office, no women and only 1,501 minors were employed.

The situation is brought out even more graphically when one examines the work list of individual mines to see how dependent they were on such labor. The Cleophas mine in 1899, for example, employed 160 women and minors out of a total crew of 1,944; the Castellengo mine in 1906 employed 213 women and minors out of a total of 2,830; the Neuhof zinc mine in August, 1912 employed 390 women and children of a total crew of 1,148.[79]

Legislation in many European countries in the late nineteenth century reflected the belief that women and children are not able to perform strenuous work over extended periods of time, and consequently there should be special protection for them. In line with this belief, Imperial Germany in a series of laws restricted the use of the labor of women and children.[80] Women and young girls were forbidden to work underground after 1868; the minimum age for children working in mining was raised to fourteen (1878); maximum hours were set for minors (1878); night work in the mines for women and children was outlawed (1878). The *Bundesrat*, however, issued a series of special edicts exempting Upper Silesian mines and smelters from certain restrictions of the employment of women (1892, extended to 1907, then to 1912, and finally to 1922). While the Dortmund mining area had banned women from the mines in the 1890s, the work force in the Upper Silesian industrial area continued to contain significant numbers of women down to the First World War.

Essentially, women and children remained a significant part of the Upper Silesian work force in the 1865-1914 period and formed an integral part of that work force even when the use of such labor was declining in other areas of Germany. On the eve of the war, they comprised 10 percent of the local working force; the foreign workers, another 10 percent. Obviously, this was no perfectly competitive labor market. The use of both women and children and of foreign contract labor expressed an attempt by Upper Silesian employers to expand production while keeping wage costs down, but even with these sources of labor the employers were at no time after the 1870s able to feel secure in having unlimited supplies; especially after 1890 real wages rose and subsistence level wages tended to disappear.[81] (See Chapter 7.) Later in this study an effort will be made to find out how the hiring of these docile elements helped or hindered the formation of a modern labor force.

One can in a few words explain why this book does not go beyond 1914. The labor market in Upper Silesia, as was to be expected, underwent a profound shock as a result of the outbreak of the war. For over 50 years, since the state had relinquished its control over private mines, mining employers had been struggling to develop large and reliable work forces. The metallurgical industries developed a short time later, and they too faced the problem of building up a suitable work force. As heavy industry went into a period of extremely rapid growth, the supply of labor proved to be an acute problem. Not only women and children were used, but also foreign contract laborers were imported to staff the enterprises of Upper Silesia. Then came the war, which absorbed great numbers of Upper Silesian workers. The Schaffgotsch concern lost 30 percent of its adult male workers in the first three weeks. The Schlesischer Bohr- und Querschlag Gesellschaft, doing work in Upper Silesian mines, lost seventy men to the army, seventeen foreigners went home, and eight men were left to do the work of ninety-five. By the end of the war the total mining force had decreased by 25 percent.[82]

Employers answered this challenge in a manner already familiar from other countries—use of foreign workers, use of war prisoners, hiring of women and children, and extension of working hours. But this is another story, and any discussion of a modern industrial laboring force in Upper Silesian heavy industry can be halted at this point.

Entrepreneurs and Managers

Who were the shadowy figures identified here as "employers," "top managers," and "entrepreneurs"? Managers are difficult to identify; owner-entrepreneurs less so, especially when they were aristocrats. In either case a shift to corporate structure and the establishment of bureaucratically-run enterprises had dissolved the individual imprint on Upper Silesian firms by the 1870s in some cases, and by the 1890s in almost all cases.[83]

Mining was nothing new for feudal lords, and the Upper Silesian magnates had managed to expand their claims of regalian rights into successful industrial enterprises in the nineteenth century. Nor was smelting unknown to eighteenth-century noble entrepreneurs, but on such a small scale and with such primitive technology that these undertakings mattered little in the industrial age. What mattered was the tradition of aristocratic involvement in industrial activity, a tradition that bore fruit in the post-1850 development of metallurgy. Of the forty-seven owners of 5,000 or more hectares in Silesia in 1887, six of the largest turned out to be important industrial magnates; of the owners of the largest coal mines in 1912, ten were nobles.[84]

Indeed there were some non-noble owners—August Borsig came down from Berlin; Georg Caro and Wilhelm Hegenscheidt made their fortunes locally; and of course there was Georg von Giesches Erben, an old Breslau commercial firm which ranked among the largest mining and smelting companies in the area.

The late nineteenth century witnessed two major trends in the structure of Upper Silesian enterprise, incorporation due to the need for capital, and concentration of ownership. Capital requirements for metallurgical ventures and even for expanded mineral mining resulted in the formation of large concerns starting around 1870 and continuing to the First World War. Incorporation and further growth by no means eliminated the individual entrepreneurs from the scene, but small companies did disappear and the great German banks did gain substantial influence in the big firms. A new group of professional general managers and their assistants now ran these companies, even though the old owners still received their profits regularly. By 1913 some 10 companies and the Prussian state mined the vast majority of coal, zinc, and lead in Upper Silesia and produced almost all the metal products marketed from there.[85] The number of independent coal-mining firms, for example, dropped from 103 in 1869 and 122 in 1874 to 63 in 1913; zinc mines, from 37 in 1869 to 16 in 1913. All the while total employment and average work force per plant climbed precipitously. At the time of the First World War the following dominated local coal and metal production:[86] Bismarck smelting works in Bismarckhütte, incorporated 1882, including the Bethlen-Falva smelting plant acquired from Prince Henckel von Donnersmarck in 1906; Donnersmarckhütte und Oberschlesische Eisen- und Kohlenwerke A.G., based in Zabrze, founded 1872 and based on the holdings of Prince Henckel von Donnersmarck; Hohenlohe works, incorporated 1905, based near Kattowitz (Prince Hohenlohe-Oehringen); Kattowitzer A.G. für Bergbau und Hüttenbetrieb, incorporated 1889 (Tiele-Winckler family); Oberschlesische Eisenbahnbedarfs A.G. in Beuthen, formed from several plants, especially the Friedenshütte (Count Renard); Oberschlesische Eisenindustrie in Gleiwitz, including a whole series of foundries and smelters; Schlesische A.G. für Bergbau und Zinkhüttenbetrieb in Lipine, founded 1853; Vereinigte Königs- und Laurahütte A.G., founded 1871 (Count Henckel von Donnersmarck); and the Georg von Giesches Erben company, owner of a long list of coal and zinc mines and processing plants. Add a few medium firms, like those connected with the Prince of Pless, Count Ballestrem, Borsig family, Hegenscheidt-Caro—this was most of local industry. However, even though the local magnates fought to retain control of the companies after incorporating, in almost every case the big German banks had by the turn of the century acquired seats on the boards of directors.

Concentration of ownership also was echoed in the increasing volubility of the Upper Silesian Mine- and Smelter-Owner Association (Oberschlesischer Berg- und Hüttenmännischer Verein). Founded in the 1850s as a loose group of entrepreneurs, this organization at first concerned itself mainly with questions of import tariffs and railroad rates. In the 1890s the dynamic leadership of Friedrich Bernhardi and changes in the exigencies of marketing and production set the organization off on a track involving price-fixing agreements, pronouncements on wages and working conditions, pressure on member firms to abide by general guidelines in relations with workers, and pressure-group tactics in Berlin. It never approached a trust—internal competition at times was bitter—but the group served as industry spokesman to the government, the press, and the middle-class public.

So much for the labor market, technology, and industrialists—the question remains of how to fit them together to understand the social shifts apparent in an industrializing region. In particular one needs to fathom the effects of potentially unlimited supplies of labor and to guage the reality of the later labor shortage. On the one hand workers are not pure economic animals, responding instinctually to market fluctuations; perhaps they acted in part on the basis of other motives, like attachment to the family plot of land or preference for particular types of occupations. On the other hand, owners and managers may have miscalculated the effort required to attract workers. The first place to turn for such an investigation is the area from which workers arrived, an area which may be considered an extension of the labor market as described in the first part of this chapter. The range of this market will imply the attractiveness of labor in Upper Silesia. Furthermore, the peculiarities of the local population can be assumed to be a relevant variable in discussing the making of a modern industrial labor force.

3

Ethnic and Geographic Origins
of the Labor Force

The modernization of Prussia entailed the sharpening of a number of social conflicts based on language, religion, and nationality, none of which had been crucial in the eighteenth century or even in the first half of the nineteenth century. It is true that the eighteenth-century colonization policy of Frederick the Great had envisaged the settlement of Germans in the newly acquired Silesia, but that governmental policy had been aimed at economic growth in a hitherto sparsely populated area and was not much concerned with the "nationality" of the settlers. Major emphasis was laid on expanding the local population base, though with little success; local Polish-speaking residents comprised the bulk of workers at the new state enterprises in Malapane (near Oppeln), near Gleiwitz, and on the site of what came to be the city of Königshütte.

Colonization of the Prussian east in the late nineteenth century was motivated by wholly different aims. It is not pertinent at this point to discuss the nationality struggle that crystallized in Prussia after 1870, but one must note that the controversy centered in Posen and West Prussia, where there existed a significant stratum of Polish landlords and professional people who comprised cadres of community leaders. In Upper Silesia, on the other hand, one can hardly speak of a Polish culture deriving from a common literature and from public life because of the truncated nature of the local community; the lack of an indigenous nobility and of middle-class groups, the traditional carriers of culture, meant that the community produced few leaders. As a matter of fact, Prussian nationalist racists (especially in the Eastern Marches Association) generally ignored Upper Silesia until after the turn of the twentieth century.[1]

Even though Upper Silesia in 1905 was the home of over one million native speakers of Polish (about 35 percent of the Poles in Prussia),[2] there were no Polish nobles resident in the area. This niche in the social hierarchy was occupied solely by Germans, among whom were to be found some of the richest men in Germany—the Prince of Pless, one branch of the Hohenlohe family, Schaffgotsch, the Henckel von Donnersmarcks, Tiele-Winkler, and others. Surprisingly, more hectares were entailed in Oppeln than in any other regency (*Regierungs-bezirk*),[3] and these local Junkers were no less eager than their counterparts elsewhere in Prussia to maintain their exalted postion.

Nonetheless, a distinct group of Polish-speaking citizens of Prussia can clearly be delineated in pre-World War I Upper Silesia. They were not merely Prussians speaking a different language, as some German scholars maintained, but they comprised a separate community speaking its own language and practicing a distinctive style of life. Aside from the Upper Silesian variant of the Polish language, the major identifying mark of the local population was its orientation toward the Roman Catholic church. To be sure, the quinquennial Prussian censuses indicated that the majority of all the inhabitants of Silesia, both German and Polish, were Catholic.[4] The Poles, however, were geographically massed east of the Oder River and from Oppeln county south, permitting the development of a separate religious life which, though restrained by the German-oriented church hierarchy, eventually became the starting point of Polish nationalism in Upper Silesia and of trade unionism among Polish workers in industry (see chapter 9). With the growth of town life around the developing industries, there began to appear Polish shopkeepers, editors, lawyers, and doctors, those groups who traditionally have spearheaded cultural awakenings among ethnic minorities. The organizational work of these men and of socialist organizers began to manifest itself in the 1890s, and after 1900 German nationalists had to take note of this hitherto quiescent area.

Not that the entire population of Oppeln regency was Polish—far from it. In 1905 over 35 percent of the population could be classified as German speaking, and the German population increased rapidly after 1900, perhaps even more quickly than the Polish group. However, this last statistic is questionable, owing to the increasingly blatant bias in the post-1900 German population censuses. In any case, there is no question that many Germans came to settle in the industrial area, and the 75,000 resident German Protestants, all relative newcomers, formed the backbone of the administrations of both government and private industry.[5]

Though many Germans lived in Oppeln regency, before the 1880s few were resident in the industrial region. They lived west of the Oder and formed no separate "Silesian" community parallel to that of the Poles. Gradually, some of these German farm and cottage workers moved into industry, joining with other Germans who migrated into the area to find employment as skilled workers and as administrative personnel. The government-sponsored school for mine technicians and foremen (*Bergschule*) in Tarnowitz drew most of its students from families of middle-class Germans, 80 percent of whom were born in Upper Silesia.[6] By 1910 German-speaking residents formed a majority in the cities of Gleiwitz, Beuthen,

Kattowitz, and Königshütte and comprised some 40 percent of the population in the regency (880,000 Germans; 1,250,000 Poles); one writer even makes the dubious claim that the German-speaking population was in the majority in the industrial region after 1910.[7]

Certainly the Germans predominated in the artisan-oriented metalworking industries, which in 1904 employed fewer than 5 percent of all working Poles in the industrial area.[8] The smelting and related industries, on the other hand, were run by a work force of both Germans and Poles; mines were manned largely by Poles, as is evidenced by some employer complaints of their inability to find a sufficient number of "purely German workers"[9] to end their shortage of haulers. At the same time, mining, particularly coal mining, was expanding its predominantly Polish-speaking labor force at a much faster rate than smelting was expanding its mixed force. Mining employment accounted for slightly fewer than 50 percent of the industrial workers in the region in 1890; by 1900, the figure had risen to a full 50 percent and by 1910 to a dominating 62 percent of the labor force in heavy industry.[10] True, the characteristics of a labor force and the issue of a shortage of labor in Upper Silesia are not automatically explained by pointing to ethnic and social peculiarities of the surrounding population. Modern industrial centers draw on extremely large areas for potential workers; long-distance migration has become practically a benchmark for an advanced economy. The Ruhr region, for example, was well known as an entrepot for workers from all over Germany and Europe; one might reasonably expect Upper Silesia to display similar characteristics. But it did not. The temper of workers in this eastern mining and smelting complex can be understood only in reference to the immediately surrounding area.

Although observers have often referred to the local origins of the Upper Silesian mining and smelting work force, little archival evidence for this assertion has been presented (except for foreign seasonal laborers).[11] At the risk of belaboring the obvious, I propose to make a few further comments on the geographical origins of these workers in order to limn in the background of recruitment for Upper Silesian industry and in order to set the stage for later discussion of the social problems involved in the formation of a modern industrial labor force.

The province of Silesia as a whole exercised little attraction on German citizens of other areas. In 1880 the largest outside contributor to Silesian population was the province of Posen, followed by Berlin-Brandenburg. Of the immigrant groups from each of these provinces, very few lived even in Oppeln regency, let alone in the industrial area. In 1900 the regency had a population of close to 1,900,000, of whom 1,750,000 were born locally. Another 60,000 came from other parts of Silesia, and no other German province supplied over 2,400 people except Posen (8,400). More specifically for the industrial region, in every census from 1871 to 1900 about 95 percent of the population of the Upper Silesian industrial area was listed as being born in Silesia.[12] As is indicated by the changes in the population structure in the local industrial cities noted above, this balance may have begun to shift after 1900, but the juggling of statistics for nationalistic purposes makes it hard to know the extent of new immigration from farther away; besides, the outbreak of the war in 1914 cut short any major shift in population trends in the industrial region. Thus the smelting industry, which had a greater need than mining to import skilled help, continued to employ primarily local workers.[13] It is apparent then that despite the potential for large-scale immigration from other areas, the autochthonous population continued to serve as almost the sole reservoir of labor in the entire period before the outbreak of the First World War.

The only group of any size not originating in the industrial area came from the nearby territories of Galicia and Russian Poland. Before the expulsions of the 1880s, there were fewer than 10,000 such workers;[14] afterwards, the number of annual migrants fluctuated, as noted in chapter 2. Moreover, the mines near the border employed a significant number of daily and weekly commuters. Besides these workers, few came to Upper Silesia from the outside. In comparison, the Berlin-Brandenburg industrial region drew migrants from all over eastern Germany, including large numbers from Silesia (over 10,000 according to the census of 1890);[15] the Ruhr also attracted hundreds of thousands of people from other provinces, including Silesia.

Inspection of worker lists at various mines in a number of localities reinforces this impression of the local area as the dominant source for industrial workers. For example, one of the Hohenlohe mines in the 1870s listed 500 workers, of whom the vast majority were born in the industrial area of Upper Silesia or in the counties directly adjacent to it.[16] Of one group of 250 workers, 175 were born in the industrial area as defined here; 60 were born outside the area; 15 were indeterminable. Of the 60 outsiders, almost all were born either in Oppeln regency or in Austria, most likely the neighboring area of Galicia. (Borders were not yet closed.) This same mine in the next twenty years hired over 5,000 workers, almost all of whom stemmed from the indigenous population.[17] Of a selected section of 89 men hired in 1876-1901, fewer than 10 were born outside the industrial region, and most of these "outsiders" came in from contiguous counties. Nor did this local orientation significantly change over time. Of another group hired in 1899-1901, 51 were locally born; 8, not local; 1, indeterminable.[18]

The localized nature of the labor force emerges distinctly from the example of the villages of Rosdzin and Schoppinitz (in Kattowitz county), which had barely 200 inhabitants in 1793, but over 21,000 by 1914.[19] Industrial workers recruited from among the local peasantry began to appear in the 1830s, and after 1850 the relevant labor market widened from northern Pless county to include of Silesia and to neighboring Russian Poland and Galicia, mainly via the railroads. Most of the workers in this industrial pocket, however, continued to come from an area bounded by a circle with a twenty mile radius from the town. In the 1890s, the supply from this small inner area, extending to Zabrze and Gleiwitz (Prussia) in the west to Będzin (Russian Poland) and Chrzanów (Galicia) in the east, still amounted to close to 80 percent of the local labor force.

That Rosdzin-Schoppinitz drew on Galicia and Russian Poland for workers gives substance to the assertion made in chapter 2 that these Austrian and Russian areas comprised part of the natural labor market for Upper Silesia. Particularly those firms near the borders employed sizable numbers of international migrant laborers who went home every night or at least every week. For example, the Morgenstern mine near Klein Dombrowka (Prussia) in the 1870s employed many workers living in Czeladź, Będzin, and the surrounding area (Russian Poland).[20] This same mine also apparently had recruiters active in Galicia, judging by the occasional hirings of groups of foreign workers simultaneously recorded in the local log books. Ironically, these border firms faced competition from mines in the adjacent Dąbrowa basin (Russian Poland), mines often owned by Upper Silesian magnates themselves. The same workers desired by Morgenstern, a Hohenlohe holding, were sought by the Saturn mine, also a Hohenlohe holding but situated in nearby Russia.[21]

Aside from the Austrian and Russian territories surrounding Upper Silesia, other parts of Germany were potential suppliers of labor. Even in the first half of the nineteenth century miners were being recruited in Lower Silesia (Waldenburg mining basin), western Germany, Saxony, western Poland (Congress Kingdom), and western Galicia. Typically for this early period, a representative of the government mining office would go to Lower Silesia and, with the permission of the local mining authorities, recruit.[22] Later in the century, employers still hoped to attract skilled miners from the nearby Lower Silesian mining basin, but few came. Before 1889 wages in Lower Silesia were higher than in Upper Silesia,[23] and after that date opportunities for migrating miners were much greater in the west than in Upper Silesia. To be sure, some people might have gone south from the Waldenburg basin; one finds, for instance, that the Lower Silesian employers' association appealed to its Upper Silesian counterpart not to make up the latter's deficit of workers leaving after the 1913 strike at the expense of Lower Silesia. On the whole, however, there is no hint of any large immigration of Lower Silesian miners. Furthermore, there is no evidence at all of movement from the other east German mining center, the Saxon lignite areas, to

Upper Silesia; contact between the two areas was practically non-existent.[24]

The other two possible sources of skilled workers in Germany were the mining and smelting concentrations in the Saar and the Ruhr. The former had a small work force, primarily of local origin.[25] The Ruhr, conversely, was forced to search all over Germany and Europe for its workers. The case for obtaining workers from the Ruhr mining region was occasionally mooted among Upper Silesian employers, but such attempts were generally disastrous. One classical case is recorded of two mines, Gottes-Segen and Hugo Zwang, which recruited 216 miners in Westphalia in 1912. Although all of these had been born in Upper Silesia, 34 never reported to work; of the rest, only 16 stayed on.[26]

Since much of the demand for labor in Upper Silesia was primarily for unskilled and semi-skilled workers, one might expect that it would have been possible to meet the needs of local industry by turning to labor exporting territories of Germany, the agricultural east, but recruiting drives into northern and eastern Germany by Upper Silesian firms were rare and insignificant in terms of the numbers of workers recruited. East Prussians and Poles from Posen who migrated in search of industrial work went in the main either to Berlin or to the Westphalian heavy industry complex; they too avoided Upper Silesia because of its reputation for low wages, poor working conditions, inadequate housing, and, for some Germans, the alien Polish environment. Other areas of the east proved no more fruitful for Upper Silesia. When 120 workers recently recruited from Stettin to replace seasonal workers who had been forced to leave by the waiting period rioted at the Ferdinand mine in 1909, the resulting scandal probably made that recruiting trip the last foray into Pomerania.[27]

Posen, the Prussian province directly to the east of Prussia, should have been fertile territory for recruitment to Upper Silesian industry because of the labor surplus in that province and because of the fairly good railway connections from Posen to Kattowitz. Still, when the need for workers became acute after about 1895, management in Upper Silesia feared the influx of Poles from an area very much alive with resurgent Polish nationalism. Not only did the Germans sympathize with the official campaign against Polish community life, but they also feared that any agitation might serve to undermine the docility of the resident labor force. In 1908 the trade office of the city of Posen wrote to the administration of the König mine that it had learned from Reichstag debates of a labor shortage in the Upper Silesian mining area; this office proposed to send some of the local labor surplus down to Upper Silesia. Although this offer was circularized in November, 1908, by the Upper Silesian Mine and

Smelter Owner Association, the association reversed itself two months later by recommending against the importation of Polish workers from Posen.[28] This is one of the few instances in which the group seemed to favor the official nationality policy over its own economic interests, although even here it might be postulated that the industrialists were concerned with the discipline of their workers, not with an overarching German national interest.

In sum, it appears that not only was the work force in the Upper Silesian industrial region recruited in Silesia province, but also for the most part was recruited within the territory of the tiny bunch of counties constituting the industrial area. The only major additions to the work force came from the border lands of Congress Poland and Galicia, which were a natural hinterland for Upper Silesian industry, but one which was shut off by Prussian immigration policy in 1885 to all but daily commuters and after 1890 reopened on a severely restricted basis.

It is entirely possible that a different relationship between Prussia and its eastern neighbors might have created a wholly different labor market in Upper Silesia, a point that might be tied in with the well-known thesis of Polish historians of the economic unity of the "Polish lands," including Upper Silesia.[29] It remains to be seen, however, how overall development would have been altered by an open-border policy. No company, no observer, no government official, no historian has ever held that Upper Silesian mining and smelting could have gone on the offensive against Ruhr coal and iron and steel had only the labor force been more numerous and reliable. Too many other factors—geological, geographical, economic, and political—worked against the interests of Upper Silesian industry.

Having suggested the parameters of the labor market in Upper Silesian heavy industry, one must be wary of treating local workers as purely economic men. Ethnic, linguistic, and religious considerations played an important role in the differentation of the local population, a situation suggesting revisions to some economists' notions about the unlimited availability of labor. Not only was there the usual lineup of workers versus employers, but there were also Poles and Germans, Roman Catholics and Protestants and later Greek Catholics, those locally born and immigrants. It is necessary to go on to study the social and economic characteristics of the local rural inhabitants in order to comprehend the social problems of a newly formed industrial labor force.

4

The Move into Industrial Employment

The large labor forces which arose in late nineteenth-century central and eastern Europe consisted primarily of agricultural workers who shifted to industry, or at least such was the case for several decades until a second generation of proletarians came of age. This was true even of Upper Silesia, despite its long tradition of mining and metalworking. After 1850, the old cadres were simply inadequate to staff the expanded mines; and the smelting industry, which developed rapidly only after the introduction of the open-hearth steel process in the early 1870s, was too new to have significant older groups to draw on. Therefore, any study of the behavior of the industrial labor force in Upper Silesia must discuss the effect of a rural background on the labor force, a type of background sometimes thought to be a significant hindrance to the formation of attitudes and behavior deemed proper for industrial vocations. Such considerations are important here too because of historians' notions about "... the long-standing tradition among Silesian industrial workers of maintaining some link with the land."[1]

Some students of the changes wrought by industrialization have pointed out four ideal-typical stages of transition from peasant to industrial worker.[2] First of all, there is the "uncommitted" industrial worker, the rural citizen who, while anxious to resume his rural vocation full time, tries to earn enough money to carry himself through hard times (for example, the drought year). In Upper Silesia the large numbers of landless workers and the prevalence of many nonviable dwarf farm holdings, a condition common in the area at least since the days of Frederick the Great,[3] impelled many of these small farmers into such temporary industrial employment. However reluctant their move into industrial wage labor, eventually they shifted to "semi-committed" status, a term referring to those who constantly wander between industrial and farm labor. Such activity in Upper Silesia dated back to the eighteenth-century peasant coal miners. Third, there are "generally committed" workers, anchored wholly in industry, and then the "specifically committed" workers, attached to a particular industry or even to a particular firm. These latter two groups began to emerge in significant numbers in Upper Silesia toward the end of the nineteenth century.

Although this schema has great heuristic value, there is a widespread tendency to reify such categories into presumed actuality. Moreover, a major objection to such a typology is precisely its ahistorical nature, which reduces the world to "pre-industrial" and "industrial" without differentiating among various societies. At least one sensitive historian has severely castigated sociologists and economists for their inability or disinclination to deal with new industrial workers in sufficiently historical and human terms,[4] and there is no denying the withering away of the worker in the face of descriptive and ascriptive norms, function-specificity, the "logic" of industrialization, and the like.

A further objection to this particular typology has been made with regard to the term "commitment," which implies a psychological reconditioning as well as a shift in observable behavior.[5] Although in an objective sense the term merely means permanent integration into the industrial labor force, one might reject "commitment" and retain the older notion of labor "discipline": "'Discipline' is the probability that by virtue of habituation a command will receive prompt and automatic obedience in stereotyped forms on the part of a given group of persons."[6] This emphasis on what men do rather than on what they think is the basis of the present study, but both terms raise problems of meaning. "Discipline" after all seems to focus on the needs of the employers, while "commitment" may imply worker behavior from the vantage point of the observer, himself committed to industrial society.

Conversely, both terms can connote more value-free outlooks if care is taken to divorce them from certain kinds of value judgments. If industrialization is taken to be good or considered inevitable, then some kind of labor discipline is required to run the resulting economy, and it is a gross error to ascribe work rules only to capitalistic avarice, as do many eastern European historians. In an article dealing with pre-World War I Upper Silesia, one Polish historian has written: "The major goal of disciplinary rules set by law and by private plants was to guarantee to the entrepreneurs an effective 'legal' tool to increase exploitation and to break worker resistance to intensifying exploitation".[7] Clearly this author (and many like him) is more interested in whipping the class enemy than in understanding what he is exposing, for he hopelessly confuses throughout this article the fact of exploitation by employers and the need of modern industry for certain rules. Ironically, at about the same time that he was berating evil capitalists for their repressive work rules, the Polish parliament received a proposed law to clamp down on unexcused absences from work.[8] This confusion of the web of rules of industrial enterprise with private ownership of the means of production reigns in the studies of many authors, whether Marxist, non-Marxist, or anti-Marxist in orientation.

Existing source materials support the often impressionistic assertion of writers about Upper Silesia that the great bulk of the mining and smelting laboring force between 1870 and 1914 was born and recruited in the small area constituting the industrial region and a few areas touching it. Given this background, one must ask how industrial opportunities affected the occupational patterns and life chances of the resident rural population. Very often scholars describe how the peasants and landless laborers in underdeveloped countries refuse to make a permanent change from agriculture to industry, but in various historical settings this generalization about lasting preference for the familiar, pre-industrial world must be modified—in West Africa, for example.[9] Besides, it is not obvious to the actors or even always true that individuals employed in agriculture will improve their lot by switching to industry.

The emancipation of the serfs in Prussia resulted in a major restructuring of the Prussian countryside. From the Stein-Hardenberg reforms of 1807 to the final decrees of 1850, noble landowners everywhere tried to fashion the execution of successive decrees in their own favor. In Silesia such attempts were remarkably successful in creating a vast impoverished and often landless stratum of poor peasants.[10]

The legally defined stratification of Silesian serfs in the eighteenth century roughly resembled that in other provinces. That is, despite a remarkable array of types of tenure, there were three major groupings: state peasants, serfs with secure tenure, serfs with insecure tenure. The question of security of tenure was further complicated by the status of the *Lassiten*, who had varying degrees of insecure tenure. The Polish population of Upper Silesia, concentrated south of Oppeln and east of the Oder River, was in an especially inferior position in this regard. After 1807 former serfs all over the province lost a sizable portion of their lands to more wealthy landowners, who benefited from Junker manipulation of the regulation decrees.

Parallel to this legal stratification of the serfs was an economic stratification, a distinction usually neglected by historians of the period, who have been overly concerned with definitions of legal status. At the very least one can discern three major levels of serf landholders: peasants with viable holdings (sufficient to support a family without significant outside income), peasants with nonviable holdings, and landless agricultural laborers. The leasing of land was quite common, and a peasant legally owning little land but leasing others' land could be one of those with viable holdings. Sometimes the legal and economic categories coincided, but the variety of legal statuses was so great and the terminology so diverse that legal questions are better left aside except where they had significant effect on shifts of economic position.

Just as the legal position of serfs in Polish-speaking Upper Silesia was markedly inferior to that of their peers in other sections of Silesia and eastern Prussia, so too their economic position in the eighteenth century was extremely precarious. Landholding in the area tended to polarize between a few extremely large estates and a mass of economically nonviable holdings, on which there lived a peasantry forced to supplement its income by outside work. Under the terms of the various emancipation decrees of the serfs, none of these were eligible for "regulation" of their land before 1850. By the law of 1850 peasant landholders more or less got to keep the land they had been farming; ironically, the sometimes destitute section of the rural population remained landholders, while many of the medium and small scale peasants had been pushed off the land under the terms of the emancipation regulations of 1816 and after.

This is not to say there were no landless agricultural laborers in Upper Silesia. There were many such local migrants staffing the farms of the area and living an undernourished existence subject to typhus and other catastrophes prevalent in relatively overpopulated areas. When the threshing machine was introduced and the expansion of arable land ceased in the 1860s, these people immediately were pushed into the ranks of an unemployed *Lumpenproletariat*, eventually absorbed by the expanding industrial labor markets of industry and the more prosperous agriculture of the Lower Silesian central plain.

It is patent that the economic stratification system was far more decisive for labor force development than was the legal system. The official abolition of serfdom in the first half of the nineteenth century signaled no abrupt breach anywhere in Germany between many mining and smelting workers and their agricultural sidelines and no massive influx of workers into these industries, despite the appearance first of mass rural pauperism and then of a rudimentary rural proletariat. In the Ruhr, most of the 12,700 mining and smelting workers in 1850, whether or not serfs previously, did not divest themselves of their small holdings; in Saxony, in the second half of the nineteenth century most of the workers spent part of the year in the mines and part in the fields. Even in Upper Silesia, where mining and smelting had begun to develop in earnest in the 1780s, there was still no strong industrial center to attract the rural masses suffering from the onerous terms of the post-emancipation land settlement. As late as the 1840s and 1850s large agriculturalists were able to press their workers very hard because industry had not yet begun to absorb labor.[11]

Nonetheless, signs of increased industrial activity were not altogether lacking. Upper Silesia had come a long way from the time when the König mine had to close down for two months in 1792 because most workers were away bringing in the harvest, and from the time in the late eighteenth century when a furnace at the Friedrich smelter had to be shut down because the smelting workers had been called to help in the lord's fishing. Fifty years later many landless agricultural workers were often employed part time as industrial workers, and in the middle of the century many peasants with draft animals engaged in hauling materials for heavy industry.[12] Thus even before the growth of a modern industry local economic conditions resulted in at least part-time work in industry by some peasants and agricultural laborers in order to augment the meager existence provided by their small holdings and by their agricultural day wages; in some ways, this admixture of agriculture and industry adumbrated the transitional situation which became dominant in the 1870s and 1880s. To be sure, one should not paint too rosy a picture of employment in early nineteenth-century industry. Aside from limitations imposed by the guild-type mining brotherhoods, positions in heavy industry were so poorly remunerated that agricultural workers avoided the mines if at all possible. Still, the inhabitants of Upper Silesia were not entirely unfamiliar with industrial work before the 1850s.

Shifting Social Patterns in the Countryside after 1850

After 1850, of course, there were no longer two independent but interacting stratification systems. All men were now officially equal citizens of the Prussian state, though continued Junker dominance of state and society also resulted in an invidious legal differentiation of the population along the lines of the earlier ruler and ruled. The three class voting system favored large landowners, who were particularly prominent in Upper Silesia and even were personally active in politics, such as Graf Franz von Ballestrem, local squire and industrial magnate, who was president of the Reichstag in the early twentieth century. This unusual combination of agricultural and industrial holdings meant that Upper Silesian agriculture was identified with industry even before the 1879 national alliance of iron and grain producers. Furthermore, Junkers generally functioned as *Landrat* and *Amtsvorsteher*, the chief governing officers in rural areas. While not always deferring to the wishes of the industrialists, such officials were often useful allies in controlling the labor force, either by making emigration difficult or by certifying the import of foreign seasonal workers.

Observers have often noted the somewhat anomalous position of Upper Silesian magnates. True, they were Junkers, exercising the patrimonial police, judicial, and administrative powers characteristic of this group throughout East Elbia. But they were also industrialists, as noted in some detail at the end of chapter 2; this kind of entrepreneurship wreaks havoc with the ordinary assumptions made about the economic conservatism of aristocrats. One might say that they had gone one step further along the road to participation in modern society than had the "pseudo-democratized" Junkers of the east who after 1873 developed a capitalist agriculture. Besides, the Upper Silesians were mostly Catholics, again a situation which differentiated them from their peers to the north and east; thus Ballestrem could become associated with the Center party, a party controlled in the main by nobles and high officials from the western areas of the empire. Other local landowners stood out in the *Reichspartei*, ordinarily identified as conservative but not so immovable as the Prussian conservatives; Silesian delegates to this *Reichstag* delegation included the Prince of Pless, the Duke of Ujest (Hohenlohe), and Count Schaffgotsch, all owners of considerable industrial holdings. Then too the Upper Silesians were rich, so rich that just before World War I seven of the ten richest men in Germany were industrialists and land barons from Upper Silesia, the list being led by Prince Henckel von Donnersmarck, Duke Hohenlohe, and the Prince of Pless.[13]

From a different angle, advances in agricultural technology, like the use of chemical fertilizers, the changeover to the four-field system, and the introduction of the threshing machine served to displace the small rural freeholder and landless laborer. Enclosure did not uproot Upper Silesian peasants so much as it did peasants in Lower Silesia, Saxony, and East Prussia, but a rising rate of natural increase of population after the mid-1850s certainly put pressure on the amount of land available to small farmers.[14]

This "push" from the countryside had in truth existed earlier in the century, but only after 1860 or so did there exist any kind of "pull" from industry to accommodate the mass of rural unemployed and underemployed and seasonal migrant laborers. The very inarticulateness of this social stratum makes it practically impossible to gauge exactly any continuing psychological attachment of new industrial workers to agriculture except through behavior that indicates a preference for the old order, and here the situation is complicated by changing patterns of supply of and demand for labor. In the Upper Silesian business crises of 1873, 1882, and 1893 industrial production declined, and workers either were laid off or could work short weeks only.[15] No doubt many workers found refuge in agricultural employment, but one cannot say that psychological longing drove them out of urban areas. As a matter of fact, by the 1890s even temporary unemployment or migration to another region tended to be more acceptable in Upper Silesia than returning to the farm, as evidenced in the emigration of a number of strikers from the Rybnik region in 1897 and again from several regions in 1913.[16]

On the other hand, the possibility of industrial workers' finding shelter in agricultural employment might be a sign of an incomplete break with the past, but this possibility is ambiguous because it may indicate a lack of opportunities for industrial employment. The great strike of 1913, to be described in more detail in chapter 9, provided examples of workers returning to their farms or to general farm work in order to ride out the crisis. Thus the Kattowitzer AG für Bergbau und Eisenhüttenbetrieb reported losing thirty-five men at the Neu Przemsa mine and fifty men (6 percent of the crew) at the Carlessegen mine. The report went on: "At the present time these people are occupied with cultivating their fields, but will certainly return to mine work in increasing numbers."[17] Industrial work was an integral part of the lives of these workers, but they were close enough to the countryside to take refuge there if necessary.

It would be extremely difficult to determine exactly how many people worked simultaneously in both agriculture and heavy industry, but some indirect evidence is to be culled from the occupational censuses of 1882, 1895, and 1907. From these, it becomes apparent that the number of people engaged in agricultural activity and in other occupations at the same time was quite large, a point that bears out what has been said about the nonviable nature of local agricultural holdings.

The Upper Silesian heavy industrial region can be subdivided into the predominantly industrial counties (Beuthen, Zabrze, and Kattowitz in 1882, later Tarnowitz, and the urban counties of Gleiwitz, Beuthen-city, Königshütte, and Kattowitz-city) and the partially industrialized counties (Tost-Gleiwitz, Tarnowitz [1882 only], Pless, and Rybnik). In 1882 the number of people claiming agriculture as an auxiliary occupation (*Nebenerwerb*) ranged from one-fourth to one-eighth of the total agricultural population in all the counties.[18] In mining and smelting (*Bergbau, Hüttenbetrieb, Salz- und Torfgewinnung*) the transitional nature of the situation was even sharper.[19] In the industrial counties, over 15 percent of the workers had an auxiliary occupation; in the partially industrialized counties, the number approached 50 percent of all mining and smelting workers based on (Table 4). Clearly, the labor force in heavy industry was still in a primitive stage if so many workers needed second jobs to support themselves (or chose to have second jobs). Indeed, this reliance on a part-time labor force indicates the rudimentary nature of a heavy industry which could be carried on with so unsteady a work force. This combination of circumstances favored the industrialists even more than the hypothetical case of "unlimited supplies of labor," in which wages at least a certain amount above subsistence level have to be paid in order to draw people out of agriculture into industrial work. Here, the pauperized local population probably needed both industrial wages and a second source of income for survival; they were on the one hand drawn into industry, on the other forced to remain in agriculture.

TABLE 4

Number of Workers in Primary and Auxiliary Occupations[a] in the Upper Silesian Industrial Region, 1882

| County | Primary Occupation | | | |
| | Mining and smelting | | Agriculture | |
	With auxiliary occupation	Without auxiliary occupation	With auxiliary occupation	Without auxiliary occupation
Beuthen	2,220	20,906	456	2,859
Zabrze	1,743	8,404	552	1,672
Kattowitz	2,849	14,356	397	3,025
Tarnowitz	3,026	4,622	1,017	3,432
Pless	1,513	1,731	4,202	20,784
Rybnik	1,013	812	3,908	15,917
Tost-Gleiwitz	1,086	2,075	3,033	15,895
Total	13,450	52,906	13,565	63,584

SOURCE: *Preussische Statistik* 76:1 (occupational census of 1882), pp. 313–316.
[a]*Haupterwerb* and *Nebenerwerb* (Center of industrial region: Beuthen, Zabrze, Kattowitz).

For 1882 more exact figures are also available, but only by regency, not by county. There were almost 69,000 workers in mining and smelting that year in Oppeln regency (Table 5), about 60,000 of whom the census found in the more narrowly defined industrial region. Of the overall total in these heavy industries, close to 14,000 had auxiliary occupations (agriculture in most cases). In addition, only about 1,000 people listed mining and smelting as an auxiliary occupation. Even if all 9,000 mining and smelting workers outside the industrial region had auxiliary occupations, some 6,000 (10 percent) of the workers in the industrial region itself were employed in a second occupation. In reality there must have been more than 10 percent in this category. It is apparent that Upper Silesian mining and smelting of the 1870s and early 1880s was still in the transitional state of using large numbers of part-time workers; one cannot yet speak of a fully formed industrial labor force.

The timing of Upper Silesian industrial development more or less corresponded with general German trends after the middle of the nineteenth century—big spurts in the 1850s, the early 1870s, and a significant expansion of production from the 1890s until 1914. More active railroads, larger cities, expanded steel production, chemical industries—everywhere a demand for power, which was supplied

TABLE 5

Number of Mining and Smelting Workers with
Auxiliary Occupations in Oppeln Regency, 1882

Total	With auxiliary occupations	With auxiliary occupations in agriculture
68,740	14,695	14,468
		(12,682 independent peasants; 1,786 others)

SOURCE: *Statistik des Deutschen Reiches,* new series, 4:1 (occupational census of 1882), pp. 90–91, 102–103, 120–121, 280–281.

almost exclusively by coal. Moreover, the advancing German economy depended heavily on metal-refining industries, which also were prospering in Upper Silesia by the late 1890s. Steel production in particular expanded from the late 1890s on because local industry had finally grown large enough to generate the scrap metal necessary to feed the area's indispensable Martin furnaces. There is no need to expatiate further on the German economy, but one should note that Upper Silesia, while losing ground relative to the Ruhr and foreign competitors, experienced an unprecedented multiplication of goods produced and workers employed. These trends were apparent in the occupational census of 1895 and even more clearly in that of 1907.

The changing demand had obvious effects on the supply of labor. Measures like those of 1882 are not available for individual counties for 1895 and 1907, but certain other information is available. From these later censuses one can learn how many people claimed mining and smelting or agriculture as their primary occupation and how many listed these as auxiliary occupations; there is no way of knowing how many workers in industry or agriculture also had an auxiliary occupation, as is possible on the basis of 1882 returns.

In 1895 the counties fell into the same two groups of industrial and partially industrial, except that Tarnowitz was rapidly becoming an industrial county. In both groups, the number of auxiliary mining and smelting workers was negligible—fewer than 1,000 out of a total of over 90,000 workers, and a large portion of these were to be found in Rybnik, a peripheral low-wage area with only a rudimentary mining industry. Peasants and agricultural workers, on the other hand, were very active in auxiliary jobs. In the partially industrialized counties, such "moonlighters" far outnumbered those without auxiliary jobs, indicating that independent farming was growing increasingly less viable economically or that rapid population growth was leading to an ever more impoverished agricultural labor force. Heavy industry, especially mining, had by now grown large enough and after 1889 was paying high enough wages to independently attract workers from agriculture.

Agriculture as a way of life became ever rarer in the industrial counties, which remained central to industrial employment throughout the prewar era; but these were joined after 1890 by newly developing areas to the north and south as demonstrated in Table 6. By 1895 Tarnowitz had joined the fully industrial counties as an area where there were more people agriculturally employed with auxiliary occupations than without. Rybnik, hitherto merely a feeder area to the inner industrial region, became something of a mining center after 1900, and by 1907 here too the peasants and agricultural workers with auxiliary occupations were beginning to outnumber their counterparts working full time in agriculture. As in 1895, so in 1907 the number of industrial workers engaged in other jobs was insignificant (tables 6 and 7). Even on the agriculturally oriented periphery the number of mining and smelting workers with auxiliary occupations was miniscule, indicating a sizable "modern labor force" as measured by the proportion of workers committed to industrially disciplined work.

TABLE 6

Number of Workers in Primary and Auxiliary Occupations in the Upper Silesian Industrial Region,[a] 1895

	Mining and Smelting		Agriculture	
County	As primary occupation	As auxiliary occupation	As primary occupation	As auxiliary occupation
Beuthen City	4,230	10	275	585
Beuthen Country	28,773	153	2,087	4,020
Zabrze	15,193	74	1,928	4,121
Kattowitz	22,379	98	3,074	6,188
Tarnowitz	8,659	77	3,643	6,829
Tost-Gleiwitz	4,552	101	15,790	6,440
Pless	3,754	96	22,955	10,367
Rybnik	3,752	370	17,827	9,525

Source: *Statistik des Deutschen Reiches* 109 (occupational census of 1895), pp. 159–166.
[a]Center of industrial region: Beuthen, Zabrze, Kattowitz; Tarnowitz transitional.

After 1890 the situation of Upper Silesian agriculture as a whole improved, thanks to more intensive cultivation of root crops and the increased use of chemical fertilizer, but such advances were generally out of the reach of the holders of tiny farms of the industrial region because they could not generate the capital necessary to make the switchover. It proved to be a good deal easier to take up mining and smelting as a primary or auxiliary occupation.

TABLE 7

Number of Workers in Primary and Auxiliary Occupations in the
Upper Silesian Industrial Region,[a] 1907

County	Mining and Smelting		Agriculture	
	As primary occupation	As auxiliary occupation	As primary occupation	As auxiliary occupation
Beuthen City	6,809	17	252	392
Königshütte	10,975	57	591	52
Beuthen Country	37,907	251	1,988	5,771
Zabrze	24,671	193	2,066	4,670
Kattowitz City	1,917	9	66	194
Kattowitz Country	34,882	324	2,669	7,233
Tarnowitz	10,978	63	4,368	10,930
Gleiwitz	2,329	41	312	287
Tost-Gleiwitz	3,215	50	16,972	9,564
Pless	6,076	196	32,227	9,924
Rybnik	3,752	370	19,156	19,453

SOURCE: *Statistik des Deutschen Reiches* 159 (occupational census of 1907), pp. 176–186.
[a]Center of industrial region: Beuthen, Königshütte, Zabrze, Kattowitz, Gleiwitz, Tarnowitz.

No wonder then that agrarian romantics[20] loudly bemoaned the passing of an agrarian dream, a vision perpetuated in Upper Silesia primarily by minor bureaucrats and German free professionals. This obeisance to a disappearing order found vivid expression in the complaint of an elementary school principal in 1902 that the new pupils in his care lacked even the most rudimentary knowledge of rural life. Of sixty-three entering little boys, seventeen had never even seen a cow, but most had a good picture of mining and smelting. All this in an area where but a generation earlier the town administration of Königshütte had complained of the daily befouling of the streets by herds of cattle![21]

The point of this brief presentation has been to show the decline of the agricultural ties of industrial workers and the concomitant growing dependence of agricultural workers and peasants on outside employment in Upper Silesia. This transformation was only part of the "flight from the land" experienced by German agriculture in the nineteenth century. True, sheep raising, at its highest point in Silesia in the 1840s, and the general turn to labor-intensive beet sugar cultivation around the middle of the century had not affected the numerous smallholders in the Upper Silesian industrial region so much as they had other areas, including the Lower Silesian fertile plain. It is also true that a large landless rural proletariat did not dominate Upper Silesia in the fashion of other eastern German areas

and that Upper Silesia continued to be marked by a large number
of dwarf farms (under two dectares) in the years from 1882 to 1907;
and only the right bank counties of Upper Silesia (including the
industrial region) witnessed no growth of large holdings in this period,
a trend associated elsewhere with enclosure and the demise of small
farms.[22] Despite all these statistical indications that the peasant
emancipation and large-scale capitalist farming had not uprooted the
peasant in Upper Silesia, it is clear that by the 1880s the local rural
surplus population was well on its way to becoming a part of an
industrial economy. Rural overpopulation was striking Upper Silesia
as well as most other agricultural areas of Germany in the nineteenth
century, and parcelization of the land without a downward shift in
the rate of the growth of population could mean only growing
economic misery in the countryside. Various areas have solved similar
problems in diverse ways: France witnessed a significant decline in
birth rates after the mid-nineteenth century; Galicia experienced a
wholesale emigration to the United States and to western Europe
toward the end of the century. In Upper Silesia—particularly in Polish
Upper Silesia—such drastic population displacement was not needed,
for the demands of industry sufficed to absorb most of those leaving
the land.

Extensive landholdings on the part of new industrial recruits may
have hindered formation of a modern industrial labor force, but it
could not halt the occupational restructuring of Upper Silesia. The
Ruhr also used workers recently removed from agriculture, but the
arrival of numerous long-distance migrants indicates that wages and
working conditions in the west were sufficiently attractive for workers to stay permanently in mining and smelting; certainly there was
no question of the numerous landholders from the east, primarily
from East Prussia, turning to agriculture.[23] In Upper Silesia, on the
other hand, sticky wages and an almost unlimited supply of labor
on the local scene in the first decades of free enterprise mining resulted
in a specific mode and rate of transition from an agricultural way
of life to an industrial one. Yet, even here continuing ties to the
land by masses of smallholders was a moribund phenomenon, as
illustrated by the occupational censuses of 1882, 1895, and 1907.

Landless Agricultural Laborers Leave the Land

Landless agricultural laborers were the most obvious choices to run
the expanding mines of Upper Silesia. As noted earlier, they were
no newcomers to the mines and smelters in the 1870s. After the
peasant emancipation of 1807, some landless rural workers worked
in industry at least part of the year, and after the final emancipatory
settlement of 1850 they moved in increasing numbers to at least

seasonal industrial employment.[24] Many of those involved worked only a few months of each year (between potato harvest and spring planting); and the mines in the 1850s continued to experience sizable seasonal influxes of agricultural laborers.[25]

The 1850s, however, also were the time of increasingly severe pressure of overpopulation in the countryside. There had been no remedy to that pressure in the 1840s other than typhus epidemics and short-term employment in railway construction; now industry began to make available extensive occupational opportunities, and in the subsequent period of industrial growth large numbers of landless laborers joined the work force. It is hard to know how many of these people worked on the farm in the summer and in the mines and smelters in the winter, but it can be said that once such a laborer joined the industrial labor force for more than a short period, he tended to stay, provided that adequate family housing was available (see chapter 6). For example, in the occupational census of 1882, only about 1,800 mining and smelting workers in the entire Oppeln regency claimed to have auxiliary occupations as farm laborers;[26] that is, once the move to industry had been made, not many landless workers were tempted into agriculture, even in a slump year like 1882.

Moreover, in the inner industrial region most men hired were probably completely free of property ties to the land, as illustrated by sporadic archival references. For a short time records at some mines included a notation of landholding. At the Fanny mine of the Hohenlohe works in Kattowitz county, only fifteen of the two hundred workers hired in 1881-1882 were landowners,[27] and this was long before extensive company housing was available.

More than likely, some returned to agriculture primarily when employment fell in mining and smelting. In 1891, for instance, total employment in Upper Silesian heavy industry dropped by about 2,500 workers in comparison to the preceding year; smelting workers were particularly hard hit by the layoffs and the shortened work week. At the same time, complaints of a shortage of agricultural labor declined. One must conclude that the furloughed workers had gone over to agriculture, thus swelling the ranks of those who annually made such a move. Two years later, a tariff war with Russia led to high unemployment in smelting, and a number of younger workers turned quite naturally to agricultural day labor for employment. Again in 1894 and 1897 a number of women workers who had returned from the Rybnik mines traveled to central Germany for the beet sugar harvest.[28]

Annual reports on the state of heavy industry in Upper Silesia give the definite impression that management tried to curb this shifting of employment by instituting shorter work weeks in slack periods rather than laying off workers. Nevertheless, wavering between the two areas of activity did not completely end before the advent of World War I. As late as 1911 the Higher Mining Office reported that the onset of good weather continued to mean that in some areas a number of miners would leave for agricultural and construction work. However, in the years after 1896, even when business was bad, there was generally such a shortage of the easily trained haulers that there were enough jobs for any agricultural workers who wanted them. It is significant that after 1890 almost all examples of such swings between the two occupations come from Rybnik and Pless counties, both of which have been noted as only partially industrialized and as paying the lowest industrial wages in the region.[29] While opportunities for agricultural employment declined to a very low level in the central industrial area, these two counties continued to be characterized by large agricultural sectors and by poorly developed mining industries. One should then conclude that labor market conditions suffice to explain a good deal of this presumably "anti-industrial" behavior, and there is no need to rely solely on explanations based on a longing for an agrarian way of life.

From 1905 on, swinging from industry to agriculture and back characterized primarily the foreign workers. Of these the Ruthenians were not subject to the waiting period, and they immediately became part of the pool of potential sedentary workers. Drawn from purely agricultural areas, these newcomers to industry were highly unreliable, and there were cases of mass switches from industry to agriculture. Yet these industrially very backward people soon in large measure came to adjust to industrial employment. It became quite common for Ruthenians to come to work in industry, quit and run away for a few weeks, and then return on a more or less permanent basis.[30]

Little detailed information on the life chances of landless laborers survives, but one agricultural worker who turned to mining but never became fully committed to his new work has related his experiences.[31] Born in Ratibor county in 1874, Antoni Podeszwa followed his six brothers to Westphalia in search of work in 1889; even though it was easy enough to get work in the 1880s in Upper Silesian mining, working conditions were bad and wages low. At first the local landowner would not let him go, claiming that labor was needed in the home area. Since the landowner also happened to be a local government official, an appeal to higher authority was necessary to overrule this continued arbitrary exercise of Junker police power. Podeszwa worked in Ruhr mining for seventeen years, but having saved 4,000 marks, he returned to Upper Silesia in 1906 and set himself up as an independent farmer. Clearly, he always had regarded his stint in the west as something temporary. Even though he had become involved enough in his new setting to join the Polish miners' union, he had never stopped dreaming of a return to the land. This biographical sketch, although dealing with a move to Westphalia, illustrates well some of the psychological barriers to the formation of an industrial labor force. If a man could go far away from the family hom and still return to farming after so many years in the mines, it can be imagined how strong was the attraction of the land to many mining and smelting workers who stayed in their local area after leaving agricultural vocations. The example given, however, represents the rare case, where psychological longing for a passing world became translated into action. Nonetheless, something must be added to the story. Presumably Podeszwa's brothers did not return to a peasant existence, making him an exceptional case; and even he worked sporadically in the Rybnik mines after settling down on his new homestead. Thus his formal mobility into the ranks of property owners did not signify his obtaining an economically viable farm holding and did not remove him entirely from the industrial labor force, but his new position does illustrate the difficulties encountered in bringing part-time peasants into the industrial sector full time.

Employers were not necessarily averse to having employees who had side interests in agriculture. In fact, management was even willing to lease out to workers small units of land from large tracts originally acquired to prevent law suits for damage due to mining-related land subsidence; this practice was intended to attach formerly landless men to a particular mine or smelter. However, the percentage of total workers who could be accommodated with these plots was piteously small in the 1880s. There were some 70,000 to 75,000 industrial workers in 1890, but the largest programs of this sort encompassed only 600 workers at the König mine, another 600 at the installations of the Oberschlesischer Eisenbahnbedarf AG, and 650 for Hugo-Artur-Lazy Henckel von Donnersmarck enterprises. Even the giant Vereinigte Königs- und Laurahütte leased only 300 plots to its workers. After 1890 the program became less important. The Prussian government, for instance, was one of the largest employers involved in such leasing, but only about 9 percent of all its Upper Silesian employees—1,533 of 17,600—participated in the program in 1906.[32]

Friedrich Bernhardi, long-time general director of Georg von Giesches Erben (coal and zinc mining) and head of the association of Upper Silesian mining and smelting employers, expressed a widespread employer view of the activity of industrial workers in agriculture as a stabilizing element in industry;[33] this opinion has not died out yet. Scholars dealing with the Ruhr and with the central Saxon mining region have more recently continued to voice the opinion that ties to the soil made the local population less mobile and therefore more reliable as a supply of workers.[34] However, these writers err in their equation of local immobility of peasant-workers with a dependable work force. In point of fact, these workers were particularly lacking in industrial discipline and not valuable in stemming the fluctuating pattern of employment in heavy industry. The course of development in Upper Silesia indicates that the fewer the connections with landowning, the more likely were the workers to remain permanently employed in industry.

Landholding Peasants in Industry

Some 20 to 30 percent of peasant holdings were viable economically;[35] their owners and lessors will not be considered separately here because it is assumed that very few of these farmers turned to industrial employment. Cities and urban life in Upper Silesia did not provide great social attractions for the local peasantry; only economic considerations could have drawn this relatively prosperous group into the mines and smelters. However, if industry must offer a wage somewhat higher than that of agriculture to attract recruits from the countryside, in this case such a transfer price would have had to be inordinately high to compensate for the loss of adequate income, landholding status, and a presumably satisfactory way of life. During the 1860s, 1870s, and 1880s, the labor market approached the condition of unlimited supply and had no need of this group; but even after the late 1880s, when management bemoaned its labor shortage, there was never a need so great as to require raising wages to this very high level. Thus in speaking of landowners turning to industrial employment, one can safely restrict oneself to that group with economically nonviable holdings.

Before the renewed surge of the 1890s, landless agricultural laborers were the prime candidates for transfer from agriculture to industry, but even in this period of relative labor surplus recruits also were to be had from the ranks of owners and lessees of dwarf farm holdings. These people were in all likelihood interested merely in augmenting their farm earnings, not in going full time into industrial employment; their farms at least provided them with a sure dwelling place and the security of a seemingly traditional way of life. Moreover, extra income was to be earned not only through the mining and smelting industries, in which industrialists had not yet broken through the illusion that only low wages would keep workers on the job, but also in the ubiquitous construction and foodstuffs industries. Ironically, the smallholders held land, a condition which made them resistant to industrial employment; but they also possessed dwellings near the sites of production, and they required additional income, a set of conditions that made them prime candidates for industrial employment.

The boundary between viable and nonviable holdings lay at around five hectares. Below this point it was practically impossible to subsist from one's own produce, a situation obvious in the statistic that in 1907 80 percent of the holders of "dwarf" farms in Oppeln regency (under two hectares) worked their own property as an auxiliary occupation only.[36] By the census of 1907 more than half of all farms in Oppeln regency were dwarf holdings. Obviously such peasants had to sell their labor in order to subsist on the land. In Breslau regency peasants in an analogous position worked on large farms; in southern Oppeln, which was not marked by capitalistic agriculture, they perforce turned to industry. In all three regencies of Silesia the trend was toward the owners of dwarf holdings to be employed primarily in industry, handicraft, and trade; but Oppeln by far showed the greatest concentration of peasants as employees in the non-agricultural sector.[37] In addition, whereas in 1895 28 percent of these men were independent farmers and 28 percent employees in the non-agricultural sector, by 1907 only 20 percent were chiefly farmers and 36 percent were employees outside of agriculture. The same trend is apparent elsewhere in the province, but nowhere to the extent found in Oppeln.

Furthermore, the territory at issue here constituted only one part of Oppeln. Prussian statistics do not allow a breakdown into counties on this point, but all other indicators point to the area of the Upper Silesian industrial labor market as being marked even more noticeably by such small plots.

The pattern of employment in these cases resembles that in other industrializing areas, both European and non-European:[38] devotion to subsistence agriculture coupled with winter industrial employment, or else more or less steady work in industry by one or more members of the family while the others tend the farm. Before 1890 employers complained about excessive labor turnover, which was often caused by harvest and other farming obligations. In August, 1863, for example, the shortage of miners became acute because ". . . the harvest period claimed a large group of workers and animals for hauling to the detriment of coal transport."[39] In addition, this complaint of the Higher Mining Office went on, a significant number of miners switched back and forth between field work and mining work. One cannot definitely know that all these workers held some plot of land, but the withdrawal of draft animals from mining work indicates that a sizable group could be classified as peasants with nonviable holdings who needed to hire out their animals to make ends meet.

As time went on, of course, the younger generation gave up on the small plots. Thus Josef Gatzki, partially disabled from his days as a smelter worker, in September, 1913, broke his leg while mining coal. Consequently, he could not bring in the harvest on his farm; and his son, employed at the Friedrich smelter, had to ask permission to return to the farm to help his father. Here is a case of the father in industry but hanging on to the old homestead while the son had moved full time to industrial work, going back to agriculture only in an emergency.[40]

On the other hand, management policies were not always geared toward the proclaimed ends of a stable labor force. Although employers apparently considered "peasant-industrial workers" as beneficial to their enterprises, a governmental commission studying the miners' strike of 1889 reported that the industrial wages of the 1880s were often so low that it was difficult to survive without additional earnings from farm work. At least some workers were aware of this dependency, and the leading Polish newspaper spoke of bitterness about management's brushing aside demands for higher pay with the comment that workers did not need high earnings because their plots of land were sufficient to support them. Even after the wage hikes of 1889, employees in mining areas on the edges of the region, such as in Mittel-Lazisk in Pless, were assumed to be able to supplement their niggardly wages with food they raised themselves—not a vast improvement over the 1860s, when a majority of miners in such areas needed home-grown potatoes and a pig to survive.[41] Such an approach —reliance on agricultural income to make up for low wages—was definitely not conducive to the formation of a full-time, all-year labor force; yet employers were loathe to abandon this notion formulated in earlier years.

The extent of the involvement of industrial workers in agriculture in the 1880s was portrayed in a very useful survey made by the local urban and rural administrative officers in 1890.[42] (See Table 8 for a breakdown by county.) At that time, some 17 percent (12,300) of all mining and smelting workers in Upper Silesia engaged in arable farming, and a few thousand more were tending kitchen gardens. About 30 percent of this group of farmer-workers owned their own land; 40 percent leased their land from the mines and smelters; and 30 percent leased their land from other private parties. Even a cursory glance at the distribution of homes and fields among workers indicates that the inner industrial area had already purged itself of a transitional labor force; Tarnowitz in the census of 1895 would show a similar trend. Only Pless, Rybnik, and the Tost area (north of Gleiwitz) carried over into the twentieth century a significant population of mining and smelting workers with strong ties to agriculture.

In general, it may be said that the more rural the area, the greater the percentage of industrial workers with ties to agriculture. Continuing a pattern noticeable in the 1870s, wages during the great expansion at the end of the nineteenth and at the beginning of the twentieth centuries remained especially low in the Nikolai (Pless) and Rybnik-Ratibor areas, a policy which was justified by managers by benefits

TABLE 8

Percentage of Peasant-Industrial Workers in the Upper Silesian
Industrial Region, 1890

| | Male mining and smelting workers | | |
County	Owned home	Owned fields	Owned animals
Rybnik (Industrial Area)	37.2	49.5	36.0
Tarnowitz (industrial Area)	30.6	37.7	25.1
Pless (Industrial Area)	22.4	40.0	22.5
Tost-Gleiwitz (Industrial Area)	13.1	15.7	5.8
Zabrze	11.2	18.3	3.5
Kattowitz	9.2	14.8	3.5
Beuthen City	7.8	9.3	2.2
Beuthen Country	4.5	3.2	1.5

SOURCE: Sattig, "Über die Arbeiterwohnungsverhältnisse im oberschlesischen Industriebezirk," ZOBH, 31 (1892):21, based on reports of local administrative officials.

in the form of "agricultural auxiliary occupations, cheap living costs ..., cheap housing in buildings owned by the mineowners, leasing of cultivable land, rent-free land for root crops, etc."[43] In the industrial portion of Rybnik county (westernmost county of the area) almost half of all workers also had their own fields to take care of, but in centrally located Zabrze county only 18 percent did so and in Beuthen, the oldest industrial county, only 3 percent. These relationships held true for home ownership and ownership of animals as well—the more industrial the county, the less closely connected to agriculture was the labor force.

Perhaps the most revealing of the relationships illustrated in Table 8 is the degree of ownership of animals by industrial workers. A farmer with no animal had but a tiny piece of land, perhaps sufficient to scratch out an increment to his income; only a larger plot, and even here not very large, would support an animal. In the 1890 survey under discussion, about 25 percent of all male mining and smelting workers (about 20,000 men) owned some animal, but only 5,000 of these had cows, the animal indispensable to any kind of independent agricultural existence.[44] Goat or pig ownership indicated that the family in question had essentially no land for farming. Only in Rybnik, Tarnowitz, and Pless did considerable numbers of workers own animals, and again and again down to the time of the First World War, these regions, especially Rybnik and Pless, figure as the mining and smelting areas most oriented to agriculture.

It is probably true that the Silesian miner before 1914 "was not completely torn away from his peasant roots," but it is also true that agricultural opportunities for mining and smelting workers had been declining before the 1890s and grew even less propitious afterwards. Often enough, ties to agriculture remained only in the guise of a tiny kitchen garden or in the form of keeping a goat, the "miner's cow." It seems then misleading to claim, as do some Polish cultural anthropologists, that "the problem of tilling land or raising animals continued to be one of the chief elements in the life of a miner."[45] No matter what kitchen gardens or farm animals or dwarf plots were possessed by mining and smelting workers, their industrial vocations were in the great majority of cases mere sidelines. Only by choosing exceptional examples can one justify the notion of the basically agricultural orientation of Upper Silesian miners.

In sum, one can hardly say that a desire to return to agricultural employment was the dominant theme of the Upper Silesian mining and smelting labor force. The behavior of the new workers (as opposed to the values imputed to them) indicates that industrial work was preferable, if only because more of it was available. Before the late 1880s, a reserve army of unemployed and underemployed rural citizens prolonged the ties between agricultural and industrial ways of life; later on, shifts to agriculture usually were induced by temporary unemployment (layoffs or strikes), not by desperate longing for a passing world. Perhaps these workers were only external conformists, "... whose performance remains satisfactory only so long as immediately available bribes and discipline suffice to win ... their compliance,"[46] but such is the stuff of which industrial labor forces are made.

True, the agricultural proclivities of at least a section of the labor force at times prevented a general commitment by some to industrial labor. On the other hand, farming was not only not preferred by workers in some cases; in both Upper Silesia and the Ruhr it was even forced on them at certain times and places by employer wage policies, especially by the low wages of areas with large agricultural populations.[47] Although the smelting labor force was also marked by these swings from one area of employment to another, it was less affected than was mining. In the 1870s and 1880s the low demand for semi-finished metal goods did not require a sizable force of metalworkers; by its very nature the industry could be run on the basis of a small skilled force supplemented by seasonal workers not acclimated to factory discipline. The layoffs of 1893 show how natural it still was for furloughed smelter workers to take jobs in agriculture.[48] However, the general business upturn after 1896 and the qualitative surge of Upper Silesian refining industries at the turn of the century meant that a more reliable labor force had to be present in order to meet the rapidly increasing market demand for high-quality goods.

Part of the answer to this need was the previously mentioned attempt to import skilled German workers from outside Silesia. There were not large numbers of them, but they were people who were presumably involved in industrial work and who had no connections to local agricultural holdings. In this sense, the industrialists framed these particular hiring policies well. Nonetheless, the outsiders were few, and local workers remained the basis of the work force; the latter, too, proved able to swiftly cut their ties to agricultural employment when adequate opportunities in industry were available.

It appears then that by the late 1890s and certainly by 1914 the phenomenon of laborers wavering between agriculture and industry was dying out. Bolstered by a generally expanding economy, Upper Silesian heavy industry was able to employ practically all those who applied, except temporarily during short cyclical recessions. At the same time, labor market pressures demanded the large-scale provision of rental housing and forced up the wages of most workers so that families could be supported—with difficulty, to be sure—by industrial labor alone. Most historians of Prussia and Germany have tradition-ally outlined the results of the peasant emancipation in terms of shifts of legal status, but it has seemed more fruitful to go beyond the common cut-off date of 1850 for an understanding of how the two systems of stratification of serf society, legal and economic, became transformed in a new legal and economic setting into a new social arrangement.

5

Recruitment of the Labor Force

Recruitment of a labor force in industrializing situations is not merely a function of communications about vacancies in factories and mines. Employers need to make strenuous efforts to draw workers into new roles; in the European context this was usually done through the medium of higher wages. W. Arthur Lewis built this situation into his model by suggesting that the wage level in industry must stand somewhat higher than that in agriculture. However, it is reasonable to assume that to draw newcomers from long distances, companies need to offer other benefits, such as good housing facilities and favorable working conditions. For Upper Silesian employers, the task became even more difficult because of competition from the Ruhr and from the Berlin area; in a way the effectiveness of such recruitment is a measure of the "modernization" of local managers. This chapter and the next are attempts to gauge this effectiveness in Upper Silesia. The Ruhr basin expanded more or less simultaneously with Upper Silesia. In the west German area, until the 1840s sons of local miners were favored in hiring and formed a large part of the work force; by the 1850s, however, employers had to reach out into the neighboring provinces, and in the 1870s to the Prussian east. By the end of the century, foreign workers were being imported in large numbers to fill out the crews. Of the Rhenish-Westphalian industrial population in 1905, over 30 percent were born in Westphalia and 50 percent in Rhineland; this contrasted markedly with 96 percent Silesian born among the Upper Silesian industrial population.[1]

In England, industrial work forces were built up at first on the basis of local supplies, for the high rate of population increase created a ready stock of rural laborers anxious for employment. When local agricultural workers moved into industry, others from farther away filled in the gaps in the countryside left by the first migrants; later the newcomers, too, moved into industry. Even the railroads did not change this pattern; their major effect at first was to induce more people to migrate short distances, but in the course of time long-distance shifts marked British population movements into industrial regions. Even more clearly in the United States, where mass immigration from distant lands formed a substantial segment of the industrial labor force in the latter part of the nineteenth century, the local labor market proved inadequate, and large numbers of outsiders had to be brought in. And in supposedly static India, about which many have long argued that the prevailing ideology and social institutions would not permit long-distance migration, distant supplies of labor were mobilized.[2]

By way of contrast, Upper Silesia never succeeded in reaching beyond its own narrow territory to attract masses of workers. With the exception of foreign seasonal labor, significant only after 1900, this far-away corner of Prussia succeeded in drawing only the local inhabitants for the formation of a modern industrial labor force. Shut off from a hinterland of unemployed or underemployed Slavic masses, unattractive to denizens of other Prussian provinces and German states, Upper Silesian heavy industry was forced to depend on the fecundity of the local (primarily Polish-speaking) population.

Recruitment Prior to the 1860s

The shortage of labor outlined in chapter 2 was not novel to Upper Silesia in the late nineteenth century; indeed, the pre-industrial and early industrial periods everywhere are usually seen as times when skilled labor is in very short supply.[3]

Frederick the Great had been very much interested in developing the mining and metal industries of Silesia. In 1769 the king issued a revised mining statute, which included the management principle (*Direktionsprinzip*), under which the state effectively controlled the running of all mines; the state was also to exercise strict supervision over iron smelting.[4] In this same year the government issued a *Generalprivilegium für die Bergleute in Schlesien*, a decree relating more directly to the problem of recruiting workers. All men taking oaths as members of the miner brotherhood (*Knappschaft*) were granted a number of privileges, including freedom from personal serfdom and freedom from service in the army. Sometimes it happened that a peasant in a difficult economic position managed to move into mining as a way of solving his economic problems and of purging himself of servile obligations. The privileges accorded to miners, naturally opposed by local landlords who stood to lose some of the services due them under manorial law, were to last only so long as the miners remained in mining.

These directives were affirmed in the Prussian General Code of 1794: "The hiring and firing of mining and smelting workers, supervisors and other employees is reserved for the mining officials."[5] Thus in a way the workers were quasi-government employees, and even though in 1816 they lost their freedom from taxation and exemption from military service, they still retained other benefits of the miner brotherhood (job security, welfare payments, prestige). In general, these decrees made the pre-industrial mining and smelting workers ". . . a privileged stratum which often stood above artisanry."[6]

Often the men working in the mines did not achieve the privileged status of "miner"; a good number remained bound by various ties of seigneurial duties. This was no novelty, for many western countries have used unfree labor in mining and manufacturing: the possessional serfs in pre-1861 Russia, industrial slaves in the United States, quasi-serf miners in eighteenth-century Scotland. Similarly, in Upper Silesian mining and smelting before 1807, the methods of mining and metal refining were so primitive that serf labor could be used profitably. Seigneurial magnates tended to use such unfree labor in their smelting works, which were not under such close governmental control as the mines.[7] Often enough, serfs were allowed by their lords to work in the mines and smelters during the winter but were recalled to the land when needed for agricultural work. The government mining office, as the major employer of free industrial labor, exerted its strength to draw such rural figures permanently into mining and smelting by holding out the advantages of membership in the mining brotherhood. As a result, the flow of serfs into mining, based on the records of the royal Friedrich smelter and Friedrich mine, was steady even before the end of serfdom, despite the opposition of the landowners.[8]

Free skilled labor was harder to come by. The Silesia of Frederick the Great was sparsely populated; Upper Silesia in particular was regarded as semi-wild, "Far from cultured men, at the edge of the Empire" (Goethe). Even many "uncultured" people hesitated to move there, as evidenced by repeated complaints of a shortage of skilled labor. This was a problem common to much of Prussia in the seventeenth and eighteenth centuries, and one can find many examples of mining and smelting installations in Upper Silesia having such difficulties.[9] The royal holdings—smelters at Gleiwitz, Friedrichshütte, Malapane, and Kreuzburg (the last two outside the later industrial region), and mines at Friedrichshütte and Königsgrube—were pioneers in importing workers from outside the area. In spite of the governmental attempt to provide adequate living quarters, the rough living conditions and Polish-speaking native population made many of the newcomers leave soon after arriving. For example, mining officials brought in about 100 miners in 1792 from Mansfeld (central Germany) and from Poland, of whom 70 soon left. Actually, such German immigrants were often unruly, vandalous, and unreliable in their work, and many of them probably came to Upper Silesia in the first place because they had lost their previous jobs.[10]

For lack of any alternative, most of the workers hired, both before and after emancipation of the serfs, were Polish-speaking peasants from the local countryside and children of mining and smelting workers. These workers did not face the problems of finding new housing, learning a new language, or accommodating themselves to new living conditions; they remained where they had farmed, continued to speak Polish, and experienced no change in their living standards.[11]

No one, not even the most hardy German nationalist, doubts that the vast majority of the population of administrative Upper Silesia in the eighteenth century was Polish speaking.[12] Although the eighteenth-century administrators of the royal mines and smelters wished to attract skilled German workers, they found this so difficult that by the end of the century foremen (*Steiger*) and the chairman of the miner brotherhood were required to be able to speak Polish. At the royal smelters, conversely, German immigrants and the German language predominated. At certain mines, too, the proportion of Germans was high, but to give exact numbers is impossible.[13] Anyone who has looked at the lists of workers in Upper Silesia knows how difficult it is to differentiate Poles from Germans by their names alone. In any event, the age of xenophobic nationalism had not yet penetrated to Upper Silesia, and the question of Pole versus German had not yet assumed great importance.

The emancipation of the serfs which began in 1807 and the freedom of occupation decree of 1810 changed the basic legal framework for mining and smelting workers. Although quasi-serf labor lingered on long after the reforms (the Donnersmarck family was using unfree labor in its enterprises as late as 1825)[14] the labor market in the first half of the nineteenth century essentially concerned free men only. During these fifty years, real wages probably fell; production remained low, thus keeping demand for labor low; technology was primitive. The work force was small, but mining and smelting workers were often scarce; prisoners were even set to work in the mines. But even at this early date, later policy was adumbrated in the administrative desire to reduce the number of Poles as far as possible.[15] The institution of the miner brotherhood thrived; membership was attractive because job security, fringe benefits, and social prestige outweighed the low pay in a country where few alternative opportunities for non-agricultural employment existed. Still, living conditions in the nineteenth century were as discouraging to potential immigrants as they had been in the eighteenth.

In addition to those workers locally recruited and trained, new men were drawn from nearby areas in this first half of the nineteenth century: skilled workers from central Germany, unskilled workers from Galicia and from the area of the Grand Duchy of Warsaw.[16]

The Slavic workers did not have the linguistic problems that faced incoming Germans, and they had no great difficulty adjusting to the local standard of living.

Such was the setting in which Upper Silesian mining and smelting met the Industrial Revolution: low outputs of mining and smelting products; some cadres of miners (mainly Poles) and smelter workers (mainly Poles, with a noticeable minority of Germans); some cadres of German supervisors and foremen. Indeed, many of the characteristics of pre-industrial Upper Silesia recurred with renewed force after 1870: shortage of workers, low level of immigration, lack of housing, nationality differences.

Recruitment in the Industrial Age

In the 1850s and 1860s the Prussian state adopted a series of laws intended to fully modernize the mining and smelting industries of the country. Had these industries remained under shackles for the next several decades, the industrial development of Germany might have taken a very different course.[17] But these laws did not come too late. The Prussia of the 1850s was already experiencing an industrial revolution: railroads were leading the way; coal and zinc mining were starting to expand; joint-stock investment banking had emerged in 1848; agriculture was being overhauled thanks to a number of technical and technological innovations.[18] In addition to coal and zinc, the steel industry grew enormously, bolsteed by the great technological advances of the 1850s, 1860s, and 1870s.

The mining and smelting industries were "emancipated" at this time, and their labor forces became important parts of the new industrial economy. The new mining laws[19] abolished the management principle, and mining and smelting became essentially private industries with but spare supervision by the government. The effect on the labor force was tremendous, if somewhat delayed, but even in the 1850s younger miners had begun shying away from the miner brotherhoods because membership severely limited their occupational mobility. All miners were soon by law enjoined to belong to a brotherhood, but at least from 1865 on (enactment of the General Mining Law) the organizations served primarily as agencies for social welfare insurance, not as a framework for a separate stratum of society.

In broad terms, one might divide the period after the passage of the Prussian mining law into two: from the end of state control over mining and smelting in the 1860s to the late 1880s, and from around 1890 to World War I. This division reflects the varying demands for labor generated by the industries involved amidst the fluctuations of the business cycle and of long-run trends. The old labor force more or less sufficed in the 1860s, but expanding markets for capital goods required more and more mining and smelting workers in subsequent decades. Pressure on the labor supply intensified to an even higher degree around the turn of the twentieth century. Ordinarily, demand in the years of the so-called Great Depression (1873-1896) sufficed to prevent large-scale layoffs of workers. When layoffs did occur, as in the slump of 1875-1876,[20] workers were still close enough to the soil to return either to their own midget farms or to agricultural day labor. Short-term declines in business in the main occasioned part-time work weeks without many actual reductions in the total number of employed since it was the part-time, unskilled, and perhaps unwanted workers who were let go.

At times employers seemed to refrain intentionally from hiring new workers in order to maintain a close-knit group of employees; such may have been the case at the Hohenlohe-owned Alfred coal field and other Hohenlohe mines in the 1860s and 1870s.[21] The courting of worker loyalty ebbed as the demand for workers multiplied in the 1860s, though to be sure this tradition of favoring already established mining and smelting families did not die out even with vastly increased production and labor forces. Thus the royal Friedrich lead smelter advertised in 1899:

> Once again a number of workers up to 25 years of age will be taken on. Sons and relatives of smelter workers, invalids or widows can until Sunday, August 19, report at the worker registration office for pre-registration or allow themselves to be registered by relatives . . .[22]

Announcements with similar preference lists were also posted around this time for workers aged 14-16; and sometimes, when there were only a few openings, they were reserved exclusively for people already connected with the smelting industry.[23] The Friedrich smelter was relatively successful in this sort of in-bred recruiting, as is evidenced in employment records for the 1895-1908 period, when approximately half of all job applicants noted that their fathers were mining or smelting workers;[24] however, Friedrich was a much smaller and more static concern than many other plants, and its hiring problems were correspondingly less pressing. Even a phenomenally prolific labor force like the one at a Gleiwitz rolling mill around 1905—families of more than five or even ten children were common—could not reproduce enough workers to satisfy current needs.[25]

Such an emphasis on industrial families was naturally easier in the metallurgical industries than in mining because mining expanded at a much more rapid rate. From 1852 to 1874, that is, before the post-1890 expansion, the total mining force grew over four times (7,400 to 33,000), and the number of miners at the König mine (largest in Upper Silesia) increased ten times; the smelting labor force expanded perceptibly but much more slowly.[26] This blossoming need for workers could not be met merely by drawing on the existing stock of labor, and the problems of recruitment, so acute after 1890, manifested themselves even in the 1860s. Still, relatively speaking, the problems before the late 1880s were small; the average coal-mine work force numbered under 500 men; and in other types of plants, even fewer.

Primitive stages of capitalistic industrial enterprise are often marked by widespread labor subcontracting, under which an employer hires a number of foremen, each of whom is to bring in a group of workers and is to maintain intermediate control over them at their jobs. English mining knew its "butty" system; textiles in India had its jobbers; United States agri-business still uses this system. In Upper Silesia, however, paternally minded bureaucrats prevented the introduction of this type of recruitment in the first half of the nineteenth century; and all through the period here under consideration mining and smelting workers were generally hired on an individual basis, with the exception of the foreign seasonal laborers from 1890 to 1914.

Finally, and perhaps most obviously, recruiting agents were sent out to bring in individual workers. There is little written evidence to show how active such men were in the industrial region; it is quite likely that the population living near the plants at an early period was easily induced to turn to industry as a natural source of employment after the exhaustion of new arable land around 1860.[27] Particularly in the 1870s and 1880s the supply of people leaving rural employment exceeded the number demanded by even a rapidly growing heavy industry. In fact, employers seem to have enjoyed practically unlimited supplies of labor in these early years; no concerted effort at recruitment was necessary in this situation.

More strenuous efforts at recruitment were made only from the 1890s on, when the growing demand for the products of local mining and smelting prompted complaints about a labor shortage. In the pages of *Katolik*, the leading Polish language newspaper of Upper Silesia, and of its supplement *Praca*, one finds little evidence of newspaper advertising as an enticement to workers. There were advertisements, of course:

> Workers will find permanent employment in the Julien foundry near Bobrek. . . .
> In the Bibiella iron mine 50 male and female workers will find permanent work. . . . The mine will search for appropriate living quarters.
> Fifty miners (haulers and hewers) are being sought for coal shaft "Lythandra" near the Frieden smelter. . . .
> Thirty hewers and thirty haulers will find immediate employment.[28]

Yet these were uncommon insertions. In fact, in the period before the First World War, the single Portland cement factory in the city of Oppeln inserted many more "help wanted" advertisements in *Katolik* than did all of the mining and smelting establishments. To be sure, a number of German language newspapers had greater circulation than *Katolik*, but the German community was not large, especially before 1900, and the newspapers serving this community would certainly not carry such advertising because the readers of these papers either were civic officials, professionals, and bureaucrats not interested in industrial employment, or were well-situated industrial employees (white-collar or high-level blue collar). There were few "recruitable" Germans in the area available for the kind of jobs which the employers needed to fill (primarily haulers in the mines).

Jobs were publicized by other methods, such as posters and one-page fliers. Occasional copies of such posters have survived, such as the case where the management of the König mine in 1906 was upset over incursions into the mine labor force by the nearby Schlesien mine.[29]

This complaint was accompanied by the copy of a recruiting poster:

For the Schlesien mine in Chropaczow near Beuthen
400 Förderleute [unskilled workers]
from 16 to 30 years old
and
200 haulers
from 21 to 40 years old
are being sought *immediately* at very good pay.
The mine is dry and has no damp sections. There are available a beautiful mine dormitory and a cheap canteen, in which are found sleeping places and beds for use, and in which cheap food and board are given. Whoever wishes to cook for himself has at his disposal a special kitchen and utensils ... [continues on about bonuses available to workers].

Good pay, good working conditions, good housing—the essence of a successful recruiting program, at least on paper.

Despite the high rate of school attendance in Prussia,[30] newspaper advertising and the written word were not the major means for recruiting workers; oral communication was apparently the most effective means of mobilizing workers, and to this end recruiting agents combed the local area, other parts of Germany, and even other countries. Unfortunately for the historian, this type of activity usually leaves no permanent record.

At times, of course, more unusual means were used. One of the most interesting in its implications was the recourse to labor purveyors. In reply to an ad in the Berlin *Kompass*, the management of the König mine in 1907 hired a Theodor Riebenstahl to recruit workers in the east.[31] Riebenstahl proved to be an effective purveyor, but the number of men he supplied hardly made any difference to Upper Silesian needs as a whole. For the König mine, these arrangements seem to have been at least minimally satisfactory, for the mine concluded such contracts with other firms, who now voluntarily offered their services to the management.[32] Other mines and smelters probably also used this method of finding needed hands, but not to the extent that employers could cease complaining about the labor shortage as production increased. One of the fallacies behind these constant complaints about labor shortage was pointed out by the purveyor Riebenstahl, who explained to the mine administration that although many industries had labor shortages, there were a number of good workers available. However, to get them, wages would have to be raised.[33] This observation merely restated in simple terms the classic law of supply and demand. Employers, however, rather than raise wages and attract outside workers preferred to change the conditions of supply by hiring foreign workers and local women and minors.

The economic state of the southern counties of Upper Silesia alleviated recruitment problems; the growing population could not support itself on the prevailing subsistence agricultural arrangement dominated by midget farm holdings. Survival demanded outside employment, and the pre-industrial existence of mining and smelting industries had accustomed the local folk to look to them for outside employment. Agents of course moved out into the countryside, particularly into Pless and Rybnik, which were essentially agricultural counties with a number of mines. Peasants and agricultural laborers were also recruited from the counties directly to the north and west of the inner area, in Lublinitz and Gross Strehlitz, and to a lesser extent from the Oder and trans-Oder counties of Kosel and Ratibor, though in the twentieth century Ratibor itself was developing a smelting industry. Evidence for the effects of local recruitment is plentiful; all extant records of employment in the area point to the local population as being the major source of workers.[34]

So long as nearly unlimited supplies of labor flocked to the mines and smelters, competition for workers remained low keyed. However, the post-1890 fierceness of local competition for workers can be imagined in the light of the prevailing shortage of labor, even if employers preferred to omit such activity from their records. One gets some inkling of that clash of interests in the complaint of the König mine about the incursions of the Schlesien mine (noted above) and in the somewhat pathetic plea of the powerful Cleophas mine that it must have foreign contract labor because it could not recruit in southern Upper Silesia due to the competition of the Eminenz and Oheim mines, the Hildebrand shaft, the many concerns in Idaweiche, and the Rybnik mines.[35] Free competition in the labor market obviously did not suit this mine, which was owned by Giesche's Erben, one of the largest concerns in the area. Government mines were not oblivious to the possibilities of poaching on other mines either, as the Donnersmarck concern unhappily noted.[36]

General competition prevailed for unskilled miners, but for highly skilled smelter workers specific individuals were personally recruited. In 1904 the Bernhardi smelter (owned by Giesche's Erben) complained to the management of the Hohenlohe enterprises that a number of good melters (*Schmelzer*) had been recruited for a new plant of the Hohenlohe smelter and that a number of others had given notice of intent to switch; the Bernhardi smelter letter went on to name specifically some of those who had given notice and left:

> The workers were induced to leave their present work by the recruiting efforts of zinc master (*Zinkmeister*) Nendza of Hohenlohehütte. Nendza previously worked in Wilhelminehütte and thus knows the people well. In addition melters (*Schmelzer*) Anton and Clemens Gormik, who still live in Rosdzin, are said to have encouraged our people to go to Hohenlohehütte.
>
> The people taken away from us by Hohenlohehütte are the melters of two Siemens ovens, that is, one-fourth of our need of melters first class, and we cannot quickly supply good substitutes. We therefore kindly request the Hohenlohehütte to order that no more melters from Bernardihütte be hired and to order the melters Gornik to stop their agitation.[37]

Obviously, haulers were not the only workers in short supply; key skilled workers in the smelting industry were not to be found so easily either.

By the 1890s, enough people in Upper Silesia had become industrial workers to place recruiting on two levels: one for peasants and agricultural workers, and another for individuals who already belonged to the industrial labor force. The first group was the focus of the discussion in chapter 4 on the social origins of the working force; the second was involved in the various plans devised by employers to tie their employees to their jobs, schemes to be discussed in subsequent chapters. Suffice it to say that by the last decade of the nineteenth century a significant portion of the population of the industrial region had accepted industrial employment as a feasible way of life. The Hohenlohe metal works, for example, from the early 1890s on were deluged with unsolicited applications for employment, both skilled and unskilled, and the Friedrich smelter experienced a similar surfeit of workers of all kinds.[38] Patently, new workers were to be had by means other than raiding the countryside; a true industrial labor market had come into being.

Little needs to be said about the recruitment of women and minors. They were either dependents living in a household with a male worker, generally also a mining or smelting worker, or were children of local farmers or agricultural laborers. In either case, employment was limited to plants within commuting distance because such workers were not free to change their residences. For instance, the vast majority of minors working in the jurisdiction 'of the mining office in Königshütte were born in the immediate area, and most of them were born in Königshütte itself.[39] Often enough, a father turned to his employer for a job for his child; the files of many firms are replete with such requests. To cite just one or two examples, the hauler Simon Nowitzki, employed for seventeen years at the west field of the König mine, had five sons aged 15 or younger. One of these had been working at the west field since the age of 14 and the father now requested employment for his second son. Or, also typically, another miner had five sons working in the mines simultaneously.[40]

Service in the mines by young people probably seemed a natural way to augment family income, and large numbers of minors already had several years of experience before being drafted into the army at 19 or 20.[41] In many cases there was no choice but to go into local industry. Thus records show one man being discharged from a Hohenlohe smelter for physical disability after eleven years of service. His three brothers were working at the same place, and it is obvious that his five children (ages 2-8) would have to seek work as soon as possible.[42] The most natural place would be in the local smelter.

The position of women was similar to that of minors. Unmarried daughters generally lived with their parents, working to augment family income, and in the main dropped out of the labor force after marriage. It was considered disgraceful for a mining or smelting worker's wife to have to take a job, an opinion still widespread among Silesian miners.[43] Often enough, wives worked the little plot of land that many miners used to supplement their incomes.[44] The unmarried women, who comprised most of the female working force in mining and smelting (4 percent in 1912; see chapter 2) in essence were limited to the area of their parents' homes.

The matter of workers from abroad was somewhat more complicated. There were two types of foreigners, small numbers of skilled workers individually recruited (for example, Italian stonecutters) and hordes of foreign seasonal laborers (Poles and Ruthenians) used for unskilled mine and smelter work and elsewhere for agricultural work.

Upper Silesian employers did do some recruiting on their own in foreign countries. Before 1885 this was not difficult because of Prussia's open-borders policy and because demand was not overwhelming. Sometimes, hiring of a number of Austrian citizens was recorded on the same day, very likely the result of activity by a recruiter.[45] As market demand for mine and smelter products increased and the labor force grew from the 1890s on, these corporations made some effort to turn outward. One mine in 1904 advertised in several Austrian newspapers for 250 miners, but with the warning of "no Poles" (probably to avoid the waiting period). Or, in 1910, an Upper Silesian recruiter was arrested in Hungary for illegal recruiting. As for other areas of eastern central Europe, proposals were made to recruit among the pockets of Germans there, but the industrialists did not generally care to expend the effort on such a campaign.[46] More obviously, the targets for recruitment abroad should have been the Czechs of northern Moravia and the Poles of Galicia and the former Congress Kingdom, but the Slavic exclusion acts of 1885 prevented any free play of the labor market here.

Czech-speaking workers played little or no role in the occupational transformation of Upper Silesia, 1865-1914, although it is not obvious why so few were to be found in local industry.[47] There was, to be sure, the mining field around Mährisch Ostrau (Moravska Ostrava) to absorb workers, and the industrial center of Brünn (Brno) was not far away. Yet some 30,000 alien Czechs were working in Germany in 1910, with only 7,000 of these in Silesia; most were in the Ruhr, where the waiting period did not apply. This does not explain why resident Czechs—some 75,000, primarily in Ratibor county[48]—hardly figured in local industrial employment. They probably would have if World War I had not interrupted industrial expansion in that southwestern section of Upper Silesia, for only in the last decade before the war did mining and smelting industries develop in Ratibor. Earlier, few workers had been brought in from the whole trans-Oder region.

Prior to 1885 the policy of open borders allowed easy migration to Prussia from Galicia and the former Congress Kingdom of Poland, but no large numbers of industrial workers came in these early years since employment opportunities were not so abundant as they were later to become. The expulsions of 1885 affected some 5,000 to 6,000 "Slavs" in the industrial region, a figure encompassing nonlaboring members of households and a sizable group of Jewish artisans and tradesmen.[49] More significant recruiting in the overpopulated east began in 1890, when the first seasonal laborers were admitted; and activity expanded significantly after 1905, when Ruthenians were eagerly sought.

The existence of Prussian border control offices gave the system of hiring foreign seasonal workers the semblance of order; but east of the border, recruitment of such workers was sheer bedlam.[50] The professional labor recruiters were interested in making money quickly, and their charges suffered from this attitude. The tsarist government attempted geographically to limit such activity, but the venerable Russian custom of bribery was often employed to circumvent restrictions. Austrian Galicia did not even have any rules, and agents, sub-agents, wild recruiters, enticers, and charlatans all had a field day at the expense of an uneducated local population.

Once across the Prussian border, a certain amount of order was established, at least until the men actually started working. Prussian authorities attempted to maintain a strict control over those admitted,[51] and more and more elaborate police and housing controls were instituted as the program was expanded from 1905 on. Still, none of these measures were intended to regulate recruiting; they were aimed rather at maintaining order in Prussia and at isolating the newcomers from other workers and from nationalist or socialist agitators.

The number of migrants admitted grew after 1900 as an ever increasing number of Prussian citizens deserted the countryside; in particular the expansion of the Ruthenian program beginning in 1905 was accompanied by a curious sidelight on recruiting methods. In 1904 a Greek Catholic priest named Hanyckyj living near Lemberg (Lwów, Lviv) wrote to authorities in Silesia that up to fifty men a day were coming to him inquiring about work in Upper Silesian coal mines.[52] This suggestion was taken up quickly by both agricultural and industrial interests in Silesia, and in 1905 a mass movement of Ruthenians began, much of it channeled through Hanyckyj and the Ruthenian National Committee in Lemberg. Soon Hanyckyj himself moved to Upper Silesia to tend his flock; his salary was then openly paid by the mining and smelting owner association, which considered him its recruiting agent.[53]

With the number of foreign workers exceeding 10 percent of the total labor force in heavy industry in 1913 (figures in chapter 2), this Ruthenian program and the foreign worker program as a whole seem to have been quite successful in adding large numbers of workers to the local industrial work force in the 1900-1914 period, albeit at the expense of severe social dislocation among these transient workers. Russian Poland and Galicia, especially the latter, were suffering under immense pressure of overpopulation, and many people welcomed the chances offered by the recruiters for Upper Silesia who swarmed through the east.

Recruitment to Upper Silesia had its obverse side: emigration of industrial workers out of the area, as opposed to the more general case of "flight from the land." This competition with local industry in its own territory illustrates how industrialists from other areas used their recruiting power to disturb the local labor market.

Emigration of Industrial Workers

The very fact of sizable emigration to industrial work elsewhere[54] indicts Upper Silesian industry for failure to meet the challenge presented by expanding production. It also gives rise to doubts about the commonly held thesis that it is the tenacity of pre-industrial rural folk to their old customs and traditions which often blocks effective formation of an industrial labor force.[55]

Occasionally, employment opened up in other eastern provinces, as when recruiters for new plants in East and West Prussia signed up a number of men in 1908, or when skilled workers were attracted to the Polish Dąbrowa basin by special premiums;[56] but usually such emigrants went to Westphalia, where most industrial jobs were to be found.

The Ruhr valley industrial complex had exhausted its local supply of workers in the 1850s and was turning to nearby provinces for workers even before steel-making became a giant industry. By the 1870s these no longer sufficed. There had been talk of sending recruiters after Lower and Upper Silesian miners in the 1850s, and by 1870 about 1 percent of the work force consisted of such miners.[57] The first recorded Westphalian recruiter to Upper Silesia came in 1871, but he enlisted only 25 workers because he spoke no Polish. Later in the year a Pole was sent, and some 500 men signed up. Complaints of such recruiting appeared in Rybnik in 1872, where the departure of 150 workers was seen as a "calamity" for the local mining industry.[58]

Despite these flurries of worker emigration, Upper Silesian industrial workers, as opposed to Silesian rural laborers, only rarely migrated to Westphalia before the 1890s. For example, a chart of the origins of the inhabitants of the all-migrant city of Erle betrays the presence of almost no Upper Silesians; Bochum, too, had few.[59] By the late 1880s, however, the attractiveness of the Ruhr was growing. Improved transportation and communications were serving to make migration to western Germany easier, and after the short but bitter mining strike of 1889 it seemed only natural to move to the west in search of a better living. The Donnersmarck management, for example, based its argument for the importation of Galician seasonal labor on the shortage of workers caused by the widespread emigration of young people to Westphalia following that strike.[60]

Whereas the isolated strike at the König mine in 1871, the largest pre-1889 disturbance, had not occasioned any migratory movement,[61] the post-strike emigration initiated in 1889 became a common feature of Upper Silesian industrial life. So in 1894 about 11 percent (some 40 men) of the crew of one section of the Charlotte mine (in Rybnik county) left after a strike, perhaps the result of employer black lists. In all, about 280 miners left the Rybnik area in the second quarter of 1897.[62] The most impressive example of this practice came in the giant strike of 1913, the largest labor disturbance of pre-World War I Upper Silesia. Even before the strike began, recruiters from the Ruhr (and from Austrian Galicia) appeared on the scene. As the strike progressed, thousands of workers emigrated to Westphalia,

France, and Russia, and continued to leave after the strike ended. One would expect a number of workers to be blacklisted by employers after an unsuccessful strike, but the prevailing labor shortage forced the owners to keep such firings to a minimum; almost all workers who so desired were rehired. Eventually a number of the emigrants returned, indicating that conditions of employment elsewhere were difficult in the face of such a glut of men.[63]

Such examples are of course extraordinary cases, but they suggest that large numbers of men had been freed from ties to the land and that Westphalia was a viable alternative to industrial employment at home. Ignorance of alternative employment was not an all-embracing state of affairs;[64] Upper Silesians could and did leave when conditions became unbearable. In less troubled times emigration was not marked by such large groups leaving at once. Few miners left in the 1870s and 1880s, but this trend was interrupted by the strike of 1889. In the peaceful years of the 1890s, there was a relapse; very few miners left, generally under 150 per year, plus a few smelter workers.

TABLE 9

Number of Emigrants from Upper Silesian Industry, 1892–1896

Year	From industry		From mining	
1892	3,373[a]	2,320[b]	92[a]	75[b]
1894	2,777[a]	2,582[b]	126[a]	117[b]
1896	1,901[a]	3,001[b]	102[a]	92[b]

SOURCES:
[a] Karol Jonca, *Polozenie robotników w przemyśle górniczo-hutniczym na Śląsku 1889-1914* [The position of the workers in the mining and smelting industry in Silesia, 1889-1914] (Wroclaw, 1960) p. 62, based on *Satistiches Jahrbuch für den preussischen Staat,* 1915, p. 69, and WAP Wroclaw, Schlesisches Oberpräsidium 2615.
[b] JRGB 1896: 146-147.

Table 9 shows clearly that this rate of migration posed no threat to local industry. Conditions changed after 1896 when the upturn in the business cycle prompted a more rapid development of mining and smelting industries in all areas of Germany. Total emigration of industrial workers to the Ruhr, now amounting to over 5,000 per year, must have included a number of miners, a surmise corroborated by indirect evidence. The local newspapers quite often cited the danger presented by recruiters from Westphalia promising much more than was actually delivered on the spot.[65]

Instead of mere individuals leaving, groups were reported: 40 haulers of the König mine leaving simultaneously for Westphalia in August 1906, and 100 more a month later. In the same year some miners left from the Beuthen area; in 1912 the employers' association

reported the loss of 600 miners to Westphalia in the course of two
months; in 1913 the labor shortage was attributed in large measure
to emigration from Upper Silesian mining to the Ruhr region. Such
figures were combined with continual warnings and complaints from
various sources about the inroads being made by Westphalian recruiters into the local mining force. In addition, the figures for total
emigration from Upper Silesia show a marked increase from the early
1890s on; over 5,000 a year were leaving in the 1890s, rising to 7,000
in 1905 (Table 10), and the rising trend continued. All of these signs
are taken to mean that Upper Silesia was losing mining and smelting
workers, at least from the 1890s on.[66]

TABLE 10

Number of Upper Silesian Emigrants to the Ruhr, 1898–1905

1898	5,087
1901	6,445
1902	5,745
1905	6,918

SOURCE: Franz Schulze, *Die polnische Zuwanderung im Ruhrrevier* (diss. Munich,
n.d.), p. 30, based on official censuses.

It seems that, like the rate of emigration abroad, the expansion
of Upper Silesian mining and smelting, the growth of the Upper
Silesian labor force, the influx of foreign workers, so too the emigration
of mining and smelting workers to the Ruhr and other places can
be divided into two periods, breaking somewhere in the 1890s. In
the 1860s, 1870s, and 1880s, some industrial workers emigrated, but
not many; from the 1890s on, the tempo accelerated. The numbers
involved were not many; after all, there were only about 43,000
Silesians, Upper and Lower, living in Westphalia in 1900 (4,500 in
1871; 10,200 in 1880; 21,600 in 1890),[67] and most of these stemmed
from agricultural Lower Silesia. Nonetheless the labor shortage was
thought to be so acute in Upper Silesia that every small movement
of population cut to the quick; when movement to Westphalia stepped
up in the 1890s and after, local industrialists grew quite upset. Thus
employers could worry about how many of their workers drafted
into the army were returning to the mines after military service.[68]
Still, no solution was ever offered other than the importation of cheap
Slavic labor, and at times the management of mines especially
dependent on the foreigners—Cleophas mine in 1909, for example[69]
—threatened to cut back production should the requisite laborers
not be permitted to enter Prussia.

That sizable groups of industrial workers emigrated indicates that
they expected more attractive conditions elsewhere. If the Upper
Silesian mining and smelting workers wanted to leave in the face

of a reputed labor shortage, certainly there should be a rethinking of the notions of labor shortage, recruitment of workers in the area, and of the more vague generalities often expressed about the anti-industrial nature of the work force in the early period of rapid industrialization.

How then does one explain the constant cry of the employers that there was a significant shortage of workers, particularly of haulers for coal mines? It must be admitted that in periods of economic expansion a shortage of workers can exist, and in developed countries one speaks of "full employment" in such situations. However, in Upper Silesia and in the Prussian east in general the countryside contained large numbers of persons underemployed in agriculture. These were the people who could have been recruited to work in heavy industry, but Upper Silesian employers were slow to draw on these reserves. While the Ruhr industries were attracting vast numbers of people from all over the east, Upper Silesian mining and smelting could hardly draw workers from anywhere beyond the immediate neighborhood and practically had to consider migrants from Oppeln county (about sixty miles north) as long-distance migrants.[70]

Upper Silesian industries in the 1870s and 1880s recruited the most easily obtainable groups in the area, and employers probably enjoyed a situation approximating that of "unlimited supplies of labor." Recruitment efforts were rather simple, as sufficient numbers of rural folk readily enrolled for industrial wage labor. When more rapid expansion came, the old conditions no longer prevailed, and old methods no longer sufficed. Even though the countryside continued to furnish vast numbers of people to all industrial regions, it was no longer so easy to build a labor force. What set in was not so much a shortage of labor, but a growth of industry so rapid that there was no longer any slack to be taken up without effort. Full employment prevailed most of the time from 1896 to 1914; that is, anybody that wanted a job in the mines or smelters could have one, and industry could almost always use more workers. It was in this sense only that there was a labor shortage, and even on this point industrialists were involved in a good deal of chicanery, as when, during the layoffs of 1904 and 1905, they continued to proclaim a labor shortage.[71]

It is understandable why an underpopulated area should be short of unskilled manpower or why a rapidly industrializing area should be short of skilled manpower, but neither of these descriptions fit Upper Silesia. The skills were usually available; the population existed. After all, the labor force in the Ruhr grew at even a faster rate than that in Upper Silesia, but the shortage in the west was of skilled miners; unskilled workers were plentiful.[72] There is no denying that Upper Silesia experienced temporary labor shortages, primarily from the 1890s on, but these were generally due to shifts in business conditions. A keen competition for labor in the expansionary period (late 1860s to 1914) did in fact exist, particularly after 1890, but this is not the same as the pleading of the Upper Silesian employers that industry was actually suffering because not enough workers were available.

The phenomenon of "unlimited supplies of labor" was of short duration in Upper Silesia. After the 1880s there was no abundance of unemployed and rural underemployed workers to force prices down to a minimum wage level. In this specific case the social context and historical preconditions helped form a labor market quite different from the one examined by W. Arthur Lewis and Karl Marx before him. In particular, the strategies of entrepreneurial advance were feeble in Upper Silesia. One can imagine higher wages, large-scale housing developments, and fringe benefits of various kinds. In fact all of these were tried, but the attempts were weak and sporadic; rather than recruit vigorously, industrialists leaned ever more heavily on women, children, and foreign workers, all of whom cannot be classified as part of the regular, long-term work force. Such a work force could be satisfactory in the very short run only; increasing reliance on such temporary palliatives over the years sapped recruiting initiative and in many ways rendered the employers unable to compete effectively for labor. Combined with the economic and geographic disadvantages outlined earlier, this retrograde employment policy severely damaged prospects for ending the acute pressure on the labor supply.

6

Paternalism and the Supply of Labor

Recruitment of new workers is merely the beginning of modern industrial labor relations. It is a truism to say that there were two inchoate groups involved, employers and workers; but that dichotomy suggests two sets of goals, two patterns of behavior, two ways of viewing the world. Contradictory trends were at work here—the first, unlimited supplies of labor, should have permitted employers to dictate whatever they wanted in the buyer's market for labor; the second, the traditional agricultural and open-air employment preferences of workers, might have made them not very amenable to industrial discipline. Essentially what happened was that employers launched a series of programs intended to draw their central core of workers away from other occupations and counted on a continuing flow of transient workers to flesh out their crews; in both cases the definition of and control over labor-management relations lay in company hands.

This issue is sometimes treated as one of paternalism, referring to the attempt by management to control the daily life of employees by supervising many of their extramural activities through measures like company owned housing, leisure time organizations, company stores, and the like, all intended to guide workers in the "correct" way of life. The Krupp firm in the Ruhr certainly stands out as an employer of this sort, but Upper Silesian magnates and managers refused to adopt any such program—not even the Prince of Pless, who administered what was in many senses a quasi-autonomous principality. The Upper Silesians turned out to be market-minded entrepreneurs concerned primarily with more narrowly defined needs of production, not feudal barons of industry controlling their serflike laborers.

In the face of a rapidly multiplying labor force and the high rates of turnover characteristic of all rapidly industrializing areas, any apparently paternalistic policies began to serve merely as ways to hinder the freedom of movement of workers and were not thorough-going attempts to control their private lives. Despite an undeniable element of concern for the well-being of employees, the effort expended by managers on building and directing welfare programs increasingly reflected the problems of controlling the supply of labor. Signs of this production orientation surfaced as early as the 1850s, when Giesche's Erben at the Wilhelmine smelter saw fit to post a list of twenty reasons for fines, not one of which was related to behavior outside the place of work.[1]

If paternalism or even paternalistic tendencies were fading before the exhaustion of ready labor reserves, it is obvious that such arrangements after 1890 would display little evidence of nonmarket interest. It should become clear in this chapter that housing, welfare policies, and similar programs came to function almost purely as recruitment techniques, with only Social Democracy and secondarily Polish nationalism standing out as the residual extramural areas over which employers felt compelled to exercise control via intramural rules.

To be sure, what may be called the social policies of each firm were not coordinated with those of other firms. For the management of a firm like Giesche's Erben it made little difference if a departing worker was going to work on the family farm, engage in light industry, or take up employment at a mine or smelter owned by Hohenlohe enterprises. So in 1904 Giesche managers were highly indignant about the spiriting away of skilled smelter workers by Hohenlohe.[2] Otto Saeger and his policymaking team at Giesche's Erben were interested in the most productive labor force obtainable, not in the long-term trends in German society. Nonetheless, a noticeable similarity marked the evolution of management policies throughout Upper Silesia, and there is no doubt that the firms may be treated as a group.

The Drive to an "Arbeiterstamm"

In order to be served by a reliable work force, Upper Silesian employers had to convince workers to take jobs in the mining and smelting industries and to stay there. Under Frederick the Great and in the first half of the nineteenth century, attractions had been framed in the form of special legal privileges such as exemption from military service and membership in the elite miner brotherhood. However, a new conception of a universal and undifferentiated citizenry materialized in the post-1850 expansion of the reforms introduced in Prussia under Stein and Hardenberg, and the newly independent industrialists of Upper Silesia had to replace legal incentives with different attractions. Especially noticeable in the first decades after the end of state control over mining was the attempt by each mine and smelter to build its own community of workers, a group labeled as an *Arbeiterstamm*, a term not easily rendered into pithy English. This concept is not identical with a fully developed industrial labor force. Often bandied about by management without precise definition, it seems to have been conceived of primarily as a group of docile individuals with unswerving faith in and attachment to the parent firm.

The small plants at the beginning of the nineteenth century had an identifiable and more or less loyal core work force bound to their work by membership in the miner brotherhoods (*Knappschaft*—including many smelting workers) and by employer supplied housing—more or less an *Arbeiterstamm*. However, developments after 1850 changed the whole picture, especially since the brotherhoods were no longer compulsory (law of 1854), and prospective workers acquired great freedom of movement at a time when the number of available jobs was swiftly rising: employment in coal mining increased from 7,400 workers in 1852 to 18,000 in 1865, the dawn of the new era of mining in Prussia.[3] The security offered by membership in a brotherhood no longer sufficed to outweigh the attractions of alternative employment, and for the first time in a century mining and smelting workers sometimes declined the opportunity to join these erstwhile elite organizations. In fact, by the 1870s the groups had become concerned solely with old-age and sickness benefits; in this innocuous form they were made obligatory for all adult male miners.

On the other hand, paternalistic ideologies of this nature are not incompatible with advanced industrial enterprises. Despite the agrarian noble origin of most of the Upper Silesian industrialists, they were not wont to develop proprietary relationships with their workers in the manner of Stumm or Krupp in the Ruhr or of modern Japanese industrialists. Prince Hohenlohe, the Donnersmarcks, Schaffgotsch, and the other old families (except for the Prince of Pless) were not extremely close to their employees. The new managers brought forth by the incorporation of many old family enterprises starting in the 1870s—men like Friedrich Bernhardi (Giesche's Erben), Gustav Hilger (Vereinigte Königs- und Laurahütte), and Adolf Williger (Kattowitzer AG für Bergbau und Hüttenbetrieb)—were inclined to plan in terms of markets, production, and labor supply, not in terms of their industrial families.

There was a sustained effort, particularly in the 1870s and 1880s, to inculcate anew into the growing labor force a sense of duty to a particular firm. At the Hohenlohe coal and zinc mines near Kattowitz, time and again separate lists of workers with many years of service, called *Stammrolle* (*Stamm*—family, clan), such as those at the Alfred mine, were set apart from ordinary lists of workers (*Arbeiterliste*), such as those at the Georg mine.[4] *Stamm* names were not added on continuously as were those on ordinary lists of workers, but apparently were compiled retrospectively with the aim of setting off the most loyal (most "committed") of the workers. In addition to standard information about name and age, these rolls purported to show a special place in the Hohenlohe "family" for these workers by giving attention to such items as names and dates of birth of wives, the number of children, and military service.

It is hard to know how conscious workers were of this effort to make them part of one big industrial community; certainly more concrete incentives, like wages, housing, and other fringe benefits were indispensable for any real loyalty to an employer. It is likely that the rolls were at first more the reflection of a pre-laissez-faire employer paternalism than they were evidence of a close relationship between owners and the highly valued workers; in later decades this incipient ideology came to be sheer cant. The earlier outlook was perpetuated by the relatively slow growth of the crews of many firms in the period when nearly unlimited supplies of labor prevailed, and even skilled miners had few chances for alternative employment. In this light the crash of 1873, which hit Giesche's Erben hard, was also beneficial for the firm in that it permitted "... the attraction of a better *Arbeiterstamm* ... through the release of inferior workers."[5] Skilled smelting and metalworkers were in a better position, but their industries were so small before the 1880s that the notion of a large-scale *Stamm* is not relevant here.

Such a convenient convergence of industrial needs and social mythology did not last long; any close relationship that did exist in these early years was undercut by the exhaustion of surplus supplies of labor in the late 1880s. The term then became either a synonym for the work force in general, as at the Schlesische AG für Bergbau und Hüttenbetrieb and at a Gleiwitz rolling mill, or a goal toward which employers were striving.[6] In these later decades the *Stamm* rolls were rarely maintained—a study published in 1915 referred to general personnel lists as "*Arbeiterstamm* rolls," and the *Stamm* rolls, like that of the Paulina mine, lost their elitist character and became quite general sometime in the 1890s.[7]

Although the idea of an *Arbeiterstamm* was part of the everyday working vocabulary of Upper Silesian industrialists, it never became the dominant ideology of the period. Actual hiring policies were more relevant to workers than was the vocabulary of industrialists. It has already been seen (chapter 4) how the management at the Friedrich smelter favored children of current workers for openings; this ability to restrict the eligible pool of labor was a sign of success in creating a work force loyal to a particular firm. It might be interesting to add that the Friedrich smelter in general, at least after 1895, was also deluged with applications for jobs by many other people, most of whom came from families of industrial workers, (see Table 11) showing that by this early date there was a sizable group of workers brought up in an industrial culture.

TABLE 11

Number of Applicants for Jobs at the Friedrich Smelter, 1895–1908

Date	Total applicants	Smelter worker	Miner	Agricultural worker/peasant	Artisan	Other
				Occupation of Father		
a. 1895–1898	162	81	12	28	11	30
b. 1899–1900	227	102	24	56	12	33
c. 1901–1902	252	93	17	53	30	59
d. 1903	200	50	30	20	14	26
e. 1904	122	46	18	20	14	26
f. 1905	159	78	10	26	18	27
g. 1906–1908	72	33	6	5	6	22

SOURCE: WAP Katowice, Friedrichshütte 698 (line a), 699 (b), 700 (c), 701 (d), 702 (e), 703 (f), 704 (g), job applications *passim.*

From 1895 to 1908 from 40 percent to 60 percent of worker applicants at the Friedrich smelter stemmed from mining or smelting families; besides these, many of those listed in "other" should be included, for almost all the numerous "invalids" in this column in all likelihood were or had been engaged in mining and smelting. One can say that more than half the applicants for jobs at the Friedrich foundry in this period had fathers employed in mining and smelting, and this in an area situated on the northern edge of the industrial region, where one would expect to find large numbers of people just coming from the countryside. Still, with so many rural people being pushed into industry, this was no *Arbeiterstamm.*

Likewise, in Gleiwitz on the eastern end of the industrial region, parts of the smelting labor force were well established. In a rolling mill investigated sometime after the turn of the twentieth century, about 45 of the grandfathers and over 90 of the fathers of the 253 workers studied were themselves smelting workers. All the sons of the 23 smelting-worker grandfathers had taken up smelting jobs, and 86 of the 356 adult sons of the workers had become smelting and metal workers themselves.[8] However, the situation in the metal-finishing industries is unclear because most workshops before 1914 did not reach the stage of large factories with an advanced industrial division of labor.

One would be hard put to match these examples from mining, particularly coal mining, where the labor force doubled from 1890 to 1913. Even when such a large firm as the Schlesische AG für Bergbau und Zinkhüttenbetrieb (over 9,000 employees in 1903) bragged of its good *Arbeiterstamm,* management also had to admit the phenomenon of a very large turnover of workers.[9] It is apparent then that one must distinguish between an *Arbeiterstamm*, tied tightly to a particular firm, and a labor force committed in the long run to industrial employment but not necessarily loyal to any one employer. A small nucleus of workers existed at each mine, but the high rates of turnover and the tremendous surge of newcomers swamped this real or so-called *Stamm*. In a few cases, there were generations of the same family working for the same employer (as at the Gleiwitz rolling mill), but the large majority of the workers were new to the industry or to the specific jobs which they held.

The disappearance of agriculture as a viable alternative way of life is born out by the marriage registers of the towns of Rosdzin and Schoppinitz,[10] located in Kattowitz county in the heart of the industrial complex. In 1875-1879 almost half the men and over one-third of the women getting married had parents engaged in agriculture, while about one-third of the men and close to half the women had parents engaged in industry. By 1895-1899, only 25 percent of the men and 17 percent of the women stemmed from agricultural families, while 62 percent of the men and 71 percent of the women stemmed from industrial families.

Once significant numbers of people had become involved permanently in industry, managers no longer felt the need to propagate this ideology. At least for the central industrial region one might contend that by 1900 large numbers of workers could be considered second-generation industrial workers but certainly not members of a core *Arbeiterstamm* loyal to a particular firm. In fact, employer hiring policies in mining hardly seemed geared to the creation of their verbally much-loved *Arbeiterstamm*. The record of the Hohenlohe administrations shows that even when two and sometimes three generations of the same family worked in a particular mine, these workers at times had problems in getting hired, or, once hired, experienced difficulties with their pensions and other fringe benefits.[11] It seems that the whole concept gave way to the exigencies of the daily need for workers and was kept in reserve for pleading a special case. Unsuccessful in its appeal, the general *Stamm* approach had been dropped by the turn of the century. For example, in 1908 the Upper Silesian mining and smelting employers' association opposed the proposed ban on employment of minors underground. The owners argued that it was necessary to employ these minor miners in order to create an *Arbeiterstamm*; without work in the mines at age 14-16, these youngsters would be lost to mining. It was after all the "moral duty" of the mining industry to provide jobs for people in the area. Such pious homilies were regularly brought forth on special occasions, but the *Stamm* concept of the work crew came to mean little for management policies except in the continued insistence on the need to educate properly workers aged 14-16. Even here, however, more

candid industry spokesmen acknowledged that the basic rationale
for hiring minors lay in the labor shortage, not in the superior moral
qualities inherent in mining work.[12]

In addition to the depressing effect of minor workers on the position
of full-time adult employees, management also demoralized any
potential industrial family by the wholesale use of foreign workers,
who disrupted favorable communications between management and
worker. Here too employers spoke of creating a *Stamm* of Ruthenian
workers, but in the end little real loyalty to a particular firm was
built among these newcomers. Even special police controls and
segregated housing did not suffice to counter what was considered
a high rate of quitting, usually without giving two weeks notice.[13]

In sum, the *Arbeiterstamm* seems to have been a product of the
days of low production and small work crews. Once expansion came
to the point of demanding large numbers of workers drawn directly
from the countryside, employers could no longer take the time to
cultivate this kind of elite labor force. Their ideology was not so
deeply founded that it could not easily be abandoned. The hope for
an *Arbeiterstamm* grew from ideas about society based on legally
established social hierarchies and on a limited freedom of mobility
and occupation. In the conditions of industrial society in central
Europe, emphasis shifted away from such abstract encouragement
of workers to more material needs, in particular to the provision
of living quarters for workers.

Housing

An inadequate supply of housing has probably constituted the single
greatest obstacle to the development of a dependable work force in
industrializing areas. From nineteenth-century Russia to Poland and
Hungary in the 1970s, workers drawn to industrial centers in central
Europe and elsewhere have experienced significant problems in finding
homes for their families and sometimes even in procuring a place
for a single man. Tales of Manchester, Vienna, Berlin have received
wide currency; Beuthen, Königshütte, Gleiwitz, Kattowitz, Myslowitz
revealed housing situations fully as tragic. The push from agriculture
must have been a mighty one to induce people to take up residences
in these urban centers.

No matter how initially successful a recruitment campaign, a
modern industrial labor force simply could not be developed without
special efforts to provide living accommodations for the mass of new
workers. Although mining and smelting employers never coordinated
their efforts in this area, so similar was their general approach to
the question that they can be dealt with as a group with a more
or less identifiable policy, especially in light of present comments

on the *Arbeiterstamm* concept.[14] Housing, after all—as the Higher Mining Office pointed out in 1896—was crucial for the creation of a "solid, reliable *Arbeiterstamm*."[15]

The desire for a permanently settled staff of workers was not new. Even in the eighteenth century housing had had to be built near Malapane, an iron center near Oppeln established under the regime of Frederick the Great;[16] farther south in the industrial region proper, makeshift quarters were the rule. As noted above, an attempt to bring a number of outsiders into local industry in the late eighteenth and early nineteenth centuries foundered on the shortage of housing. Even without immigrants, population growth far outstripped the supply of housing, a situation leading to the expansion of such abuses as the zinc workers living under the ovens. To be sure, one might explain that anyone working in the foundry all day would not mind a little humidity at home,[17] but such conditions were hardly calculated to entice newcomers to seek work in Upper Silesia. Not that all the fault lay on the side of "wicked" employers; often enough, as the chief of operations in Tarnowitz reported in 1818, the worker preferred his old comfortable hovel to new company housing. Why? "... Because he does not feel at home in such a house [new company housing], because he cannot bury his cabbage and potatoes in the hut; he must keep his cow outside and thus must go out of the house to see the cow; in a word, because the living quarters are too good."[18]

In the late eighteenth century, the primary motivation for building worker housing had been to assure that the scarce workers would not quickly change their places of employment. Here was the motive of a "settled down" labor force that was to emerge so strongly later in the nineteenth century, when employers again felt pressure on labor supply. In between these two periods, however, employer attitudes had less of a sense of urgency. For instance, the Wilhelmine smelter, founded in 1834, did not at first build worker housing because the workers were "children of landowning peasants" and consequently were assumed to be able to find quarters with their parents on the farm. A similar reliance on pre-existing housing appeared when the Schlesische AG für Bergbau und Hüttenbetrieb was formed in 1853, but as early as the late 1850s the company had to relent and started buying land on which to build worker housing.[19]

By the 1860s expansion of arable land had stopped,[20] and a marked growth of industry had begun. Housing projects for employees were then geared toward the complementary policies of settling down the workers and in many cases giving them local roots by helping them acquire small pieces of property. It was considered "... highly desirable that a *settled down* and where possible *propertied* working class be created."[21] Docility or at least loyalty to a particular firm was no doubt envisaged as a product of landholding by workers.

Acquiring a house with land was no easy task, and it was common practice for companies to give workers loans or grants for construction of individual houses (*Beihülfehäuser*). By the early 1890s about 11,000 dwelling units were available in the form of subsidized housing, with the majority of the units being connected with the government owned mines and smelters,[22] but the total could hardly provide for a rapidly increasing labor force, which amounted to over 80,000 individuals in 1890.

Local industrialists had to do more than simply underwrite mortgages; they obviously had to provide rental housing if they hoped to form some kind of stable labor force. At first, rather than becoming mere landlords, they made available a number of agricultural opportunities to make industrial work more appetizing—thus a number of workers in government plants in the 1870s received as leaseholders a small parcel of land each for plowing, and more than twenty firms in the 1880s rented out dwarf-size farms (under three hectares) to some six thousand workers.[23] The provision for part-time agricultural activity was aimed at a potential work force still attracted by farming; by enabling some workers to hold small plots, management hoped to draw into industry many of the marginal agricultural types being pushed off the land by the shortage of arable land and the effects of new agricultural technology. However, land in the area was too dear for employers to be able to provide large numbers of such parcels. Although some observers in the early 1890s looked to houses with kitchen gardens as the answer to the pressure on labor supply, even these were not plentiful.[24]

The work force increased steadily, and fewer and fewer firms felt it necessary to provide such added incentive. Some of the largest firms in Upper Silesia—Vereinigte Königs- und Laurahütte, Giesche's Erben, Schaffgotsch, Borsig—had very few plots for plowing and only a minimal number of kitchen gardens; most of their company housing was devoid of such accoutrements. Even the keeping of cows, so popular in the 1860s, declined rapidly because space was no longer available. Some industrial workers continued to farm all through the prewar period, but such activity was less common among smelter workers than among miners because a larger proportion of the former stemmed from non-agricultural families and because the smelting plants did not possess as much open land as the mines.[25]

Despite an optimistic government claim of having attained a settled labor force by 1873, after a short time it became apparent that encouraging workers to possess their own houses was not sufficient to ensure a pool of labor. The trend in the late 1880s began to turn to company built and company owned housing. While in 1890 about half of all company housing took the form of subsidized private homes, in 1912 only one in eight company associated dwellings fell into this category; the rest consisted of housing rented to workers.[26]

Company rental housing was of two basic types: apartments for families and dormitories for individuals, each type presenting its own particular social tensions. It would not serve any purpose here to chronicle the details of the housing programs of various companies; a few remarks on the general pattern of post-1890 housing should prove satisfactory to illustrate the broader implications of the projects.[27]

Recurring complaints by both management and workers about the housing shortage accompanied the post-1890 expansion of the work force.[28] With labor in short supply, even in years of economic retrenchment, emphasis in housing came to rest on multiplying the base number of available dwelling units without bothering about making permanent an *Arbeiterstamm*. The provision of company land for tilling practically disappeared in the built-up central counties, and even in the outlying regions little attention was paid to the leasing of midget farms to workers, though many in these peripheral areas did maintain their farms while working in industry and mining. The administration of the royal mines and smelters, the largest single employer in Upper Silesia, leased land to fewer than 10 percent of its workers in 1905; at the rural Bielschowitz field in Rybnik county, where one would expect a great deal of vacant land, only about 15 percent of the miners leased agricultural land.[29] Not that employers were any less interested in having their chimerical "settled" labor force; this wish kept resounding all through the period.[30] It is just that provision of land for farming no longer seemed important—the days of the peasant-industrial worker combination for the most part were over.

Even the workers were becoming leary of the traditional way of life. For example, Giesche's Erben in 1906 opened the much publicized colony Gieschewald, where 642 families (including those of 600 workers) were placed in individual houses designed in traditional Upper Silesian peasant style, including a garden and good water supplies for each house. The whole arrangement was intended to make industrial workers feel at home in a peasantlike environment. Yet so alien had the old ways become that the company had trouble getting workers to stay on![31]

Urban conglomeration was the order of the day. While a Gleiwitz drawing mill in 1910 might still employ a number of workers who were supplementing their incomes through truck gardening or animal husbandry, there could be no question of such activity in the heart of the industrial area. Thus the entire city of Königshütte (population 77,000 in 1913) retained few vestiges of its rural past and took on the face of a contemporary city with great blocks of tenements and with 75 percent of its area built up.[32]

In sum, simple dwelling units for worker families formed a prime answer to labor shortage, although judging by other attempts to change conditions of labor supply (hiring women, minors, and foreign laborers), one would surmise that this one answer did not suffice. In fact, by expanding the use of women and minors, management was able to increase output without bearing the burden of providing new housing. These employees stood outside the regular labor market because they lacked the mobility of adult males; by residing with their parents, the two groups presented no housing problem.

So far the present discussion of housing programs has focussed on housing designed to keep families together, but in a parallel effort to meet the demand for labor, industrialists, especially after 1890, expanded the building of worker dormitories.[33] Nowhere does the absolute priority being accorded to the provision of simple sleeping space for workers come out more clearly. Designed with rooms averaging thirty to fifty beds each, the dormitories were run with the strict discipline apparent in the Deutschland mine in the 1880s, where residents of dormitories were expected to stand at attention when representatives of management entered the building.[34] Though this martial atmosphere was lightened in ensuing years, rarely was any consideration given to individual preferences or to privacy, let alone to provisions for farming land or truck gardens for the residents of these barracks. Originally intended for single male workers, these accommodations were soon taken by married men who commuted home on Sundays and holidays and were later also occupied by the growing number of foreign seasonal workers.

Because of the skewed nature of the dormitory population, this housing was not as popular as other types, though by 1913 one in five single male workers lived in such barracks. The low dormitory occupancy rate (70 percent in 1913) often reflected poor administration—one dormitory reported 90 percent occupancy with a good housemaster and 70 percent with a poor one—and a refutation of the self-serving claim by management that the Upper Silesian workers preferred the barracks atmosphere over small semi-private rooms, which were held to resemble jail cells. In all likelihood, the lack of family atmosphere determined the unpopularity of the dormitories. Management nonetheless perceived a need to concentrate on this socially turbulent form of housing. In 1890, companies had provided family quarters for 11,000 workers and dormitory space for 3,000, but according to one source by 1913 the 28,000 dormitory spaces almost equalled the family units available.[35]

One should not neglect to mention that both in 1890 and in 1912 a majority of workers did not live in company owned or company sponsored housing. At the end of the period close to 50 percent of married employees and 20 percent to 25 percent of single male workers lived in company housing.[36] The others lived either in private rented housing, with their parents, or on their own property. Propagandists for employers were happy to see both in 1890 and 1912 that well over 60 percent of single male workers lived with their parents, a phenomenon regarded as much healthier than the "appallingly large number of subtenants" in the Ruhr. Living at home was also regarded as being settled down; dormitories were regarded as a necessary evil, and subtenancy was to be avoided if at all possible.[37]

Family life, however, remained essential to most mining and smelting workers, and adequate housing had to be provided for dependents of workers. Whereas in agriculture women were expected to share the work, once in heavy industry wives (or at least mothers) tended to drop out of the labor force.[38] Consequently a large number of people who would be classified as surplus labor in the countryside had to be housed when their families moved into industry even though they themselves were not available for industrial work. Worker dormitories were an attempt to answer this problem by leaving dependents outside the area of employment, but the high rate of vacancies there and the experience of Russian factories in the pre-World War I years indicate that this solution was not wholly successful.

Those women who were indeed a part of the labor force presented no special housing difficulty. They, and children in the labor force too, were not mobile like the adult men. These workers were recruited in the neighborhood and continued living in their parents' homes, or, less often, as married women with their husbands. Seasonal foreign workers were a different matter. For the most part, housing was the official responsibility of the employer, and most of these workers wound up in dormitories. Judging from complaints about job turnover, one might also guess that some of them took up lodging as subtenants in private dwellings.

Throughout this discussion there has been no reference to the quality of housing offered in Upper Silesia, on the assumption that sheer quantity was at that time of primary importance in building a committed labor force. The only exception has been the remarks on the worker dormitories, basically different in kind because of the break-up of the family. It seems that the average apartment in industrial Upper Silesia was a good deal smaller than the Prussian average and very much smaller than the average flat in Westphalia and the Rhineland, but to discuss the crowded interiors and the widespread disease in local housing would go too far afield from the present topic and would mainly repeat what has been said elsewhere.[39]

Was the housing program a success? Quantitatively there was progress: in 1890 only one in six workers could be placed in company housing; in 1912, one in four. From this angle of vision employers had a positive recruitment program, particularly effective in drawing in the men on the margin between agriculture and industry and between migrating to southern Upper Silesia or northward. Very likely the various programs were effective in holding down turnover of workers, based on experience in other mining regions.[40] But what of creating an *Arbeiterstamm*? Promoting a "committed" labor force? Here no unqualified answer can be given.

Before the 1890s employer-sponsored housing was aimed at a small group of workers who might evolve into a worker elite by means of their propertied status; however, property mobility in Upper Silesia never became a widespread phenomenon. On the peripheries, many miners owned tiny farms, but these peasant-industrial workers hardly could qualify as the mainstay of a reliable labor force. On the contrary, the breakthrough from semicommitted to generally committed industrial workers came first among the former day laborers, who after 1860 were ever more forcefully being pushed from the countryside. These no doubt were people who responded to employer schemes of leasing bits of farmland to industrial workers. However, in a short time the pace of industrial development canceled out the necessity and even the possibility of offering land to workers, and attention had perforce to be turned to finding places to live for new workers.

To be sure, company housing was used not only as an inducement to workers, but also as a weapon of coercion. For example, the Bismarckhütte management retained the right of inspection of company housing at any time; no doubt this was typical of most firms. In periods of labor unrest, certain workers were evicted; and if a worker quit work, he had only two weeks to vacate company housing and to find new quarters, an extremely difficult task in Upper Silesia.[41] Housing could be used not only to entice workers to a firm, but also to force them to remain at their jobs.

Despite rural overpopulation and a continuous stream of migrants from rural to urban areas, Upper Silesian employers did not enjoy unlimited supplies of labor, at least not after 1890. Unlimited supplies depend on two major conditions: (1) an unimpeded flow of labor from the countryside to industry, and (2) the lack of alternative employment for the masses of people wishing to leave the countryside. The housing program was an attempt to assure that unimpeded flow, and as such it must be judged a qualified success. That is, the proportion of workers housed in company dwellings rose appreciably from 1890 to 1912 while the work force as a whole grew enormously on the basis of new workers drawn primarily from the local region. On the other hand, the acute housing shortage never ended, and at no time could all potential workers be cared for. Together with low wages, this housing shortage made Upper Silesian rural inhabitants receptive to hopes of employment elsewhere, primarily in Berlin and the Ruhr. So the second condition for unlimited supplies of labor remained unfulfilled: competition for workers among the major

German industrial complexes appreciably increased the blandishments required of industrial recruiters. Therefore, Upper Silesian industry could not offer only a bare minimum to potential workers; potential newcomers had to be actively persuaded to come to take employment locally. In this sense worker dormitories were not enough; real family housing had to be made available on a large scale. The post-1890 housing program was an indication that unlimited supplies of labor were no longer a possibility; no major firm could contemplate any expansion without provision for worker housing.

Paternalism in Upper Silesia: Employer-Sponsored Welfare Organizations

Company housing alone would not suffice to develop loyalty to a particular firm; employers had to use other weapons in the struggle to form a structured, stable, committed labor force. Besides giving preference in hiring to relatives of current workers, industrialists established a series of welfare institutions designed to make employment by an individual firm desirable. So the Borsig smelting complex in 1912: The Borsigs "have always been conscious of the fact that they owe their workers somewhat more than mere bread and wages; they have continuously thought of caring for and furthering the well-being of their workers and the working population in general."[42] One should not make out the employers to be completely cynical; they probably did believe such things of themselves. However, even such well-intended rationalizations were usually formulated only when required by the contingencies of labor supply or on the occasion of some company celebration.

More than bread and wages—that vague promise covered a variety of circumstances, often determined on an *ad hoc* basis. On the structural level, management made many formal commitments to employee welfare, and the numerous local jubilee publications invariably boasted of these marvelous fringe benefits.[43] There were, first of all, deliveries of coal free or at reduced prices, available under certain circumstances. At the government mines, this meant being married and having three months of service. This battle against a higher cost of living was augmented by low-priced potatoes, cabbage, rye, fish, meat, or other staples, particularly in years of relative scarcity. Sometimes there were even direct money grants, such as those vaunted by the Vereinigte Königs- und Laurahütte.[44] Other methods abounded, including food-purchase cooperatives and subsidized cafeterias.

Although payment in kind had been outlawed for industry in the middle of the nineteenth century, these food stores and canteens were in a sense a continuation of that method of remuneration. At

Bismarckhütte in 1901 some 10 percent of the workers' pay was deducted for the reduced price food sold by the company. Instead of raising wages, a step which no doubt was felt to be an encouragement to be lazy and to skip workdays, employers chose this wage supplement method, doubly attractive because it was probably cheaper and because it served to bind employees to a particular firm. At times workers were even forced to join the cooperatives.[45]

How enticing these arrangements could be, at least in the early decades of free-enterprise mining, came out clearly at the Mathilde mine (near Schwientochlowitz) in 1863. Cheap meals were furnished at the company restaurant, but married workers had access to the facilities only if they boarded an unmarried worker.[46] Clear evidence of the ever pressing need for housing!

Wage supplements had a tradition going back to the early nineteenth century, but other programs evolved mainly after 1890, when the focus shifted from the simple recruitment of workers to the retaining of workers at a specific firm. Not all firms were equally diligent in these matters, Donnersmarckhütte being generally regarded as the pacesetter. There were pension plans, supplementary accident insurance, free use of hearses, old age homes, vacations (rarely with pay), libraries, vocational schools, schools for girls, kindergartens, parks, bath houses (though not without pressure from the government),[47] and many others varying in size and scope.

The immediate needs of workers were not disregarded either. The König mine noted proudly its 331 underground toilet buckets, averaging out to one 0.06-cubic-meter bucket for every 6.4 men, while above ground there were twenty-five buckets plus four toilet areas with twenty-one seats, coming to one bucket or seat for every seven men. The primary motivation of all such programs found expression in the official mining and smelting journal in terms already familiar as the creation of a "settled-down body of workers" (*ein sesshafter Arbeiterstamm*). Of course, this 1902 report went on, the "most effective means" of accomplishing this end was to build "good and cheap worker housing," but all the various welfare policies came into play in this regard.[48]

Mining had its brotherhoods as a basis for retirement benefits, but the lack of tradition about pension funds allowed the well-organized smelter owners to impose their own conditions on the administration of these monies. Although one should not completely dismiss the employer-operated pension funds in smelting as without benefit to workers, there is no denying that these institutions were in large measure designed to undercut worker job mobility. Financial retribution ranked high in the list of steps taken to reduce labor turnover; certainly such considerations underlay the passionate efforts of the Upper Silesian Mine and Smelter Owner Association to resist any change in the restrictive nature of the welfare funds.[49] Just as mine owners before 1905 vehemently opposed the free transfer of drawing rights from one mining brotherhood to another, so employers in the basic metal industry would not allow those leaving employment to recover their pension fund contributions.

Eventually some big smelting employers (Hohenlohe, Donnersmarck in some cases) did institute such refunds, and after 1900 a few (Kattowitzer AG für Bergbau und Eisenhüttenbetrieb, Borsigwerk, Bismarckhütte) allowed transfer of funds to a new employer, but on the whole complaints of this no-refund practice continued to be voiced all through the prewar period. In addition, a certain amount of mismanagement reigned, as in 1904 when five private pension funds in Upper Silesia went bankrupt.[50]

Ironically, turnover was hardly affected by this threatened loss of money. At six large smelters surveyed in 1902, very few of those quitting (273 of 9,196 workers) had put in the five years necessary for eligibility.[51] It turns out then that the refusal to return contributions affected younger workers least because they had little to lose; but they were the ones who, as will be discussed presently, were the most mobile and the most prone to change jobs. Would more of the established workers have quit had there been no accumulated pension rights? Perhaps. But pension funds certainly provided no anchor for the free-floating younger men.

The actuality of some of these employer policies might better be grasped by looking at the experience of individual workers. Theodor Wyderek, employed by the Friedrich lead smelter, received this wage receipt for June, 1908:[52]

Shifts	Per Shift	Total
22.2	3.25 marks	76.16 marks

Deductions		
Sick Fund	1.12	
Advance on Salary	30.00	
Invalid and old-age insurance	.48	
Pension fund	2.75	
Coal	22.00	
	56.35	
	Net wages	15.81 marks

The large sum for coal probably represents storing up for the winter; still the 16 marks hardly seems adequate for living for two weeks, considering that 30 marks had been advanced for the previous two weeks.

Another worker at the same firm fared even worse. August Kupka in December, 1908, received the following wage receipt:[53]

Shifts	Per Shift	Total	Total
20	2.75 marks	55 marks	61 marks
2	3.0	6	

Deductions

Sick fund	1.60
Advance on salary	25.00
Death fund	.75
Invalid and old-age insurance	.72
Pension fund	3.25
Coal	10.00
Potatoes	9.00
Food	7.29
	57.61 marks

Net wages 3.39 marks

Even with the food, not much left after a full month of work!

Both of these men were full-time workers, apparently not given to excessive absenteeism; it is hard to concur with employer apologists that wages for such men would have been completely adequate had it not been for the tendency to skip workdays. There was no doubt that the Upper Silesian worker "... eats better, is dressed better, and lives much better than 50 and 100 years ago,"[54] but this statement would not have been great consolation to Wyderek, Kupka, and their tens of thousands of fellow workers in an age of marked rises in the cost of living.

Not all paternally distributed "fringe benefits" fit into categories of programs of one sort or another. In particular, Upper Silesian firms maintained a tradition of one-time or longer-term money grants to workers and their survivors. Requests to management show that widows and orphans could apply for direct grants; disabled workers, for money or for light jobs; workers, for a convalescence grant or a stay at a health spa; even regular workers, for extra money simply to support their families.[55] The list of special occasions is long.

Not that the big firms were easy spenders. The prevailing attitude made applicants more like supplicants, like the Hohenlohe worker who was refused a grant to take care of his children for a period because he had "... prosperous relatives who could take care of them." This remarkable close watch over the details of everyday living emerged quite often, for paternal care also included paternal strictures. A widow of a smelter worker applied to Hohenlohe for aid, but the administration refused because she had two unmarried sons to support her; besides, she was ". . . addicted to drink and on that account not worthy of a grant."[56]

In a militaristic state like Prussia, army service could determine whether one was hired or not, but even more, political or quasi-political activity did not escape the purview of the management bureaucracy. K. Wider, "formerly quite a good worker," was fired by the government mines in 1878 for insubordination in regard to directions given about the recent Reichstag elections.[57] Eighteen years of service at Hohenlohe did not cancel out one man's presumed political activity in a Catholic church organization in 1901. Naturally, more open "subversive" political interest was also punished. At the Deutschland mine and other Donnersmarck properties, twenty-five-year service awards were denied criminals who had lost their civil rights and all those who ". . . furthered anti-German or anti-monarchy efforts," meaning, of course, Polish nationalists and Social Democrats.[58]

Employer paternalism spread beyond the physical boundaries of the mine and smelter works, particularly when it came to combating the twin bogies of trade unions and Polish nationalist groups, both of which were considered to be disruptive elements in the push toward a loyal labor force. Besides, they were unpatriotic, a charge of special significance in Imperial Germany.

Trade union and socialist party members were persecuted, but these groups, as will become clear in a later chapter, attracted little long-term support until shortly before the outbreak of World War I. The commitment to oppose all forms of minority nationalism permitted employers to assume an even more righteous air, for they were opposing the latest challenge to the unity of the Second Empire: "Upper Silesia must now and in the future be the most important battleground of 'Germandom' and 'Polishdom' (*Grosspolentum*). In this battle Upper Silesian mining—which from head to foot is a German industry—is the strongest mainstay, the most effective support of Germandom." In pursuit of this missionary purpose, which also had the useful by-product of a quiescent labor force, the employer association from 1900 on printed and many firms distributed free a thrice-weekly newspaper, "Der oberschlesische Freund," which was intended to "spread the German language" and "work against Polish nationalist agitation." The run reached 26,000 copies and was soon supplemented by the annual "Arbeiterfreund-Calender." These publications, in addition to emphasizing worker loyalty to their employers, devoted much of their space to praising the German state.[59]

Although local heavy industry deviated at times from this xenophobic chauvinism—particularly in its desire to import seasonal Slavic workers—there was also a good deal of pressure on workers to join patriotic groups like the "Veterans' Organization" and the singing groups, which had as their avowed purpose the inculcation of German patriotic ideals. By 1912 some 225 chapters of veterans and 41 of singers existed. Polish workers formed a minority in such organizations, usually dominated by the German white-collar workers and the German-speaking labor aristocracy. Although practically any list of miners in pre-1914 Upper Silesia is dominated by Polish surnames, German names were predominant in the list of charter members of the singing group founded in 1911 at the Cleophas mine. Moreover, of the fifty-six men, there was only one hauler; all the rest were skilled workers of some sort. Those Poles who did join used the groups as tools for occupational and social mobility, for only those could join the groups who were "patriotic Germans." Often the singing clubs were condemned as German "Tingel-Tangel" clubs, but the very idea was attractive enough to prompt the founding of rival Polish singing groups, like "Echo" in the town of Domb in 1896. Here the local government administrator bid the Hohenlohe works discourage their employees Richard Gajowski and Ernst Szczekalla from establishing a Polish singing organization; it was in the "public interest to battle Polish propaganda with all legally available means." Gajowski and Szczekalla did not withdraw, but a few months later Johann Plonka's activity in "Lutnia" cost him his job at a Hohenlohe zinc smelter, and Joseph Frącek went so far as to get the club to submit an affidavit that he was not the Franz Fronczek mentioned in the membership list. There is no evidence and little likelihood of the existence of parallel clubs of Polish veterans of the German army. The national component in this reluctance to join is emphasized by the readiness of Lower Silesian miners, who were German speakers, to join such groups, even though they received no obvious material benefit from their membership.[60]

Magnate influence over local government abetted control over workers. Not until 1898 did Graf von Tiele-Winckler relinquish his feudal rights over the mining police in the Herrschaft Myslowitz-Kattowitz, which had been exempted from many of the provisions of the mining law of 1865. Some noble entrepreneurs or the corporations which succeeded them controlled mining and smelting areas classified administratively as "estate-counties" (*Gutsbezirke*), an arrangement which implied extensive police and administrative powers over the local population. In 1910 Gieschewald (Giesches Erben) with 4,350 inhabitants and Emanuelsegen (Prince of Pless) with 3,000 were among at least eight such communities in the industrial region with over 42,000 population, all of which appear to have been officially controlled in some way by the local industrial magnate or corporation.[61]

In sum, a grab-bag of motives and methods characterized the list of welfare opportunities made available to workers in Upper Silesian heavy industry. The extensive housing program constituted the major nonwage enticement offered by management; but the basic economic desire to control a loyal, disciplined, and obedient labor force was also fed by employer paternalism, exaggerated fears of socialists, and exclusivist German nationalism. Other brands of paternalism, these demanded by government legislation, were not so popular among top managers because they raised the possibility of outside supervision or of independent worker action. Their hesitations notwithstanding, local employers managed to a certain extent to manipulate these required arrangements to the ends of a less mobile labor force.

Paternalism in Upper Silesia: Required Welfare Organizations

The 1854 law concerning mining brotherhoods and the 1867 law on trades transformed the centuries-old institution of the miner brotherhood into an agent for administration of sickness, old-age, and accident insurance; the social welfare legislation of the 1880s merely incorporated these groups into the national scheme.[62] In the smelting industry, state-initiated schemes were organized through the Silesian Iron and Steel Cooperative Association (*Schlesische Eisen- und Stahl-Berufsgenossenschaft*), created by the laws of the 1880s. Metalworkers in the main worked in small workshops and were not covered by the new arrangements; although comprising a sizable segment of the industrial labor force, these men were of little direct concern to the great entrepreneurs and managers of Upper Silesia.

The statist tradition of government involvement in Prussian industry did not evaporate when the mining laws of the 1850s and 1860s transferred responsibility for hiring and firing from government administrators to the mine owners proper. In the welfare area, the mining brotherhoods continued to enjoy legal support and guidance. They had once signified a separate stratum of society, but the new mining laws eliminated all vestiges of the estate tradition, culminating a trend begun in the early nineteenth century.[63] The law of 1854 ended for all time the special social position accorded those allowed to join the brotherhoods (including a few smelter workers but also excluding large numbers of miners), and from then on the organizations in Prussia functioned as obligatory social insurance groups for all miners. Benefit funds were built up by contributions from both employees and employers, but one practical effect of the 1854 law was to give employers control of appointment of delegates to the boards of directors; subsequent interpretations of the law gave mine directors substantial control over brotherhood activities, including the right of disapproving the president and two vice-presidents of

the brotherhood and even extending to the point of deciding when
and if the board of directors could meet. More drastic measures could
also be taken, as when the administration of the Castellengo-Abwehr
mine, disapproving of the workers' choice for the board of directors
of the brotherhood in 1909, fired the man to prevent his serving in
the post.[64]

Indirectly, this overseeing of the brotherhood boards of directors
entailed a limitation on the freedom of movement law of 1860, for
any mining or smelting worker member of a brotherhood leaving
his job with a particular firm risked losing his membership in a
particular brotherhood and his accumulated sickness and old-age
benefits. Even after all the various Silesian brotherhoods were united
into two units in the 1870s, the large Upper Silesian Miner Brotherhood and the much smaller Pless Brotherhood, employers were
able to exert great pressure to prevent labor migration out of the
region. In this case, no worker's contributions were transferable if
he left Upper Silesia; this situation was alleviated only by the mining
law of 1905, which permitted such transfers. At no time were worker
payments returned if workers left mining work. All of this control
stemmed from one aim: to cut worker turnover, which owners felt
would be multiplied by "the so-called miner brotherhood freedom
of movement"[65] allowed by the 1905 law.

Undeniably, workers were helped by sickness, old-age, and sur-
vivor benefits; however, the monetary benefits of all these arrangements is not at issue here. It is clear that the brotherhoods after
the 1860s no longer conferred high status on members; increasingly
management exerted control over general policy, a situation matched
by developments in the smelting industry pension funds established
under the social insurance laws of the 1880s. All these various funds
came to function as part of a general paternalistic scheme in which
employers, even when concerned with benefits to workers legislated
by the Prussian and German governments, attempted to influence
the patterns of life of the workers.

The labor unrest manifest in the waves of mining strikes of 1889
and 1905-1907 convinced the Prussian state authorities to expand
social welfare legislation beyond benefit funds. To be sure, mine and
factory inspection had turned out to be relatively innocuous. The
reports of the factory and mine inspectors indicated little friction,
with emphasis lying on the employment of women and minors.[66]

The possibility of worker participation in the framing of work rules
proved to be more threatening; management classed this threat
together with the influence of trade unions as undermining the
established and necessary hierarchical relationships in local industry.
Their uneasiness was mixed with apprehensions about monetary
losses, as in their opposition to the 1905 mining law, which forbade

employers from arbitrarily not paying wages for inappropriately filled coal wagons. However, the fear of loss of authority was most marked in the case of the works councils (*Arbeiterausschüsse*), made voluntary in 1892 and compulsory in 1905 for all industrial plants employing more than 100 people.

Despite the example of the Prince of Pless, who had introduced such committees into his mines even before the 1892 law, the sphere of competence of the councils was ill defined. Tasks included the ambiguous assignments of commenting on work rules and forwarding the complaints of workers, but local employers prevented the development of this role into a significant power position. Elections were manipulated, if necessary by transferring popular candidates to another mine shaft, a tactic fought in court by workers of the Hohenzollern mine (Schaffgotsch concern) in 1910; topics of discussion were limited, even to the point of considering the exclusion of all debate on wages, clearly one of the chief points of worker interest. Although occasionally council members like those at Hohenlohe's Neue Helene zinc mine would throw off their docility, timidity generally reigned; industrial archives are replete with minutes of management-dominated meetings, including some called to order and then immediately adjourned for lack of business. The most common report on the councils sounded like this: "There is nothing noteworthy to report on the activity of the works councils. . . ."[67]

Perhaps employers were correct in mistrusting the worker committees and the safety inspection men provided for in a law of 1908; perhaps they realized by this time that their conception of a *Stamm* of workers was chimerical and that workers would not elect the pliable men prized by management. In 1912, for example, a local newspaper maintained that the safety inspection men at the mines were almost completely controlled by the Social Democrats.[68]

Similar distrust of arbitrating institutions was displayed in the workers' hesitant attitude toward industrial courts (*Gewerbegerichte*). Set up in the late nineteenth century, the courts, including representatives of workers and employers, dealt primarily with claims of unfair labor practices, such as quitting or being fired without two weeks notice. These tribunals might eventually have proved helpful in acclimatizing workers and managers to settlement of disputes without violent or work-disrupting protest; but employers adamantly opposed greater participation by mere hired hands, and workers in the main hesitated to trust government institutions to completely resolve work issues. Experience in other industrial societies has indicated that such grievance procedures do not wholly satisfy participants in modern industry.

In the final analysis, the grievance procedure turned out to be so much pap, and the workers knew it. They expected little of the arbitration courts, as evidenced by complaints about the court in the *Gazeta Robotnicza* of July 21, 1906, and in letters to the regency president in Oppeln in 1907;[69] at the same time works councils and plant safety men were effectively throttled by plant directors. Thus before the growth of labor unions wildcat strikes were almost the only method of manifesting protest, except through individual disruptive procedures like turnover and absenteeism and the resultant long-term low productivity.

Given this myriad of employer-sponsored funds, organizations, and activities, it is relevant to ask what "paternalism" actually meant in the context of Upper Silesia. Paternalism does not merely involve the granting of extensive fringe benefits and the sponsoring of extramural activities, for these all may be developed in an atmosphere of purely market-oriented company policies. The crucial question is how such programs were manipulated to exert control over the workers' entire way of life. It does not suffice merely to list a series of measures intended somehow to benefit workers; one must investigate the implementation by employers of their extensive welfare programs. Though records on the 1870s are sparse, enough information exists to show that the group of Upper Silesian industrialists and top managers made an obvious attempt in this decade to direct the daily lives of the workers. The *Arbeiterstamm* concept was in essence a way to build the industrial community inerent in a paternalistic arrangement, but this particular effort quickly ebbed in the face of the rapidly growing labor force required by expanding market demand for local ores and metal products. It proved quite difficult to maintain close supervision over the home lives of the members of a rapidly changing labor force regardless of employer intent.

Only in an unusual case could real paternalistic policies be maintained down to 1914. This was particularly so at the mines of the Prince of Pless, where there was even a separate miner brotherhood for the small mining crew (about 1,000 people) and where the first and only employer-initiated works councils in Upper Silesia were found. Still, this was a special case, made possible in large part by the location of these mines on the periphery of the industrial area and by the very slow growth of this particular labor force, conditions that enabled management and workers to establish a close relationship lacking elsewhere in the region. The wealth of the prince also enabled him to avoid incorporation and to maintain a more personalized regime.

So it turned out that neither company owned housing nor the post-1890 development of extensive welfare institutions could serve to manipulate closely the style of life of the mining and smelting workers. Upper Silesian employers, like their peers in the Ruhr and in other industrial countries, never willingly ceded the slightest bit of rule-making power and apparently never considered any of their concessions as permanent; their welfare projects became simply tools in attracting and keeping employees and perhaps were useful in limiting the latter's occupational and geographic mobility, though even this control was severely restricted by the miner brotherhood freedom-of-movement law of 1905. From the mid-1880s on there could be no question of a "paternal" relationship between worker and boss, for the hard issues of wages and hours and the less clearly defined issues of rule-making authority came increasingly to dominate labor-management relations. What is important here is that top management, because of its immense power over the mining and smelting workers, could afford to perpetuate modes of dealing with workers which had been developed under earlier labor market conditions; as the realities of production shifted, the use to which these programs were put changed, but their partly outmoded form remained.

7

The Definition of Labor-Management Relations: Wages and Hours

Even in the urbanized fully industrial countries of the modern world, workers are not attracted to jobs by wages alone, for a host of extramonetary considerations weigh heavily in decisions about where to work. In order to take account of these other factors, the present study has dwelt on recruitment, housing, and welfare policies. It should be clear by now that I consider "paternalism" to have been extremely important before the 1890s and to have become less decisive in the quarter century before World War I. No doubt so-called traditional attitudes remained important to large numbers of workers, and one must be careful to differentiate first and second generation unskilled industrial workers from craftsmen with a longer memory of industrial work. But one of the chief lessons of Upper Silesia lies in the observation that Upper Silesian mining and smelting workers could indeed learn to function well in a new situation, regardless of where their long-term preferences lay. As the character of the labor market shifted and as the local labor force adapted to an industrial life style, wages, hours, and control over rule-making in the mine and on the shop floor dominated the conflicts between employers and employees. The rest of this book revolves around these points of conflict.[1]

Wages

The record of the absolute level of wage rates of coal miners in Upper Silesia is easy enough to find; wages for other types of mining and smelting are not so readily available, though some material does exist.[2]

As indicated by Figure 3, before the 1880s wage rates in Upper Silesia moved very unfavorably for coal miners. In the crash following the boom of 1873, expansion of the labor force slowed considerably; production flagged; and wages of hewers and haulers fell precipitously the rest of the decade. Wage rates for other mining workers remained more or less steady; had they fallen any lower, these low-ranked people might have dropped out of the labor force altogether. The industrial cyclical recovery after 1879 turned out to be advantageous for hewers and haulers only; the wages of women, minors, and other underground workers proved to be extremely sticky. Only with the production upswing of 1888 did the wages of these other groups join the now rising trend of mining wage rates,[3] though gains of women and minors proved to be transitory. After another period of stagnation in the early 1890s, the wages of women and children rose very little (real wages fell), while the money wages for all other miners rose sharply, except for dips in 1902-1904 and 1908-1910. Thus any talk of improved standards of living cannot refer to those unskilled employed at the bottom of the pay scale.

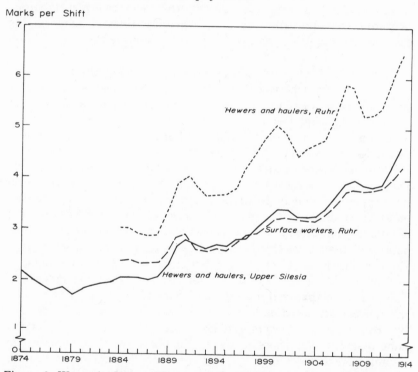

Figure 3. Wages in Upper Silesia and the Ruhr, 1874-1913, in marks per shift. Source: ZBHS, annual statistics, for 1889-1913 collected by Gerhard Bry, *Wages in Germany*, 1871-1945 (Princeton: Princeton University, 1960), pp. 342-343, 389-391.

Figures for other mining industries are not so clear as those for coal mining. Zinc, lead, and iron miners were few in comparison with coal miners; the iron miners in particular were a dying breed due to the exhaustion of local ore deposits. From a high of some 4,300 iron miners in 1890 (4,300 in 1872; 2,400 in 1880) the work force declined to 3,000 in 1900 and 1,000 in 1913. Zinc mining averaged 7,500 workers in the 1870s, and 10,000 thereafter; lead miners numbered fewer than 1,000.[4]

All three groups were paid less per shift than coal miners. In 1905, for instance, hewers in coal mines received an average 3.79 marks per shift; in zinc and lead, 3.10 marks; in iron, 2.36 marks. Haulers in coal earned about 3.25 marks a shift, in the other three types of mines they got 2.63, 2.63, and 2.27 marks respectively.[5] On the other hand, many coal miners worked ten hours, while the others ordinarily worked only eight. It is hard to know how contemporaries weighed leisure versus extra pay. Still, coal miners do seem to have been the most prosperous of all these; the lead, zinc, and iron mines could apparently attract newcomers only from the immediately surrounding areas and from among the alien seasonal laborers. Migrants, even short-distance ones, gravitated toward higher-paying coal and iron-smelting jobs, which in any case were the most readily available positions.

Two types of wage disparities existed in Upper Silesian mining and smelting: that between the skilled and unskilled, a gap cutting across all industries but masked by the unavoidable use of average wages, and that between the stagnant or moribund endeavors of zinc, iron, and lead mining on the one hand and the semi-finished metal industries and coal mining on the other.[6]

No great inter-industry wage differential appeared among zinc smelters, iron and steel foundries, rolling mills, blast furnace operations, pipe and nail factories, and coal mines (hewers and haulers only). In contrast to the great distinctions between different types of mining, semi-finished zinc and iron and steel (1887—first available data) presented a relatively uniform wage front. Some areas jumped ahead of others for brief periods, but none stayed ahead so long as to draw off large numbers of workers from neighboring industries. Table 12 shows that coal-mining wages were comparatively low before the strikes and raises of 1889, but the gap then started to narrow. By 1896 wages for hewers and haulers in coal-mining were of the same magnitude as those in the metal industry; they remained in a similar bracket down to the war. The very low wages for surface workers indicate the problems faced by the unskilled everywhere in the area.

Even though coal mining employed a rising percentage of workers, the smelting and metal industries by the 1890s had grown sufficiently large to present some potential employment alternatives to local seekers; but by that time coal-mining wages were competitive. About 50,000 persons worked in the smelting and metal industries in 1913, but it is difficult to interpret their average wages because available figures do not permit a breakdown by skill. In addition, one must approach the owners' statistics with a certain reserve. For example, only average annual wages were given, and it seems that some supervisors were included in this average. Besides, in all these areas women and minors, who constituted a significant element of the labor force, earned appreciably less than adult male workers and received raises at a much slower pace. The situation for these underprivileged employees was similar to the one in coal mining, where these immobile groups hardly shared in the general prosperity.

It is also important to note that iron and steel workers in Upper Silesia were paid less than iron and steel workers anywhere else in Germany, receiving wages far below those prevailing in any other section of the country in the period 1888-1912.[7] That is why figures on money wages are important; comparison of rates in industrial regions suggests why long-range migrants rarely chose to move to Upper Silesia for work.

Though wage rates in Upper Silesian coal mining rose over time, those in the Ruhr (and in the Saar) consistently stayed a good deal higher than those in Upper Silesia. As a matter of fact, average wages per shift in Upper Silesia in the 1889-1914 period were lower than the average in every other bituminous mining area of Germany except for Lower Silesia;[8] almost until 1900 even the Ruhr surface workers, the very lowest people in the hierarchy of adult mine workers, earned a shift wage higher than the hewer-hauler average in Upper Silesia, and until the World War these Ruhr surface workers continued to be paid at a rate not much less than the Upper Silesian hewer-hauler average. Wages per shift in the Ruhr were much higher than in Upper Silesia, despite the more difficult geologic conditions in the western area and despite the fact that Ruhr miners worked fewer hours per shift for this higher pay. These relationships are presented graphically in figure 4. Comparative wages for all German mining areas are then given in tabular form with the aim of pointing to the inferior competitive position of Upper Silesian coal mining in the German labor market, for Upper Silesian hewer-hauler wage rates consistently lay below the all-German average. Lignite workers in Halle, bituminous miners in the Saar, even hewers and haulers in Lower Silesia (before 1900) outdistanced Upper Silesia in wages.

It would also be interesting to compare Upper Silesian annual wages with the national average, but this has proved impossible. Hoffman and his associates have reckoned an annual all-Germany mining wage, but they arrived at their figures by assuming 310 shifts per year per worker. The Upper Silesian coal miner, however, rarely averaged over 290 shifts per year, and the Ruhr workers fluctuated considerably between 300 and 320 shifts.[9] Thus Ruhr miners worked shorter workdays and received more pay per shift than the Upper Silesian workers, but the Ruhr miners also worked many more shifts per year.

Industrialists defended themselves against the charge of low wages by pointing out that it was unfair to compare average wages because

TABLE 12

Annual Wages in Upper Silesian Heavy Industry, 1887–1911

(Marks per year)

Year	Coal mining: hewers, haulers[a]	Coal mining: surface workers[b]	Blast furnaces[b]	Iron and steel foundries[b]	Iron and steel rolling mills[b]	Zinc smelting[b]	Wire, pipes, nails, etc.[b] (adult males only)
1887	548	437	656	617	684	677	578
1893	728	591	806	744	780	804	757
1899	899	683	930	859	922	922	869
1907	1112	852	1085	1027	1069	1119	1056
1911	1106	888	1169	1048	1147	1172	1127

SOURCES:

[a]ZBHS, 1887–1914, for shift wages, multiplied by average number of shifts worked annually (also from ZBHS).
[b]ZOBH, 1887–1912.

Marks per Shift

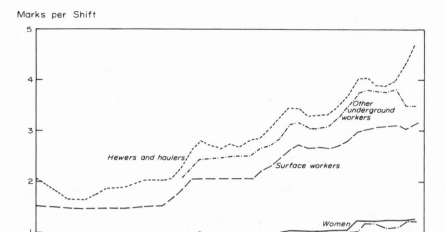

Figure 4. Wages in Upper Silesian mining, 1874-1913, in marks per shift. Source: ZBHS: 1875-1914, for 1889-1913 collected by Karol Jonca, *Polozenie robotników w przemyśle górniczo-hutniczym na Sląsku w latach 1889-1914* [The position of the workers in the mining and smelting industry in Silesia, 1889-1914] (Wroclaw: 1960), pp. 154-155.

the Upper Silesian work force contained proportionately more unskilled, and hence lower-paid, workers than did other areas; consequently, the average wage was dragged down. In 1912, 34.2 percent of the mining force was unskilled in Upper Silesia; 22.9 percent in the Saar; 22.8 percent in the Ruhr.[10] In addition, the lower paid, semi-skilled haulers comprised a larger segment of underground workers than in other areas, again lowering the average wage. However, it was not only the popular image of a low-wage area that hampered recruiting efforts; in actuality Upper Silesian wages did lag behind other regions, as exemplified in the fact that the wages of Ruhr surface workers kept pace with the rates of the most highly paid Upper Silesian miners. (See Figure 3.) It is particularly striking that as the wages of hewers, haulers, and surface workers began a continual rise from 1888 on, the pay of women and minors rose only very slowly (Figure 4); and it was precisely among the lower-paid groups that significant expansion of the work force took place after the turn of the century. The loudly heralded labor shortage was apparently not the only reason for hiring women, minors, and foreign workers; the ability to pay extremely low wages proved very attractive to employers at a time when other rates of pay were rapidly moving upward.

Another excuse for niggardly wages lay in the wage supplements granted by many firms. The employers' association reacted indig-

TABLE 13

Wages in German Mining, 1874–1913 (Selected Years)

(Marks per shift)

Year	BITUMINOUS[a]							LIGNITE
	Ruhr[b]		Upper Silesia[c]		Saar[b]	Lower Silesia[c]		Halle[b]
	Hewers, haulers	Surface workers	Hewers, haulers	Surface workers	Hewers, haulers	Hewers, haulers	Surface workers	Hewers, haulers
1874			2.17	1.53				
1878			1.84	1.32				
1882			1.96	1.46				
1884	3.08	2.36	2.02	1.46				
1886	2.92	2.35	2.03	1.58				
1889	3.42	2.57	2.31	1.83	3.44	2.40	2.03	2.60
1893	3.71	2.70	2.74	2.15	3.83	2.60	2.21	2.83
1896	3.90	2.81	2.82	2.16	3.73	2.68	2.24	2.94
1899	4.84	3.18	3.27	2.44	3.99	3.04	2.49	3.32
1903	4.64	3.29	3.37	2.65	4.12	2.93	2.59	3.42
1907	5.98	3.87	4.00	3.00	4.57	3.57	2.99	4.10
1911	5.55	3.97	3.98	3.13	4.60	3.54	3.08	4.16
1913	6.47	4.34	4.85	3.19	5.18	3.84	3.09	4.31

[a]Bituminous—*Steinkohle*.

SOURCES:

[b]ZBHS 1875–1914, 1885–1914, after 1889 compiled by Gerhard Bry, *Wages in Germany, 1871–1945* (Princeton, 1960), pp. 343–348, 389–391.

[c]ZBHS 1875–1914, after 1889 compiled by Karol Jonca, *Polozenie robotników w przemyśle górniczo-hutniczym na Śląsku 1889–1914* [The position of the workers in the mining and smelting industry in Silesia, 1889–1914] (Wroclaw, 1960) pp. 154–157.

nantly to the cost-of-living bonuses granted at the Friedrich smelter in 1905. This action, the association felt, affected the wage level; cheap meat should have been sold rather than making money grants, for these tended to affect wages elsewhere.[11] The modern observer can only note that this was a form of wages in kind, characteristic of more primitive stages of capitalism.

To be sure, emphasis here has been laid primarily on the level of wages offered by employers, but one of the arguments running through the present study is that only through management initiative could there come about the gradual acclimatization to industrial work and the Stakhanovite labor force desired by employers. Very commonly management complained that higher wages, instead of inducing increased effort, merely resulted in fewer days worked; since workers lived "from hand to mouth," once the desired earnings level was reached in a given period of time, a day off seemed in order. Yet strangely enough the average number of days worked per year remained relatively constant at least as far back as 1886 (see chapter

8). One suspects that much of the fuss was feigned, or at least exaggerated, and that the "backward bending supply curve of labor" had ceased to operate in Upper Silesian mining and smelting before the 1880s (if it had ever been operative). About the 1870s little can be said except that management complained of carousing at night which resulted in absenteeism the following day,[12] but such behavior certainly did not stem from the leisure afforded by excess wages. Indeed, the 1870s constituted the nadir of local wage trends in the period of rapid industrial development.

Wages and prices in Wilhelmine Germany in recent years have been the topic of several noteworthy studies,[13] but regionally specific information on Upper Silesian real wages is hard to obtain.

The cost-of-living is an elusive figure, particularly when dealing with a region which might well deviate from national averages, especially in the costs of rent and fuel.[14] Upper Silesian employers always contended that the low food prices of the region justified their comparatively low wage rates. Situated close to major grain-producing areas, Upper Silesian residents probably enjoyed lower prices for such products than did workers in western Germany, but consumers also purchased meat products, as well as demanding clothing, light, fuel, and housing. Meat products had no such geographical advantage, and clothing centers were certainly no closer to Upper Silesia than to other heavy industrial centers. Fuel, naturally, was obtained locally; but the well-known shortage of housing certainly drove up rents, despite lower rents in company owned housing. Lastly, one must realize that a considerable number of Upper Silesian workers had supplemental incomes from kitchen gardens, barnyard animals, and from small farm plots. Suffice it to recall chapter 4, where it was pointed out how common it was for local industrial workers to retain some small connection with farming. All of these factors make it extremely difficult to speculate on average rent.

Another important problem is that available price series refer to national averages. One author, for example, has gathered material on the changing price of rye in the six major cities of the industrial region; but for prices of other food products he was forced to rely on national averages, which often enough were computed on the basis of figures taken from other regions. This bias is even more pronounced in statistics on rents, which no doubt differed markedly from city to city; here historians have examined only the very big cities, none of which were situated in Upper Silesia.[15] The great firms of Upper Silesia were happy to boast of their extensive housing programs, but one finds practically no mention of prevailing rents. Besides, the majority of workers lived either in privately rented quarters, which are notoriously high-priced in densely populated areas, or on their own plot of land, in which case rent was not a significant element in their expenses.

Using a cost-of-living index derived for Germany as a whole[16] (Table 14), one sees that mining wages moved in the same general pattern as rent, food, and clothing in the period 1871-1900. Real wages exhibited no significant rise before the late 1880s. The 1870s and 1880s witnessed a sharp decline in all prices and wages after the crash of 1873, leaving workers in their practically subsistence situation. From 1888 to 1900, wage rates moved upward while prices held more or less steady. After 1900, however, the increase in real wages was stemmed by skyrocketing prices.[17] That Upper Silesian wages followed the national pattern indicates how well integrated the area was into the national labor market and how management assertions of a significantly lower cost of living in the area were distinctly unimpressive to prospective immigrants.

TABLE 14
Cost of Living Index in Germany, 1871–1913
(1895=100)

Years	Food	Clothing	Fuel	Lighting	Rent	Total	Upper Silesian Mining Wages (All-Miner Average)
1871–1875	112	123	174		97	115	73
1876–1880	108	92	99		93	103	64
1881–1885	104	94	97		92	101	67
1886–1890	100	86	116	112	100	100	86
1891–1895	104	95	107	96	100	102	101
1896–1900	102	103	108	101	109	103	112
1901–1905	109	110	112	102	112	109	125
1906–1910	121	119	123	103	125	121	144
1911–1913	129	129	123	101	133	129	150

SOURCES: Cost of living—Ashok V. Desai, *Real Wages in Germany, 1871–1913* (London, 1968), p. 117, here converted to 5-year averages (except for rent, which is given for every fifth year) and to a 1911–1913 average. Wages—ZBHS 1874–1913, for 1889–1913 compiled by Karol Jonca, *Polozenie robotników w przemyśle górniczo-hutniczym na Śląsku 1889–1914* [The position of the workers in the mining and smelting industry in Silesia, 1889–1914] (Wroclaw, 1960), p. 154.
(All numbers rounded to nearest whole number)

This survey is bolstered by such scattered evidence as the fact that Upper Silesian workers seemed to use their increased wages to purchase goods other than rye and wheat, indicating that they could afford a better diet, or at least a more varied one.[18] Or, to take another case, after 1890 the increased availability of company housing mentioned in chapter 6 may have meant lower average rents, thus raising the average real wage.

Employers were not averse to a rise in real wages if it did not cost them very much. They were not unaware of the connection between rising food costs and labor unrest, and they hastened to alleviate the pressure by means other than raising wages or by the more ordinary granting (or selling cheap) of potatoes to workers. In 1896 and again in 1903 the Upper Silesian mining and smelting employers' association sought special permission to import Russian swine to combat high meat prices; in 1896-1897 they supported lower tariffs on potatoes and cabbage. Note that the organization desired government intervention to counter the effects of the high cost of living; employers were loath to increase wages, as evidenced in their rebuke of the Friedrichshütte employers mentioned above.[19]

In conclusion, the exigencies of production, the shortage of labor, and pressure from the workers themselves all combined to effect an improvement in money and real wages for underground miners from the late 1880s (or at least from the mid-1890s) to the turn of the century; real wages rose slowly after 1900. Employers learned, albeit reluctantly, that the formation of an industrial labor force required not only a change in the life style of the worker—from farmer or peasant in the factory to proletarian—but also required increased remuneration and improved working conditions. Where wages lagged behind the average, workers were inclined to be less productive. While demand for industrial products was slack (1870s, mid-1880s, early 1890s), employers could afford to ignore worker habits that indicated dislike of industrial life (for example, absenteeism); when demand started to rise markedly and workers became more militant, incentives had to be provided to ensure a more regular work force. Among these incentives, wages stood out as one of the most important. It is doubtful that higher wages alone can generate worker loyalty to one's employer and diligence at one's job, but there can be no ignoring the importance of wage relations. One might even suppose that the post-1900 inflation contributed to an increasing unrest among workers, unrest which fed the strike of 1905-1907 and the somewhat successful unionization campaign beginning in 1908.

On the whole it seems that Upper Silesian heavy industry continued to be much less attractive to prospective workers than were the other major industrial areas, the Berlin-Brandenburg and the Ruhr regions. After all, local wages lagged behind those of the other areas; the old problems of housing and language remained; and the workday in Upper Silesia remained appreciably longer than in the Ruhr.

Hours

Quite often modern discussion of the propensity of new industrial workers to limit severely the number of hours worked focuses on the attitude and behavior of workers in relation to the prevailing wage rates; yet the development of the labor force of the Upper Silesian mining and smelting works was shaped in good part not only by the question of earnings, but also by conditions of work, including the question of hours. Employers sought to regulate hours and work rules by fiat; but the government, the workers, and fluctuations in the business cycle all played a role in determining how these working conditions evolved in Upper Silesia.[20]

It is easy enough to see a general shortening of working hours in coal mining after 1889. This process was less noticeable in other types of mining and particularly absent from smelting. Evidence for the 1870s and 1880s is hard to find, especially since a pre-1889 work "shift" in Upper Silesia referred to a specific amount of product, not to a certain number of hours.[21] Still, it seems that in the first quarter of 1889 over 97 percent of all coal miners worked twelve hours per day, and only 2 percent worked eight hours. Given the oversupply of labor and the sluggish market prevalent in the 1870s and 1880s, one might expect this situation in early 1889 faithfully to reflect conditions of the previous twenty years. However, following the great nationwide mining strikes of 1889 and the accelerated pace of labor force expansion, by the fourth quarter of the year only 64 percent worked twelve hours; 32 percent, ten hours; and 4 percent, eight hours.[22] From then on the number of hours worked by most categories of workers declined steadily; by the end of the first decade of the twentieth century, large numbers of most groups of workers officially worked ten-hour shifts, with the trend toward shorter hours being evident in all categories except among surface workers. Quite likely the stickiness in hours for this one group lay in the presence of foreign seasonal laborers, most of whom were employed as unskilled surface workers; due to their presence, full-time employees could exert even less leverage than usual on the mine administrations. For all categories of workers, the eight-hour day proved to be much more elusive; it was not reached for most workers by the time of the outbreak of the war. (See Table 15.)

Upper Silesia, even with slow reductions in working time occasioned by prosperity and by a shortage of workers, stood out as the German mining region with the longest working day. In 1902, for example, Upper Silesian coal production per man per shift (1.118 tons) was appreciably higher than in the Ruhr (0.828 tons) or the Saar (0.726 tons), but in the western German areas the length of an underground shift was eight or ten hours, whereas in the east large numbers of miners worked twelve-hour shifts.[23]

TABLE 15

Hours Worked by Upper Silesian Coal Miners, 1891–1910

	Percentage of Workers		
	1891	*1900*	*1910*
Hewers and Haulers working:			
8 hours	11.4	9.7	20.4
10 hours	34.5	59.3	70.2
12 hours	45.1	31.0	9.4
Other underground miners working:			
8 hours	7.4	7.5	18.7
10 hours	46.5	46.5	54.0
12 hours	46.1	46.8	27.3
Minors working:			
8 hours	25.2	23.9	25.0
10 hours	20.1	52.0	48.5
12 hours	54.7	24.1	26.5
Surface miners working:			
8 hours	4.2	3.8	4.2
10 hours	32.7	33.8	29.5
12 hours	63.1	62.4	66.3
Adult women working:			
8 hours	7.9	1.4	7.8
10 hours	23.9	59.5	47.7
12 hours	68.2	39.5	44.5

SOURCE: ZBHS, statistical section, 1892–1914, compiled by Karol Jonca, *Polozenie robotników w przemyśle górniczo-hutniczym na Śląsku 1889–1914* [The position of the workers in the mining and smelting industry in Silesia, 1889–1914] (Wroclaw, 1960), p. 124.

Such slow change was illustrated in the form of the model work rules published by the Upper Silesian Mine and Smelter Owner Association in 1905, where auxiliary workers above and below ground were marked for twelve-hour shifts, while hours for hewers and haulers were left to be filled in by the individual employer.[24] In a year when over 75 percent of the local hewers and haulers worked ten-hour shifts, Upper Silesian employers displayed no willingness to make ten hours the general rule.

The situation was not so advantageous for coal miners as these percentage changes indicate. Employment trends showed that although the level of employment of women remained steady after 1889, the relative number of workers with shorter hours (especially hewers) was declining, while the relative and absolute number of haulers, minors, and foreign laborers was increasing rapidly. This situation allowed employers to speak of "shorter hours" while at the same time maintaining the old standard. At the König mine near Königshütte, largest in Upper Silesia and reputedly ahead of all others in concern for workers, the 1898 work rules acknowledged a nine-hour day for hewers, but provided for "up to 12 hours" for haulers and a definite twelve hours for auxiliary workers both above and below ground.[25]

Evidence is lacking concerning hours in zinc and lead mining, but one suspects a situation similar to that in coal. For example, the underground workers of the Neue Fortuna lead mine in 1889, 1890, and 1891 worked nine and one-half to ten and one-half hours daily, while all surface workers worked twelve hours, even though the work rules of 1892 spoke of nine hours for hewers and twelve hours for others both above and below the surface.[26] Here again the increasing differentiation between the skilled hewers and the other workers emerges.

On the general German scene, the eastern mining regions lagged behind the Ruhr in terms of hours. Once the reductions of 1889 had been made, the Silesian workday declined much more slowly than in the Ruhr. After 1900, the length of shift declined markedly in the Ruhr but stagnated in Upper Silesia. In fact, in a number of mines the twelve-hour day and the twenty-four-hour swing shift (the change made twice a month from day to night shift) remained in effect all through the prewar period. Even where working hours had been shortened, there was no guarantee that employers would not attempt to alter the situation when management felt strong enough to do so, as when in 1896 government mines lengthened the work day from nine to nine and one-half hours. When the administration of the Donnersmarkhütte coal mine in 1908 instituted a one-hour pause between the eight-hour shifts, the reputation of management was such that the miners struck, fearing this move as an opening to a nine-hour work day.[27] (The change was rescinded.)

Although existing evidence on smelting is not conclusive, it seems that similar trends emphasizing the role of workers with lower pay and longer hours marked these industries also, except that there the working day traditionally exceeded the mining day. To understand that situation, a few remarks must be inserted on the technological development of smelting.

The mining laws of the 1850s and 1860s did not mark a caesura

TABLE 16
Lengths of Shifts in German Mining, 1904–1907
(hours)

Mining Region	Average Length of Shift			
	1904[a]	1905[b]	1906[b]	1907[b]
Upper Silesia	8–12	8–12	8–12	8–12
Lower Silesia	8–12	8–12	8–12	8–12
Dortmund (Ruhr)	8–9	7–9	6–8	6–8

SOURCE: H. Imbusch, *Arbeitsverhältnisse und Arbeiterorganisationen im deutschen Bergbau* (Essen, n.d.), p. 70
[a]1904: including descent into and ascent out of mine.
[b]1905–1907: excluding descent and ascent.

in smelting as they did in mining because local entrepreneurs had not been so totally subject to extensive government control over their activities. The technology of smelting was, of course, quite different from that of mining.[28] While western Europe in the 1860s and 1870s was experiencing a revolution in steelmaking, Upper Silesian smelting continued to be dominated by puddling. Local iron ore was too high in phosporous to use in the Bessemer converter but too low in phosporous to use in the Thomas-Gilchrist furnace; the Siemens-Martin open-hearth process could be used only with the addition of large amounts of scrap metal, which was not plentiful on the local level. Puddling therefore dominated until the late 1890s, when the import of higher grade ores began; after 1900 the local machine industry was mature enough to generate sufficient scrap for the open-hearth furnaces. Only in the 1890s and for reasons not inherent in any business cycle did the puddlers begin to disappear from the Upper Silesian landscape. In short, the differentiation between skilled and unskilled workers, always more marked in smelting than in mining, was perpetuated by technological circumstances; this was reflected in working hours.

Before the Prussian government sold the König smelter to private interests in 1870, the royal smelting plants had dominated Upper Silesian metallurgy; even after the formation of the now privately owned Vereinigte Königs- und Laurahütte, royal production remained important. According to the work rules of 1861, the workday at the government-owned Friedrich smelter was thirteen hours in summer and twelve in winter; women and minors worked twelve-hour shifts in all seasons. In 1890 the work day in government smelters was officially cut to twelve hours; however, Sunday work (seven-day work weeks) and twenty-four-hour swing shifts continued to be common. The only exception to this strenuous regimen was made for certain unhealthy jobs, for which three eight-hour shifts were instituted.[29]

The three-shift system (eight hours each) made little headway among Silesian iron and steel industrialists.[30] On the whole, the twelve-hour day at both private and government smelters remained the rule into the twentieth century; at the Guidotto zinc smelter near Chropaczow, for example, the work day at blast-furnaces lasted from 6 a.m. to 6 p.m. and from 6 p.m. to 6 a.m. On Sundays, those changing shifts worked a twenty-four-hour day. Other workers toiled from 5:30 a.m. to 6:30 p.m., though women were allowed to quit work an hour and a half earlier.[31]

By taking advantage of legal exceptions for enterprises requiring nonstop work, Upper Silesian smelter owners managed to sustain the twelve-hour day in the major operations of iron, zinc, and lead smelting all through the prewar period.[32] Indeed, the demand for an eight-hour day in iron smelting on the eve of World War I was countered with the plea of labor shortage; should the work day be cut, warned the journal of the employers, artisanry and agriculture would be decimated in the ensuing competition for workers in metallurgy. Therefore, the journal piously proclaimed, the introduction of the eight-hour day into the iron smelting industry would be a calamity for all German industry.[33]

The official working day does not reveal the entire situation, for Sunday work (seven days) and forced overtime were common. Few data exist for the period before the 1890s because Prussian factory inspection was not concerned with these problems before the enlargement of the inspection force under the factory inspection law of 1892. Even then inspectors could check on Sunday work only with difficulty; forced overtime was not proscribed by law and could merely be noted in the factory inspector reports. As industries grew, authorities attempted to limit such work except in plants requiring twenty-four-hour operation, principally the blast furnaces and roasting ovens in the iron, zinc, and lead industries. Still, in 1900 factory inspectors continued to voice complaints that the Sunday rest rules were not being complied with satisfactorily in all Upper Silesian industries, light and heavy, one indication that employers in heavy industry were not the only ones making it difficult for workers to commit themselves to a particular job. Despite the promised enforcement by factory inspectors, forced (and illegal) Sunday and holiday work continued into the twentieth century, as witnessed by a 1903 strike at a zinc roasting smelter in protest against such seven-day weeks.[34]

Just as forced Sunday work might promote turnover by creating unpleasant working conditions, so might forced overtime, a practice common to all the Upper Silesian mining and smelting industries in periods of peak demand. Again, no records exist for the years 1870-1888, but the ubiquity of required overtime from the 1890s until 1914 indicates that employers most likely would have acted similarly in the 1870s and 1880s had the demand occasioned. However, a labor shortage did not appear until the late 1880s (chapter 2), and it is reasonable to assume that forced overtime was a reaction to a shortage of labor; therefore, most cases of extended hours are likely to have occurred from the late 1880s on.

It is difficult to document specific cases of forced overtime, but complaints of this practice were so general that there can be no doubt of its widespread existence, even after it was outlawed in 1905. Occasionally, embittered workers would complain very strenuously, as when workers at the Deutschland mine were said to be quite rebellious about increased working time in 1898. In 1908 the Higher Mining Office in Breslau felt constrained to warn mining officials in Beuthen that labor shortage, demand for coal, and needed repairs were not sufficient to merit the very high number of extended shifts required of miners. Such warnings were not overly effective, as revealed by worker complaints in 1913 in this same area about being required to work one and one-quarter shifts or be punished. The metallurgical industries, because of the indulgence of the *Bundesrat*, were even legally able to maintain a high level of overtime. In 1910, for example, about 40 percent of the 32,000 workers surveyed often put in added hours.[35]

In light of constant employer complaints that higher wages induced Upper Silesian workers to work less, it is almost laughable to read the note of the Samuels-Glück lead and zinc mine to local officials: "Because of the notorious shortage of workers, we place great value on the voluntary working of at the most four-hour extra shifts by willing workers." Such cant did not stem workers' complaints. Other, more feasible defenses were also thrown out for public consumption, particularly the contention that the excessive absenteeism of the "high-living" Upper Silesian worker—in this case, smelting workers— necessitated compensatory overtime. Perhaps so, but the same factory inspector report laying the blame on irresponsible workers also pointed to the shortage of skilled workers as the basis for overtime in the metallurgical industries.[36]

In conclusion, one should not omit mention of the relative position of working hours in Upper Silesian mining and smelting vis-à-vis German industry as a whole.[37] Bituminous mining had the shortest average work week in all of German industry from 1885 to 1914 (earlier years not available). Averaging 51 to 53 hours weekly in the 1880s and 1890s, the mean work week dropped to 46 hours in 1900-1905, 48-1/2 hours in 1905-1910, and 50 hours in 1910-1914. All of this is paltry in light of the Upper Silesian work schedule. Six days of 10-12 hours each meant 60 to 72 hours weekly in coal mining, as opposed to the 51 to 53 national average before 1890; even after 1890 significant numbers of local workers put in 10-hour shifts in mining.

As late as 1912 over 70 percent of the hewers and haulers and many more than half of all other miners worked 10-hour days, while in the Ruhr, Lower Silesia, and the Saar over 98 percent of the hewers and haulers worked only 8 hours daily. Only surface workers in these areas continued to work longer shifts of up to 12 hours.[38]

All other industries had longer days than coal mining, in most cases by significant amounts; however, only scattered data are available for smelting and metalworking (table 17). German smelting workers averaged 66 hours weekly in 1875-1880 and 1885-1890 (77 hours for blast furnace workers), dropping to 63 hours in the 1890s and 60 hours in 1910-1914 (no data for 1900-1910). Metalworkers fared slightly better: 65 to 66 hours in 1880-1890, 61-1/2 hours in 1895-1900, and 56 hours in 1910-1914. Even more than in mining the 10- and especially 12-hour day predominated in Upper Silesian smelting, signifying once again the inferior position of the Upper Silesian metallurgical workers (compared to other parts of Germany), though not in so gross a measure as in coal mining.

TABLE 17

Hours Worked per Week in the German Metal Industry, 1875–1914

Years	Smelting workers	Metalworkers
1875–1880	66 (blast furnace workers:77)	
1880–1890		65-66.5
1885–1890	66 (blast furnace workers:77)	
1890–1899	60	
1895–1900		61.5
1910–1914	60	56.0

SOURCE: Ruth Meinert, *Die Entwicklung der Arbeitszeit in der deutschen Industrie 1820–1956* (diss. Münster, 1958), as cited by Walter Hoffmann et al., *Das Wachstum der deutschen Wirtschaft seit der Mitte des 19. Jahrhunderts* (Berlin, 1965), pp. 213–214.

In terms of hours worked, it seems then that mining concerns attempted to overcome their shortage of labor by requiring extended working days, while smelting plants used a loophole in welfare legislation to force workers to report on Sundays and holidays. Here again it appears that conditions at work militated against a loyal work crew which would tend to stay at one job. High rates of absenteeism and turnover, while due in part to drunkenness and instability in industrial society, very likely were also based on the physical need for rest and recuperation from strenuous labor. If a committed labor force connotes a feeling of responsibility to one's job on the part of workers, the development of such feeling requires reciprocal action on the part of employers in the form of hospitable working conditions, particularly in terms of hours of work. Such reciprocity did not appear by the time World War I broke out, at which time the state itself required longer hours of work to support the war effort.

In this sense vacations too would have relieved physical strain on workers, but hardly any mines or smelters were prepared to grant such things to workers. That people were aware of the problem is clear from factory and mine inspectors' reports from 1907 on,[39] but little progress was made. There were a few exceptions, usually in the form of leave for a limited number of workers, as at the Brandenburg mine (near Beuthen), the König mine, and at the Heinitz and Blei-Scharley mines, but these were generally cited as unusual cases. A few workers also qualified for "rest leaves," but in the main vacations, paid or unpaid, figured hardly at all in pre-World War I mining and smelting in Upper Silesia. Most firms found such leave unnecessary, sometimes justifying their policies by remarking that workers got their needed rest on the numerous Catholic holidays, which were not work days.[40] Official time-off was augmented, of course, by continual high rates of absenteeism on days after payday.

The necessity for periodic vacations was barely discussed by 1914. Given peacetime, vacations, at first without pay and later perhaps with pay, might have become an ordinary condition of employment in local heavy industry. In the meantime, employers were so obsessed with a supposed general shortage of workers and so intransigent about wages and hours that progress was slow. Only continued years of prosperity, in turn meaning a continuing labor shortage and consequent rising wages, would have served to bring industrialists around to the notion of vacations.

There is no aspect of the Upper Silesian work force that can be discussed without reference to the role of women, minors and foreign workers. Women and minors, the subject of welfare legislation as early as the 1860s and 1870s, were supposed to work fewer hours under less strenuous conditions than were fully-grown men. As detailed in chapter 2, women, though not permitted to work in the Dortmund mines after the early 1890s, continued to form a significant though declining proportion of the Upper Silesian mining force. In iron smelting at the turn of the century they formed almost 7 percent of the work force, performing jobs executed in western Germany by men.[41] Children too performed extensive tasks in both mining and smelting.

Certain legislation to control the hours of these two groups was passed at various times, mainly in the law of 1892—the prohibition on night work, a maximum ten-hour day, and prescribed rest periods. The records of most employers contain numerous references to government concern over hours and working conditions of these specially protected workers, but occasional admonitions to employers and the recognized shortage of inspection personnel imply that the laws were often transgressed. Certainly in the total number of annual shifts worked women and minors were regular workers. After 1885, women averaged the same or slightly more than hewers and haulers; children, slightly fewer.[42]

Women and minors at least had the attention of the state; foreign workers received no such sympathy. Before the expulsions of 1885, resident alien Poles in mining and smelting were not many; when the number of seasonal laborers swelled after 1900, employers gained another tool with which to force regular workers to accept the terms of work outlined by these employers. These foreigners did not enjoy even the minimal legal protection offered other industrial workers; in addition, work on the surface, which the foreign workers usually did, entailed more working hours than did underground work. In all ways the foreigners were worse off than the natives; in addition, they detracted from the bargaining position of the local workers.

In sum, the story of the development of trends of wages earned and hours worked resembles tales of situations elsewhere in Europe—a long period of low wages and long hours, then a breakthrough to higher wage levels and shorter hours, a steady rise in money and real wages and something of a decline in hours worked, and then the erosion of some of the gains by inflation. In comparison with the Ruhr workers, Upper Silesians advanced at a slow pace. Wages proved sticky, especially for those not at the top-paid levels of mining and smelting, and working hours remained long. The general absence of unions and the pressure of workers amenable to management policies (women, minors, foreign workers) served to slow the improvement of the position of the workers and also helped perpetuate the reputation of Upper Silesia as a bad place to work. The patterns of recruitment furnish ample evidence for the continuing preference of long-distance migrants to choose other areas of employment over Upper Silesia; company policies on wages and hours illustrate quite well the substance of the migrants' aversion to Upper Silesia.

8

Workers Confront Management:
Labor Discipline

Regular attendance at a steady job is generally considered one of the primary measures of modernity of an industrial labor force, and the *Arbeiterstamm* idea was directed toward this goal. High labor turnover and frequent absenteeism together might be taken as a sign that labor "discipline" in Max Weber's sense had not yet become part of the ethos of the body of mining and smelting workers in Upper Silesia. On the other hand, one cannot automatically assume that such evidence of ill-discipline proves the existence of any phenomenon often conceptualized as "peasant mentality," uncommitted or semi-committed workers, peasant-workers, and the like.[1]

Two qualifications must be made to the assertion that the acceptance of factory discipline implies an acceptance of a new work order. First, traditionally employers and their spokesmen have defined the problem, and they have not been prone to admit in writing that an informal give-and-take always exists in any confrontation of management and free labor; that is, less than perfect obedience comes out as disruptive, reactionary, and unsuitable for industrial organization. Second, ill-discipline—in particular high rates of turnover and absenteeism—is often construed as protest by new industrial workers against their general social situation as urban factory workers.[2] However, such patterns of behavior in Upper Silesia lasted long after the 1860s and 1870s, decades when the work force consisted primarily of people just off the farm; and it is plausible to maintain that such action represented an attempt by workers to improve their conditions within the developing industrial order, not to withdraw from that social nexus. Prior to the strike of 1889, which signaled a change in the character of the labor market, this question of work attendance probably outranked wages and hours as the center of the struggle over rule-making authority; in later decades the more familiar wages and hours came to the forefront.

Turnover

Dissatisfaction with industrial work and the resultant effect on efficiency have proved to be extremely intractable problems in most societies.[3] Although high labor turnover posed a problem all through the years from 1870 to 1914 in Upper Silesia, one must seek to explain the persistence of this trend in two different ways. In the 1870s and 1880s the supply of labor exceeded the demand, and turnover was probably due to worker reaction against the new factory type discipline, to the pull of agriculture, and to the low wage rates which the market allowed employers to pay. By the 1890s there existed a large nucleus of workers accustomed to industrial occupations (primarily mining and smelting but also construction and craft industries); when the call for labor began to outstrip supply, these workers could easily be tempted to change jobs. In addition, newly hired workers are ordinarily the most prone to quit; and when those newly hired are also fresh migrants from the countryside, one might expect fo find a high rate of turnover. From the 1890s on Upper Silesian mining and smelting labor forces displayed two general groupings: an older, usually married, stable core and a younger, often single, frequently just recently arrived transient body of unskilled laborers.

Before the 1850s employers had been able to afford to prefer the stable worker to the skilled one, but once expansion of mining and then of smelting had begun, management had less control over the situation. Assume that working one year or less was a sign of rapid turnover. Based on Hohenlohe records for 1863-1891 (Table 18), it is apparent that from the very beginning of large-scale heavy industry in Upper Silesia a large proportion of newly hired miners—in these cases, 25 percent to 50 percent—tended to quit their jobs after working one year or less.

On the other hand, a large number of employees stayed at the same job for more than a year and in quite a few instances remained five years or more. In other words, high rates of turnover affected primarily the younger segments of the work crews; a more experienced group of older workers maintained the continuity necessary to keep the plants and mines functioning.

Two additional rolls reveal little hiring in the 1870s but expanding work forces and increasing labor turnover starting about 1880 (Table 19). Of course, turnover, necessarily measured here by the number of those working less than two years, may have been intentionally understated in order to give the impression of a *Stamm*, but there is still some use in examining these records. The results for the 1870s are startling—practically no turnover. There might have been a certain tampering by management to achieve the desired *Stamm*, at least on paper; yet the figures are not inconceivable, for there was high unemployment in the mining region in 1873-1879. As employment grew, the rolls began to look more like ordinary lists of workers, and turnover became similar to that at other mines; by

TABLE 18

Turnover of Workers at Selected Mines, 1863–1891

Date	Total hired	Number leaving after working:			Name of mine	Volume number and entries in Hohenlohe records
		one year or less	1–5 years	5 or more years		
1867, (Mar.–Dec.)	83	24			Fanny	2664, 219–302 (earliest year available)
1869[a]	56	23			Fanny	2664, 387–442
1871[a]	75	23			Fanny	2664, 507–581
1873[a]	173	48			Fanny	2664, 725–897
1876[a]	174	65			Fanny	2664, 1168–1341
1878[a]	303	169			Fanny	2664, 1479–1781
1881[a]	245	123			Fanny	2664, 2403–2647
1884[a]	294	91			Fanny	2664, 3000–3293
1885[a]	147	78			Fanny	2664, 3294–3440
1886, (Jan.–Mar.)	45	23			Fanny	2664, 3441–3886
1863–1868	26	7	13	6	Fanny	2664, 163–188
1869–1870	26	10	16	0	Fanny	2664, 439–464
1875–1877	26	7	19	0	Fanny	2664, 1096–1121
1878–1880	26	13	13	0	Fanny	2664, 1506–1531
1881–1883	26	11	15	0	Fanny	2664, 2500–2525
1886–1887	25	14	11	0	Fanny	2664, 3450–3474
1872–1877	274	136			?	2652, 1–274
1878[a]	141	15	117	32	?	2652, 1–141
1879	151	74			?	2652, 119–370
1879–1889[a]	480				Georg	2659, all entries
1879–1891[a]		295	277	214	Georg	2659
1889–1891[a]	82	18			Georg	2660
1879–1901	89	40	19	30	?	2653, 1–89 in first third of volume

SOURCE: WAP Katowice, Hohenlohe, volumes as indicated.
[a] All entries for the year/years involved are included.

the late 1880s and early 1890s, large number of employees had been working less than two years.

The steel industry was younger than mining and may have experienced more difficulty in these early decades. According to a contemporary survey made by the Organization of German Iron and Steel Industrialists, turnover in 1888 in the entire German iron and steel

TABLE 19
Turnover of Workers at Two Mines, 1870s–1901

	Paulina Mine		Alfred Mine	
Year	Number hired	Number working less than two years	Number hired	Number working less than two years
all 1870s	216	0		
1876			9	0
1880			22	0
1886	315	162	239	71
1891	271	156	320	190
1896	226	141	296	186
1900	317	177	313	177
1901			331	184

SOURCE: WAP Katowice, Hohenlohe 2658 (Paulina); Hohenlohe 2655 (1876–1896), 2657 (1900–1901) (Alfred).

industry would approach 100 percent, leaving a very small *Arbeiter-stamm*.[4] It should be noted though that technological advance in metals was still novel; the Bessemer steel-producing process was displacing puddling in Upper Silesia only in the 1880s, and much of the turnover no doubt stemmed from a settling-in period observed in most new industries.

From the 1890s on demand for workers greatly increased; workers found it even easier to change jobs if they so desired. Employers were too hard pressed to close ranks and enforce a policy of not hiring those coming directly from another mine, as was done in the smaller Saxon mining region. By the turn of the century, complaints of frequent changes of employment were common in Upper Silesia and continued to dominate reports of worker conditions up to the time of the World War.[5]

These complaints were often mixed with remarks about high rates of absenteeism, to be examined subsequently. Still, one is hard put to know how to take these claims. For example, records for 1901 and 1902 of some of the largest steel plants in Upper Silesia and for 1903 to 1905 for several zinc plants show the results listed in Tables 20 and 21.

In most of these cases, the percentage hired in iron smelting in 1901 and 1902 varied from one-third to over three-fourths of the total number of workers; in zinc smelting after 1900, the percentage was usually much higher. In both branches of industry there was a lively rate of movement into and out of employment. The two groups can in this case be confidently regarded as typical of Upper Silesia, for these smelters were some of the largest in the region, employing about half of all iron and steel workers, and these Hohenlohe zinc plants

TABLE 20
Turnover of Workers in Smelting, 1901–1902

Plant	Year	Total number of workers	Left employment	Hired
König smelter	1901	6,991	2,807	2,184
	1902	6,099	1,837	1,550
Julien smelter	1901	2,104	1,395	947
	1902	1,613	1,255	1,139
Bismarck smelter	1901	3,155	2,828	2,772
	1902	3,080	2,654	2,635
Bethlen-Falva smelter	1901	1,747	1,344	1,182
	1902	2,220	1,164	1,201
Frieden smelter	1901	3,082	2,460	2,375
	1902	3,596	2,364	2,833
Hubertus smelter	1901	687	425	418
	1902	687	488	475
Total	1901	17,766	11,259	9,878
	1902	17,295	9,733	9,833

SOURCE: JRGB 1901:104; 1902:143.

TABLE 21
Turnover of Workers in Zinc Plants, 1903–1905

Plant	Year	Total number of workers	Left employment	Hired
Neue Hohenlohe zinc smelter	1903–1904	917	196	261
Theresia zinc smelter	1903–1904	110	30	29
	1904–1905	109	46	45
Hohenlohe zinc rolling mill	1903–1904	188	33	60
	1904–1905	195	47	70
Total	1903–1904	1215	259	350
	1904–1905	304	93	115

SOURCE: WAP Katowice Hohenlohe 321: second p. 234-second p. 241 (1903–1904); Hohenlohe 322: 28 October 1905ff. (not paginated) (1904–1905).

employed close to 15 percent of all zinc workers. Such exact figures are not available for mines, but the annual reports of factory inspectors, mining authorities, and employers all indicated even greater turnover in mining, especially in the rapidly growing coal mining sector.[6]

It is difficult to know whether these figures indicate "high" turnover. Is a crew composed of 25 percent new workers considered to have high turnover? Fifty percent? What did the term mean to the Ruhr mine owners, who also complained of high turnover as early as the 1860s? It is claimed that in 1907 every second miner in the Ruhr changed his job; in the Lugau-Oelsnitz region in Saxony from 1888 to 1913 the annual number of miners leaving their jobs never fell below one quarter of the total labor force.[7] Are these cases of high turnover?

There is no one standard by which to judge "high" and "low" turnover, for much depends on the type of industry involved, the point of economic development of a particular society, and the social context within which labor functions. More narrowly, turnover also tends to fluctuate from plant to plant and is often affected by changes in the business cycle. German mine owners and smelter operators, moreover, often used "turnover" to mean the number hired plus the number fired, by which means very high percentages were attained, reaching well over 100 percent of the work force in the Ruhr in a number of years.[8] Not that the number quitting was not great, but employers tended at times histrionically to exaggerate their problems.

In addition, turnover in smelting industries (and presumably in mining) was concentrated among those recently hired. For example, in the Gleiwitz and Kattowitz factory inspection areas over 35 percent of those leaving lead smelters in 1905 had worked for less than one month; and another 60 percent of the quitters, less than one year.[9] This same pattern emerges in iron, zinc, and coke plants. These figures are presented in Table 23, along with data from some other industries which were not so new to the area and not technologically changing. The similarities in rates of turnover suggest that all industries have a settling-in period which is not automatically to be attributed to general dissatisfaction with industrial life.

Furthermore, these data clearly indicate that industries were served by crews with long experience at their jobs—witness the high percentage of workers with over one year and even over five years of service in heavy industry. Of the 12,000 iron smelter and rolling mill employees included in the survey, over 10 percent had over twenty-five years of service at the same job[10]—and this in the same industry about which employers seventeen years earlier had talked of 100 percent turnover!

Employers in Upper Silesia and the Ruhr may have been subject to an illusion of how stable an industrial labor force could or should be in a period of rapid expansion. To make only very gross comparisons, General Motors, reputed to be one of the most efficient companies in the world today, in 1968 lost one-third of its new workers; and the American electronics industry had a turnover of some 40

TABLE 22

Turnover and Length of Service of Workers in Several Industries
in the Gleiwitz and Kattowitz Factory Inspection Areas, 1905

Industry	Turnover (percent of workers leaving)			Length of Service of Remaining Crew (percent)		
	Under 1 month	1 month to 1 year	Over 1 year	Under 1 year	Over 1 year[a]	Over 5 years
Lead smelting	35.4	59.8	4.8	51.7	48.3	20.4
Coke plants	24.4	51.1	24.4	34.2	65.8	40.9
Briquette factories	27.6	72.4	0.0	69.0	31.0	4.2
Iron smelters and rolling mills	16.8	57.8	25.4	23.7	65.6	6.7
Zinc smelters, roasting smelters, and rolling mills	14.3	46.3	39.4	20.4	79.6	48.6
Metal finishing plants	17.4	58.3	24.3	30.0	70.0	34.7
Textile industry	9.7	50.5	39.8	47.8	52.2	14.2
Leather industry	0.0	80.0	20.0	29.4	70.6	35.3
Foodstuffs industry	24.5	58.0	17.5	27.2	72.8	30.4

SOURCE: JRGB 1905: 162–163

[a] Includes those listed separately in last column (Over 5 years).

percent in the same period. Or, to take a modern example closer
to the present subject, over 20 percent of the miners in Upper Silesia
in 1958 were employed less than one year in their present jobs. On
a national scale, 34 percent of the 19,000,000 employed persons in
the Federal Republic of Germany in September, 1957, had changed
jobs at least once during the year.[11]

It seems that relatively high rates of turnover are common in the
years of growth of particular industries (for example, U.S. electronics
today), and varying rates of turnover are compatible with a labor
force completely divorced from a rural setting. There is no one rate
of entering and leaving industrial work which marks a modernized
labor force. Some of the turnover was due to rural people reacting
unfavorably to their experience in industry, but employers failed to
consider that under conditions of full employment workers are easily
tempted to change jobs, especially when they are conscious of
relatively low wages, as the Upper Silesians were. When economic
conditions worsened, turnover declined, as in 1902 and 1910, indicating
that workers were aware of the conditions of an industrial order and

a free labor market. Employers could do little to discourage job-hopping; they wanted the workers too badly. When a recession hit Westphalian mining in 1908, the miners returning to Upper Silesia were eagerly rehired by local firms.[12] All of this suggests that the workers had a rather keen understanding of the industrial labor market.

Besides, much of the employer claim of extreme rates of turnover was grossly exaggerated because it was based on the sum of those hired and those leaving work. Upper Silesian heavy industry (and that of the Ruhr) doubled the total number employed from the late 1890s to 1913 and grew considerably even earlier; thus it is obvious that the number of those hired would be very large. For instance, at the Alfred field of the Hohenlohe coal mines only 9 people were hired in 1876 and 22 in 1880. In both years there were practically no workers with less than two years of service. However, in 1886, 239 were hired; in 1896, 296; and in 1901, 331. At the same time the number of other workers with under two years of service rose to 200.[13] In addition, many of those hired were also counted as leaving from somewhere else. When one also considers the number of young men drafted out of the mines into the army (worker lists indicate that almost all miners served in the army), the problem of turnover assumes lesser proportions.

In order to place the question of turnover into perspective, one must not forget that from the earliest days of free enterprise mining a disproportionate number of the quitters were young people.[14] Recall, too, that in general there was a shortage of haulers, the positions filled by younger workers. Combined with an admitted tendency of young workers to be highly mobile from firm to firm, this shortage—more precisely, full employment, particularly after 1890—allowed the haulers many alternative job opportunities; the bonuses offered for longer periods of service hardly affected such a group not yet burdened with family responsibilities. Clearly turnover had many causes—to name only the most obvious, the preference of young people for leisure over savings, the many opportunities for change of employment offered by an expansive labor market, a settling-in period frequently encountered among new employees, bad working conditions and low wages, and the lack of decent housing. Besides these younger workers, there were a number of older seasonal workers who moved from one kind of industrial job to another; despite their impermanence, they too could be counted as part of an industrial labor force.[15]

One special problem of concern to mineowners was the phenomenon of leaving work without giving the required fourteen days notice, which more than any other single practice might be considered as a sign that workers were not yet adjusted to the demands of industrial life. Employers were vehement in their condemnation of this practice, and their association spent a lot of time discussing it. In retaliation, employers paid salaries with a one or two-week time lag and would not pay these back wages to those who quit without giving notice. Furthermore, the model work rules (*Arbeitsordnung*) drawn up by the Upper Silesian Mine and Smelter Owner Association in 1905 explicitly sanctioned this forfeiture of pay.[16] (The practice was curtailed by the mining laws of 1905 and 1909.)

On the other hand, one recent student of Upper Silesia has pointed out that before the mining law of 1892 employers themselves often fired workers without giving two weeks notice.[17] Increasing government pressure on employers to publish and follow work rules helped to restrict this no-notice policy, and firings with cause as elaborated in the work rules became much more common.

One might think that quitting work without giving notice is a sure sign of a work force being "undisciplined," yet this picture must be qualified. First of all, the numbers involved were small. Aside from employers inveighing against the practice, evidence is fragmentary at best, but it is still instructive. In 1902, only 264 workers out of 9,200 leaving work at six smelters broke their contracts; at the Hohenlohe zinc complex (three smelters and a rolling mill) in 1904, barely 3 percent of those leaving work gave no notice, and in 1905 virtually none were guilty of this practice. Furthermore, even those quitting without notice seem to have been taking advantage of full employment; when business took a downturn, not only turnover in general but also contract-breaking declined. This impression is buttressed by figures from the Ruhr, where the same kind of bitter complaints were heard. Yet each year from 1910 to 1913 the number of those quitting without notice was never above 8 percent of the total leaving their jobs and was usually much below that figure. Data from the Ruhr metal industry in 1905 indicate again that the younger workers presented the greatest problem in this too; those aged 16-25 were twice as prone as other age groups to break their contracts.[18] Although Upper Silesia and the Ruhr differed in many ways, this comparison should be revealing because the problem seems to have been worse in the Ruhr, at least according to the official government reports published in the *Zeitschrift für das Berg-, Hütten, und Salinenwesen*.

After 1890, and particularly after 1905, much of the concern with contract-breakers in Upper Silesia centered on Polish and especially on Ruthenian workers. Frequently, large groups would shift from industry to agriculture, as in 1906, when 4,200 Ruthenians were hired for industrial work in the first half of the year, but in June only about 1,900 remained at their jobs. With time, however, it became clear that even here the question of adjustment was not entirely one of agricultural people confronting industry; soon they would return to the mining and smelting jobs they had recently left. It may very well have been that the high rate of mobility of these workers lay in their difficulties in adjusting to the foreign German environment, as well as to industrial employment. After all, the rate of leaving without contract was high among the Slavic agricultural workers in Pomerania as well as among the industrial workers in Upper Silesia.[19]

Employers spoke a great deal about blacklisting workers who left other firms without giving notice, although the Ruhr and central German owners were better organized in this respect than the Upper Silesians. The latter did attempt to set up a worker identity card system with which to control workers, as is evident in the case of Tomasz Rybok, an old miner whose troubles seemed to stem from secret code marks placed in his workbook;[20] but on the whole, this effort failed.

It must be emphasized that contract breakers could flourish only in an area where there were plenty of possibilities for jobs. Complaints of contract violation increased markedly whenever industry picked up;[21] employers did not usually quibble over the source of their workers when the labor market was tight. Therefore, this whole problem of labor turnover and quitting without notice should be viewed from the perspective of a lively demand for labor, a labor shortage if you will. One of the hallmarks of a modern labor "market" is improved communications, resulting in a knowledge of alternative job opportunities for workers. During periods of prosperity, such alternatives were plentiful; employers had to learn to live with that fact.

In conclusion, one might ask whether labor turnover was injurious to mining and smelting and whether it was a sign of an uncommitted labor force. No doubt there were many cases of inefficiency and very likely of increased accidents, but these may have been due to other causes as well (for example, long hours, use of untrained foreign workers and minors).[22] There was never any consideration of the idea that working conditions may have contributed to a propensity to turnover and absenteeism. None of this is to deny a problem of rapid change of employment, but it must be kept in mind that the unstable qualities of the workers were not the only contributing factor to this situation. So, for instance, where workers obtained company housing, it is extremely likely that turnover declined precipitously, assuming that Upper Silesia resembled the Ruhr in this respect.[23]

The problem of turnover does not seem critical when compared to expansion and profits in mining and smelting which were achieved by many firms even under these labor conditions. One is tempted to say that what was lacking was not so much a labor force committed to industry but rather a group of owners and managers who knew how to deal with the labor relations problems of the industrial world. In a way, one of the major problems of the big firms was the limited outlook of management who did not know how to make jobs attractive to workers; personnel difficulties were not due solely to the unstable nature of the work force. For example, the improvement of safety conditions at the Rybnik mine effected a marked decline in the rate of turnover; workers had gotten their message across to the mine administrators.[24]

Finally, it should be recalled that mining before World War I in certain respects resembled pre-industrial cottage industry.[25] Miners worked in small teams in individual rooms within the mine; only with postwar mechanization did there appear the large working groups usually associated with industrial production. Even though the miners were working in a modern industry, arrangements for work were such that a high rate of turnover could be tolerated without essentially disturbing production. Besides, the nature of the work was so similar from mine to mine that the influx of new employees hardly disturbed the rhythm of production.

Smelting was more vulnerable to fluctuations in the labor force than mining, but here too the problems of turnover were easily overcome so long as key employees could be retained. The discussion of recruitment in chapter 5 indicated that the skilled smelting workers were the object of keen recruiting competition. Such a situation implies a group of highly skilled smelter workers who were relatively settled in their jobs but who could be hired by other firms given sufficient enticement. This is certainly not the same as voluntary quitting and seeking of a new job, as was the case with miners and unskilled smelter workers.

High rates of turnover were not peculiar to mining and smelting alone. Other industries, even those with long pre-industrial traditions, sometimes had worse performance records than did heavy industry. Thus in 1905 iron and zinc smelters and rolling mills in Oppeln regency experienced a change of about one-third of the work force; the metal working industries, about one-half. Older branches of industry had greater problems of retaining workers; textiles, and woodworking had fully 100 percent turnover, and foodstuffs, two-thirds.[26] It was not only the novelty of modern industry that encouraged workers frequently to change their jobs. (See Table 22.)

Absenteeism

There is hardly need to document the assertion that early stages of industrial development have traditionally been plagued by high rates of absenteeism, particularly on Mondays, days after holidays, and days after paydays.[27] Absenteeism (*willkürliches Feiern, Bum-*

melschichten, bumelki) was certainly nothing new to Upper Silesian mining and smelting. In 1860 the chief local administrator condemned the phenomenon of irregularity in mining in terms reminiscent of those heard years later:

> If complaints about low wages are becoming loud, it is primarily because the complainers, and among them the haulers, are disposed to skip 1-2 shifts per month. So it results that many of them earn scarcely 20 shift-wages monthly. Since every opportunity is granted to work a shift every weekday, it must be concluded that they think to earn a sufficient living with a lower shift-wage. And that is the case because the haulers are with few exceptions unmarried young people, who reckon their laziness as enjoying life.[28]

Such was the employer picture in the 1870s and 1880s: wages were so high that workers did not feel like working every day. That explanation rings oddly when measured against the number of mining and smelting workers who were also engaged in auxiliary occupations in these years, for numerous people were needy enough and energetic enough to hold two jobs in order to raise their meager wage level.

In the first decade of the twentieth century miners were condemned in the annual report of the Upper Silesian mining and smelting employer association in terms quite similar to those used by the local official in an earlier age:

> ... Unfortunately the reverse side of the medal has not been missing in conjunction with these wage raises [1889-1907], and the very interesting absentee statistics ... have shown how little in general our Upper Silesian workers understand about utilizing the times which are presently so good for them. ... The raises in pay have led not to *increased* output, but to *less* output and thus to a heightening of the existing shortage of workers.[29]

For employers little had changed in the attitude of workers toward industrial work. The latter were expected to show an insatiable desire for higher earnings, but they inexplicably continued in their hedonistic ways.

More specifically, when business conditions improved in the second half of the 1890s, the complaints about worker absences were unending, especially right after paydays. Rather than save up for emergencies and old age, mining and smelting workers were said to prefer to live "from hand to mouth." Capricious absenteeism was considered by employers to be the chief reason for low incomes, and as late as 1913 it was claimed that Upper Silesian workers were losing up to 10 percent of their pay for skipping work (a claim perhaps inflated by including days lost in the 1913 strike). In general, Upper Silesia was known as the German mining region with the highest rate of unexcused absences.[30]

In 1905, Josef Czernetzki, the 18-year old son of a smelter worker, was fired from a Hohenlohe zinc smelter for this pattern of attendance:[31]

worked	June 1-7
unexcused absence	8-9
worked	10-12
unexcused absence	13-14
no record	15
worked	16-22
no record	June 23
worked	24-28
no record	29
unexcused absence	30
unexcused absence	July 1-10

Of the 26 work days in June (June 4, 11, 18, and 25 were Sundays, hence probably not work days), Czernetzki missed 5 by unexcused absence. Apparently the need for workers was great enough for this to be excused, but skipping the first 10 days in July proved to be too much for management; he was fired July 11. Similar examples can be found, such as a smelter worker fired for missing 70-80 days following paydays in 1892.[32]

These are sorry records indeed, but it is unlikely that huge numbers of workers behaved in quite the same manner. At three of the fields of the König mine, management in 1897 complained of absenteeism running to over 5 percent or 6 percent of the total possible shifts per month. True enough, but the force of the complaint is lessened when one examines the records and finds that most of the absentees were excused ("*mit Urlaub*"). Of 2,175 absences at the west field in October, 1897, only 268 were without leave; at the south field, only 442 of 1,554 absences were unexcused; at the east field, only 557 of 1,964 absences. Corroborating data might be sought in the Ruhr, where in 1910 and 1911 less than 30 percent of all absenteeism was unexcused;[33] not good, but certainly not crippling in effect. Such information inclines one to reevaluate thoughts of widespread labor ill-discipline.

The pattern of annual shifts worked in Upper Silesia also mitigates the accusation of gross absenteeism. From the mid-1880s through 1911 (no earlier figures are available), the Upper Silesian miner averaged between 275 and 284 shifts worked per year;[34] the Ruhr miner, 305-313 shifts. (Note that 52 weeks times six shifts per week equals 312 shifts per year.) In both areas the years 1912 and 1913 witnessed unprecedented increases in the average number of man-shifts worked. Except for a tendency toward slight increase in shifts worked in Upper Silesia, there is no observable trend in the annual figures nor is there any noticeable fluctuation in accordance with the business cycle. In fact, the steady record of Upper Silesian workers illustrates that on the average higher wages did not result in fewer days worked (or more days either) and also indicates that despite a supposed acute shortage of haulers, the hewer-hauler average of shifts worked did not fluctuate wildly, as one might expect on the basis of management complaints(see Table 23). Unfortunately data for hewers and haulers are grouped together, and there is no way to judge the validity of employers' complaints that haulers were particularly prone to be absent from work. As for declining output, difficult geological conditions seem to have been more decisive than absenteeism.

TABLE 23
Average Number of Annual Shifts Worked in Coal Mining,
1886–1913

| | All Miners | | Hewers-haulers |
	Upper Silesia	Ruhr	Upper Silesia
1886–1890	277	309	270
1891–1896	275	305	266
1897–1901	280	313	275
1902–1906	280	305	275
1907–1911	284	309	278
1912–1913	311	328	306

SOURCE: ZBHS, statistical section, 1887–1914.

In order to combat both absenteeism and turnover, management used two major kinds of countermeasures. First, punishment, centered on fines and other monetary measures. In the 1870s and 1880s, advances on wages, so necessary for workers who were paid only monthly, were withheld if a shift was missed. In addition, payment of wages before the mid-1880s was made not to individuals but to teams of workers who then divided the pay among themselves. This system, incidentally, was used to force workers to discipline their comrades since their pay was determined by the output of the group as a whole. Paydays were also kept infrequent until the 1890s in order to exert pressure on workers to appear regularly and on time. Fines for unexcused absences were assessed all through the period, and after 1890, when paydays were becoming more frequent, fines became the major form for punishing workers for absenteeism. These were often arbitrarily imposed, such as when the Hohenlohe firm unilaterally halved the earnings of a mine crew for low productivity due to "laziness."[35] Actions like this caused great resentment among workers and were not at all geared toward making workers any less prone to skip shifts.

Second, rewards, which took the form of bonuses given for regular attendance at work: the Bibiella iron mine paid 10 Pfennigs daily for regular attendance, a practice followed by other mines; the Silesia mine attempted to recruit workers away from other mines by offering a 10 percent bonus for regular attendance at work, a policy in common use; a Rybnik mine sold midday meals at 15 percent discount to those who worked a full month without unexcused absences.[36] Such examples could be multiplied.

From local officials in 1860 to the Upper Silesian Mine and Smelter Owner Association in 1913, bureaucrats and employers underlined high wages as an incentive for workers to skip shifts. Instead of laying away money for emergencies and for old age, both mining and smelting workers tended to cut their work time as soon as they reached their desired consumption level. This observation—the so-called "backward bending supply curve of labor"—is a charge often hurled at workers in early industrial situations. However, this preference of much leisure over higher earnings can be understood only in its social context.[37]

First of all, although it is true that many workers skipped work without permission, one must realize that even disciplined workers did not necessarily think it bad to miss some time at work:

> The employers now claim that we workers skip work (bummeln). If I stay out 2-3 shifts, I am told on the next day, "You are a damned malingerer" (Bummler). If you are in the hospital, the doctor always comes and asks if you are better. The worker then says, "Yes, I am better," upon which he is discharged from the hospital; when he comes to work, they say to him. "Nu Sie Bummler."[38]

Thus did a miner express his outrage at being reprimanded for missing some time in the mines and being accused for malingering when on sick leave. He was committed to industrial work, even to the point of joining a miner's union, but this commitment did not mean adopting a standard of behavior prescribed by the employers. An industrial work ethos need not be that set down by the employers, who are as liable as workers to misunderstand the needs of industrial enterprise.

In addition, most of the absenteeism as noted in the sources above occurred among younger, unmarried workers, whose life styles had not yet been adjusted to the needs of family life. Their preferences were for more leisure—that is, their indifference curves had different shapes from those of older workers; but they also had an idea of what industrial employment meant for their existence. When business was off and jobs not so plentiful, absenteeism and turnover declined. In such actions workers acknowledged that they did not dominate the labor market; but when prosperity and full employment came, collectively they flaunted their power over employers in this one area where they could do so. From this perspective, it is harder to take at face value such industrialist claims that had it not been for absenteeism in 1906, the Upper Silesian market area need not have suffered any coal shortage—and this complaint despite a 6 percent rise in productivity that year in coal mining![39]

None of this is to say that the work force was ideal and that the employers completely fabricated their labor problems, nor is it to say that absenteeism was not at least in part due to workers rebelling at the new industrial order. Newly opened areas sometimes provided the stereotype of reluctant industrial workers. The Rybnik region, mentioned here several times as a low-wage semi-agricultural area, had an extremely high rate of absenteeism to go along with its closer ties to agriculture. In that area, developed for mining after 1900, increased wages did indeed seem to result at times in fewer shifts worked.[40] On the other hand, unexcused absences may also in part be accounted for by the long hours prevalent in mining and smelting; workers probably used these days off as a means of recouping their strength spent in arduous 10- and 12-hour days, periodic double shifts, and forced overtime.

Despite the actuality of absenteeism, it was not the major hindrance to greater production, as one might infer from the claims of industrial management. In conjunction with earlier comments about labor shortage and recruitment, considerations of both turnover and absenteeism lead one to believe that Upper Silesian employers tended to blame their economic problems on their labor forces, in turn leading to a magnification of the problems of labor relations. Even within the limited framework of regular hours and regular attendance at work, it seems that the Upper Silesia of 1870-1914 was similar to modern underdeveloped countries in that "... the 'labor problems' of industrialization are really in large measure 'management problems.' "[41] Both absenteeism and turnover must be evaluated in terms of labor market conditions and working conditions and cannot be dismissed as mere manifestations of the agricultural origins of workers. To the contrary, in certain contexts they may reflect a labor force well versed in the methods of industrial life.

9

Workers Confront Management:
Authority Relations in Industry

The specific nature of a "modern" industrial labor force becomes clearer if one emphasizes patterns of industrial bureaucracy in early industrial situations. In terms of an ideal type, a prebureaucratic labor force is marked by personal relations between workers and owners, without an extensive layer of intermediate officials; wages flexible because of grants in kind, varying rates for similar work, irregular bonuses and other fringe benefits, and arbitrary fines; total absence of or a minimum of written work rules, with changing situations usually defined unilaterally by foremen or owners; and an authoritarian social order within the factory, with the worker more or less completely at the mercy of the employer. Behavior by workers and employers is not totally capricious and unpredictable; vague contractual obligations and a number of unwritten, often unarticulated expectations exist, but the whole situation is in general most irregular, without firm routine.[1]

In contrast, the bureaucratized labor force is marked by impersonal lines of authority between workers and owners. In big firms this situation is complicated by a large hierarchy of intermediate supervisors, often culminating in a corporation board of directors rather than in a single person. A regular schedule of wages prevails, or at least generally accepted methods exist to regulate wages in an industry such as mining, which has shifting pay rates due to variable geologic conditions; bonuses, payments in kind, and fines are still to be found, but they generally appear as peripheral items, not basic to the pay packet. Detailed work rules not only are drawn up, but an effort is made to inform every worker of their content, and foremen are expected to supervise on the basis of these explicit rules. Codes of discipline are based on production and safety needs and are not subject to arbitrary decisions by the boss. As in pre-bureaucratic times, workers in particular retain a whole list of vaguely perceived expectations; now, however, these must be disguised behind more formal demands relating to quantifiable elements such as wages and hours.

Bureaucracy, it is true, is essentially a method of imposing authority in a manner intelligible to all concerned. Given the demands for increased efficiency and higher production built into an industrial economy, it is no wonder that a kind of bureaucratic structure has evolved in all those firms with a sizable group of employees, including those in mining and smelting.[2] Small firms too have in the main gone over to such an arrangement, but that process often moves more slowly and is of no direct concern to this study. Were evidence available, contrasts with the small metal-finishing workshops of Upper Silesia and Congress Poland would be highly instructive. Perhaps another time.

Consequently, any attempt to understand the creation of a modern industrial labor force must deal not only with the behavior of workers but also with the acts of managers, not only with absenteeism and turnover but also with working conditions and fringe benefits. Most of these points come together under the evolution of some type of industrial bureaucracy, for lines of authority between workers and management form perhaps the most crucial area of the amorphous relationships subsumed under the term "working conditions." In addition to the more publicized clashes over wages and hours, conflicts about rules governing daily activity on the job have generally constituted a key point in the evolution of modes of labor protest. Often enough this type of dispute is attributed either to the kind of rapacious capitalistic exploitation otherwise expressed in long hours and low pay or is traced to the unwillingness of new industrial workers to adjust to the efficiency demands of modernizing industry. However, one can probably better comprehend the evolution of a modern labor force by regarding labor-management relations not merely as an adversary process but as a mutual learning experience for both groups in a total industrial context.

Employers and Their Policies

Broadly, how did pre-1914 Upper Silesia fit into this idealized picture? Mining for coal, zinc, and lead had a long tradition and was not so given to the bureaucratized order as smelting. Producing units were still organized on something like cottage industry lines because of slow-changing technology and the hoary traditions of miners, but the capital and organizational requirements of the industry as a whole precluded any small workshops with tight owner-worker relations. Smelting, on the other hand, was transformed by nineteenth-century technology into an industry with such enormous capital requirements and such significant economies of scale that small plants were out of the question.[3] Only the metal-finishing shops retained a heavily artisan work force, and the leading role of metalworkers in German unionization (not in Upper Silesia) clearly suggests a wholly different kind of labor force. One of the most disputed points in this evolution lies in the distribution of authority: to wit, what is the role of workers in the industrial rule-making process?

In a certain sense a pure pre-bureaucratic organization of the labor force never really existed in Upper Silesian mining and smelting. Even in the first half of the nineteenth century mine crews could number several hundred, though groups engaged in charcoal smelting of iron might be much smaller. Most of the giant firms that consolidated near the end of the century were large even before amalgamation; most grew out of the extensive landholdings of local magnates, who, unlike their peers elsewhere in Europe, engaged actively and success-fully in industrial development—the Kattowitzer AG für Bergbau und Eisenhüttenbetrieb in 1889 (earlier, holdings of Count Tiele-Winckler, who continued to be chief stock-holder); the merger in 1887 of the already large holdings of Wilhelm Hegenscheidt and Georg Caro into what became the Oberschlesische Eisenindustrie für Berg-bau und Hüttenbetrieb; the incorporation of the holdings of Prince Christian von Hohenlohe-Oehringen into the Hohenlohe-Werke in 1905. Some firms had changed to the corporate form earlier—the Schlesische AG für Bergbau und Zinkhüttenbetrieb formed by Prince Guido Henckel von Donnersmarck in 1853 (but note that the prince continued to serve as chairman of the general supervisory board until his death in 1916) or the giant Vereinigte Königs- und Laurahütte, put together with a purchase from the government in 1871 by Count Carl Hugo Henckel von Donnersmarck (a second branch of the family). Some did not incorporate at all before 1914—the holdings of the Borsig family, though direct family management ended with the accidental death of Arnold Borsig in 1897, and the mining works of the Prince of Pless, reputedly one of the richest men in Prussia. The extant records of these firms show no significant difference in treatment of employees before and after incorporation. Working conditions were in no way a function of the personal capitalization of Upper Silesian heavy industry, with the single exception of the Prince of Pless, in whose mines a number of experiments were tried, such as works councils in the 1890s. Still, these involved only about 2,000 men. On the whole, local workers had no contact with owners or with general managers even before specific contracts replaced whim as a basis of industrial relations.

In some cases the magnates' personal control lasted for a long time; in others, general directors took over the business. General directors, mine and smelter directors and their deputies, personnel directors, and a whole bureaucratic hierarchy existed in embryo in the 1860s and grew rapidly in subsequent decades. Paternalism and changing working conditions, however, did not correlate with type of ownership. Bernhard Stephan, general director of the Schaffgotsch enterprises, had the reputation of being very interested in welfare activities, and certainly the well-known Friedrich Bernhardi of Giesche's Erben maintained a lively interest in his employees' life styles.[4] Other important directors differed little in their approaches; Gustav Williger of the Kattowitzer AG and Ewald Hilger of the Vereinigte Königs- und Laurahütte, two of the most powerful men in the industial associations of the region after the turn of the century, administered properties that developed bureaucratic relationships in a way similar to those produced under lesser known figures like Franz Pieler at Ballestrem. The big metallurgical firms, whose capital requirements often resulted in having the German big banks represented on their boards of directors, did not deviate from the widespread patterns of labor relations.[5] The crucial variables remained labor supply and market demand for local products, the latter closely tied to technological advance; these trends moved independently of formal ownership of firms.

Local enterprises in the 1870s and 1880s in retrospect seem incredibly small. The employers' association, after 1882 comprised of institutional members, in 1885 listed many mines and factories with under 100 employees; most places had at the most 600 or so. The vast holdings of Prince Guido Henckel von Donnersmarck showed the Deutschland coal mine with 622 workers and the Bethlen-Falva blast furnace works with 235. The Schaffgotsch Godulla zinc smelter had 629, and the Hegenscheidt Baildon iron smelter, 672. These were among the largest; only the Prussian state mines and the works of the Vereinigte Königs- und Laurahütte exceeded them by any significant number. Subsequent decades witnessed the disappearance of most of the midget workings and the rise of huge concentrations of workers. By 1913 the numbers employed in various firms dwarfed earlier figures.[6] The Prussian state alone employed over 21,000 workers. Others, not all quite so large, stood as enormous conglomerations of workers, like Bismarckhütte with 7,500 employees; Georg von Giesches Erben, 19,000; Vereinigte Königs- und Laurahütte, 24,000; plus some others. Fewer than 25 firms each employing over 1,000 people accounted for almost all of the local mining and smelting production and the vast majority of the workers.

Lines of authority and rule-making were of course centralized, but small subdivisions of large firms might conceivably influence worker attitudes and management policies. However, even local sections of large firms often numbered thousands of subordinates. The Blei Scharley zinc mine (Giesche) listed 3,400 workers in 1913; the Richter coal mines (Vereinigte Königs- und Laurahütte), some 3,300; Max coal mine (Hohenlohe), 2,550; the Huldschinsky metal-refining plant (Oberschlesische Eisenbahnbedarfs AG), 1,700. True, some were very small—59 coal miners at the Pless Heinrichsfreude mine; 87 smelter workers in one section of the Bethlen-Falva smelter (Bismarckhütte).

But the essence of the situation remained the same; even where firms maintained small working units, the latter lay in close proximity to larger sections with working conditions outlined from the top. For example, repeated references in the Hohenlohe archives point to top management supervision of the activities of local supervisors. In this same collection of papers one continually finds appeals of workers addressed directly to Prince Hohenlohe as though he were their ombudsman—for instance, a letter in 1896 from the crew of the zinc roasting ovens at the Godulla smelter (47 men signed) asking for higher piece-work rates because of difficulties encountered in mining low-quality ore.[7] Other appeals came in normal times without work stoppages, but invariably all such requests were evaluated and answered by officials in the bureaucratic hierarchy.

Clearly, local mining and smelting establishments did not experience the kind of close owner-worker relationships often found in small workshops of industries emerging into a new technological era. The charcoal smelting industry had been small,[8] but it bore little organizational relationship even to puddling, let alone to the incredibly fast-growing Bessemer and open-hearth steel-making plants.

Management did not consist solely of general directors and their assistants. Except for supplications to the highest authorities, contacts with "management" meant dealing with low-level supervisors and with local directors like the *Steiger* and *Obersteiger* of mines, and in many cases these contacts were not pleasant. One eyewitness reported that as late as 1910 mine overseers resorted to corporal punishment as a means of stifling resistance to company orders.[9]

Nonetheless, the formal definition of working conditions lay in the hands of top management, and local officials could do little more than aggravate what was already an arbitrary system of control. By unilaterally imposing rules on subordinates, management tended to create an impersonal system of production far removed from the tightly knit social groupings of the "management-principle" era. In many cases the regulations were not motivated by any clear-cut economic need but by the attempt to exercise authority over many facets of the lives of workers. Such was the case in the 1880s when roomers in the Deutschland mine dormitory had to stand at attention whenever a company official entered the room or whenever the workers met such an official in the vicinity of the dormitory.[10] Extant records indicate that with the instituting of such a "punishment-centered bureaucracy"[11] a good deal of resentment appeared against foremen and their superiors, but to have contented workmen was a goal secondary to that of increasing output and of inducing the "proper" docility in the work force. So, for example, a Johann Slawik complained to this employer (Hohenlohe) that he had received pay for only two and one-half shifts for February, 1894, even though he had worked five. In response, the Hohenlohe administration pointed to absenteeism and to the "laziness of the local crew" in producing only half the required output; therefore, all hewers had been fined half their pay.[12] It is true that five shifts indicates very irregular work, but it is unlikely that employers could ever build the kind of loyalty they were seeking with so arbitrary a system of punishment.

Working conditions before 1850 cannot be considered determinants of later developments because of the "management principle," the system whereby Prussian government officials controlled hiring and firing even at privately owned mines. However, after this system was reformed in favor of private enterprise in the mining laws of the 1850s and 1860s, private firms, both individually owned and incorporated, attempted to impose tight, unilateral control over their employees, as though nothing had changed except the individuals in charge of personnel matters. A good deal of conflict resulted, in the main centering around perceived changes in traditional rule-making relationships. In fact, some workers, like those at the Baildon smelter (near Kattowitz) around 1870, were still inclined to look to government officials for redress of grievances brought on by what were considered high-handed acts of employers.[13]

It quickly became apparent that government bureaucrats would now abstain from interfering in the web of rules being established in private industry; from then on "bargaining" of all sorts could be carried on only at the plant level without interference from higher authorities. In fact, even the government-owned facilities—mines near Königshütte and Zabrze and smelters in Friedrichshütte and Gleiwitz —after 1865 were administered by bureaucrats who applied standards of management indistinguishable from those used by private mine and smelter administrations.[14]

Upper Silesian industrial entrepreneurs and managing directors sometimes competed with each other, as in sales of iron and steel, and sometimes cooperated with each other, as in positions taken on railroad tariffs or activities of the Upper Silesian Mine and Smelter Owner Association. On labor policy there was little rift; they wanted an ever improving standard of output and its prerequisite, labor discipline. From this last point of view these policy makers undoubtedly formed a kind of group about whom general statements may be made.

One should not omit some comment on the role of the Prussian state as an entrepreneur, especially since in the eighteenth century the various state-owned enterprises in Upper Silesia had been known as pacesetters for local industry. It is true that miners at the König mine received slightly higher wages and somewhat greater benefits than other Upper Silesian miners; it is also true that the safety equipment at the König and Laura mines was exceptional, but little else marked off the complex of state-owned mines and smelters from other plants. Marketing policies were indistinguishable from other firms, and their employment policies in the main were identical with those of other employers: foreign workers were used; women and children were employed and subject to abuse; working conditions sometimes fell below the standard prescribed by law. In addition, the local administrators participated in the employers' association, as observers in the 1880s and 1890s and later as active participants with an extremely large bloc of votes.[15] In sum, the state enterpises in Upper Silesia were not the paragon of progress against which others could be measured.

Problems of Steady Work

Strains in relations between managers and workers used to revolve and still revolve not only around wages and hours, but also around those relationships involved in a transformation to a bureaucratically organized labor force, one in which both parties to the industrial process have learned to recognize and articulate the spheres of competence of the other side. These spheres can indeed change, but unwritten expectations also change and for a while decline in importance as issues of labor protest. One can probably correlate types of protest with stages of industrialization: clashes over working conditions in the early years of factory work, often settled on an individual level by paternalistic treatment; over wages and hours as workers adapt to the industrial life style, with negotiations in large plants such as those in Upper Silesia tending toward an adversary process as the most common form of settling issues; and finally the reemergence of unrest over working conditions once workers reach a certain level of affluence, with the adversary process remaining important.[16]

The opposing groups changed their respective modes of behavior at varying tempos, and one finds that many of the complaints in the pronouncements of employers appeared before the late nineteenth century. An 1858 list of fines for the Guido Henckel von Donnersmarck mining and smelting works indicates very well the kind of problems met by employers striving for a disciplined labor force. In addition to fines for being absent without leave, large fines were levied for coming late or leaving early, for feigned sickness, for malingering, for drunkenness, and for insubordination. Even though all the fines were heavy (at least one-quarter of a day's pay), the heaviest punishments were reserved for extended absence (two-three days' pay) and insubordination (one-two days' pay).[17]

It is not difficult to understand how such punishable practices would limit production, but other prohibitions are not so easily linked to labor productivity. The requirement of being present at morning prayer (abandoned around 1890) was obviously a vestige of an earlier age, when the mining brotherhoods practically formed a separate social stratum; again, the fine of half a day's pay for failure to appear at a comrade's funeral hardly seems appropriate at a time (1889) when mining and smelting labor forces had grown far beyond the point of small, intimate groups dedicated as much to social community as to production of industrial products.[18]

Since the factory system is based in the main on a hierarchy of authority organized to maximize production, then insubordination must certainly appear as a threat to the efficient functioning of an industrial plant. Consequently, employers were very much concerned with punishing such offenses as failure to obey superiors and cursing and threatening supervisors, examples of which occur frequently in company records.[19] Such events did not, however, comprise a formidable obstacle to increased production or heightened productivity; they were generally isolated incidents, not unlike those that occur today in advanced industrialized countries. There were few, if any, cases of group disobedience (outside of strikes).

A far more serious problem was encountered in the phenomenon of drunkenness. Although workers in iron and steel had a reputation for an especially strong liking for drink, miners could hold their own. Not only were mines and smelters plagued by celebrations of "Blue Monday"—large-scale absenteeism after a weekend binge—but drinking even while on the job posed noticeable problems. "Drunk on the job" was a common enough reason for reprimanding or fining a worker, and management was upset but not unusually surprised over the case of some workers who "... sat down behind an oven and were drinking *Schnaps*."[20]

Employers were often reluctant to act in their own interests in questions of worker behavior, in particular in the matter of drinking. In the 1870s many workers were forced to go to taverns to change the large bills with which they were paid and to divide their wages paid to them as groups. Finally, from the 1880s on, workers were paid individually. In all fairness, it must be pointed out that a number of remedies were tried to break this debilitating habit. Substitutes like seltzer water, lemonade, and coffee were offered, and the purchase of a new-style seltzer water machine by the Friedrich smelter attracted wide attention from employers all over Germany. However, a much more widespread practice evolved of legally requiring all taverns to close on paydays. The government, not the employers, took the lead in this matter; some mine and smelter administrators were dubious about the efficacy of such a measure, and local officials sometimes had to force compliance by industrial plants to pay workers on prescribed days (those days when taverns were closed), as in the case of the Neue Helene and Brzozowitz mines in 1902.[21]

Such palliatives did not stanch the drinking urge of local denizens, and the outbreak of a major miners' strike in 1913 occasioned a tremendous fear on the part of county officials that the strikers would turn their idleness into a drunken binge. In Pless county, at least, all taverns were summarily kept closed in April and May, 1913.[22]

These signs of noncooperation with industrial organization—insubordination and drunkenness in particular—figured less and less prominently in labor-management relations as free-enterprise mining and smelting became increasingly well established in the five decades after the promulgation of the Prussian mining laws. Insubordination of course continued; nor did excessive drinking disappear from the Silesian scene, as even the most casual observer can note to this day.

Still, it is important to differentiate between social problems (drinking) and individual cases of industrial ill-discipline (insubordination) and a pattern of such behavior which would militate against the efficient functioning of a mine or smelter. Even in the 1870s Upper Silesian workers were able to participate in large numbers in a more or less unbroken process of industrial production; industry could function and function well, regardless of any traits among the workers which might be labeled "pro-industrial" or "anti-industrial."

Patterns of Labor Protest

Among the various forms of labor protest, the most visible is a mass refusal to work. In early periods of industrialization—in Upper Silesia the 1870s, 1880s, and sometimes later—spontaneous strikes of workers hinged in part on questions of wages and hours but in large measure also concerned changes in traditional rule-making relationships. In a period of excess labor, it is not feasible vigorously to protest matters of pay; friction centers on other matters.

Strains in relations between workers and employers appeared quite sharply even in the business prosperity before 1873 when owners began to rationalize the old, nonprofit-oriented work rules in order to promote greater production. Following the 1873 crash and in the ensuing depression the trend toward cutting costs accelerated, a process that included laying off the most inefficient sections of the still relatively small labor force.[23] Now, more stringent work rules swept aside older patterns of condoning unwritten perquisites of employment and laxity at work, the "indulgency pattern."[24] Such implied benefits included leniency in cases of absenteeism, the hiring of invalids for light tasks, the selling of coal or food cheaply, and outright grants to workers in times of need. In the early 1870s and probably later miners used to carry coal home each day. They did not consider this to be serious, looking on the practice as analogous to stealing small amounts of wood from forests.[25] However, when such practices were curtailed, workers grew very restive. So the largest pre-1889 strike in Upper Silesia, at the König mine in Königshütte in 1871, resulted from the introduction of a more efficient system of checking daily attendance at work. One should be careful to note, though, that production problems in those early years did not result simply from the unwillingness of mining and smelting workers to abide by a new sort of industrial discipline, but also from difficulties of adjustment on the management side—the supervisors on the plant level often beat their workers, and the level of fines deducted from wages was so great that on paydays police had to be on duty at some mines to forestall rioting.[26]

The local social structure exacerbated these clashes; in particular the dichotomy between the Polish and German communities runs as a leitmotif through the pre-1914 period in Upper Silesia. For example, Hugo Solger, the chief government official of the area of the mining and smelting basin (the then Beuthen county), blamed disorders at the König mine in 1871 on the conflict between the Polish Catholic working masses and the German Protestant officials.[27] Only some two decades later did German workers become more numerous, but even metallurgy, where they were most prominent, continued to employ enough Poles to be split into national communities.

A critically minded economist might raise here (and in other places) the objection that such conflicts, while seemingly over rule-making priorities, actually resulted from changes in the commodity market or in technology—for example, a market demand for coal that workers had previously taken home with them might have triggered the new rules about coal perquisites at Königshütte in 1871. And it is true that coal prices did increase considerably from 1870 to 1871 (6.82 to 8.02 marks per metric ton[28]), perhaps transforming formerly unprofitable coal into a marketable product. However, price fluctuations did not always trigger social unrest, and we know that various kinds of perquisites continued to exist for decades thereafter, only slowly being eliminated as a form of payment in kind. What was happening was that employers were learning swiftly how to deal on the commodity market, but over this half-century their actions on the labor market hardly developed so rapidly; they consistently regarded workers as a passive force when instituting changes suggested by shifting levels of demand and prices.

Although occasional references to other labor disturbances in these first decades of free-enterprise mining and smelting appear in available sources, it is difficult or impossible to differentiate between clashes based on further restrictions of the indulgency pattern and those prompted by a call for higher wages. In all likelihood the two were mixed in such affairs as the 1873 strike at the Scharley zinc mine, where workers "went limp" in the face of the police. The ineffective strike at the nearby Cäcilie zinc mine in the same year signaled the end of work stoppages for a while because widespread unemployment set in with the "Great Depression." For the next sixteen years archival sources mention only some thirteen small strikes plus hints of a few others. Despite a long-term trend of expanding output in the coal and iron industries, the shorter-term business lag of those years undercut potential strike action because of the likelihood of unemployment at the slightest downturn of demand, such as that witnessed at the Friedrich smelter in 1878.[29]

During this wrangling over control of the workplace, preliminary efforts at unionization were made by socialist and Hirsch-Duncker (anti-Marxist) union organizers, but they met with little success. The short-lived mining unions of the late 1860s were opposed by Karol Miarka in his influential newspaper *Katolik*, which was designed to counter the pernicious, atheistic appeal of the socialist-oriented trade unions. This incipient nationalist feeling remained quite crude in the 1870s as *Katolik* stressed anti-Semitism and a rigid kind of Polish Catholicism, apparent in articles like "Secrets of the Talmud." By the early 1880s anti-Semitism was no longer its primary concern, but attacks on Jews were still common; by the 1890s, a Christian union became permissible; and Polish nationalism, Catholicism, and anti-socialism came to constitute the basis of most articles, with anti-Semitism falling by the wayside.[30]

The lean years of the 1880s were not devoid of attempts to organize workers—for example, the St. Barbara Verein der Berg- und Hüttenarbeiter zu Königshütte, the Chrześcijański Związek Robotników w Katowicach (Christian Union of Workers in Kattowitz), and others.[31] All of these groups faded quickly, in the main due to the supply of labor significantly exceeding demand. Conflict on the plant level remained far more important than industry-wide organized protest, at least until the last few years before the outbreak of World War I.

Employment and production began to rise in the late 1880s, and by the early 1890s Upper Silesian mining, and to a lesser extent smelting and metallurgy, had reached the point in their expansion where they employed more than 75,000 workers (about half the local labor force); heavy industrial employment increased to about 200,000 in 1913 (still about half). The rapid absolute growth is apparent not only in global figures but also in the beginning of a management complaint about a shortage of labor, a complaint that was to grow ever stronger from the late 1880s to 1914 (see chapter 2). The strain in the labor market gave an impetus to two major trends: one, from management, an effort to bypass the regular labor market by using women, minors, and annual seasonal migrants from Russia Poland and Austrian Galicia, and two, from workers, a rising labor militancy.

Employment policies of top management need not be discussed here at any length. As elaborated in earlier chapters, women and minors played significant roles in Upper Silesia, but their number remained constant after 1895. The number of Slavic workers, however, was a variable on which employers set great hope. The social implications of the seasonal importation of workers into Imperial Germany are complex. Suffice it to say here that agrarian pressure groups were the primary force that brought about the changes in state policy allowing this population movement, which eventually included hundreds of thousands of people, the majority of whom were employed in agriculture. However, a number of heavy industrial employers also profited from this program, including seven mines which at one point had work forces composed of 20 percent or more foreign workers. The total number of migrants in the 1890s was small, never above 3,000 (2 percent to 3 percent of the mining force—few worked in smelting).[32] After 1900 the labor market grew even tighter, and urgent managerial requests for seasonal workers punctuated periods of prosperity. In 1904 the Poles from abroad (from 1905 Poles and Ruthenians) numbered over 4 percent of the mining force and from 1908-1913 constituted 15 percent or more of the labor force in mining. It is hard to gauge the impact of these potentially strike-breaking foreigners on the natives' labor action, but at the most, labor unions were delayed and strikes weakened, not decisively blocked. After all, the strikes of 1905-1907 took place despite the foreigners, and the largest strike in the entire prewar period occurred in 1913, exactly when the number of aliens reached its peak.

The second major effect of the labor shortage, one more to the point at issue, was the rise in labor militancy. In all the major German mining areas 1889 was the year of significant strike activity. Although the Upper Silesian action lasted only five days, it involved about 15,000 men (30 percent of the coal miners and 13 percent of the ore miners) and engulfed about half the coal mines and one third of the ore mines in the area.[33] The smelting and metalworking industries lay quiescent for many more years, or at least disturbances in that area have not been noted in the materials now available for study. Furthermore, that year saw the formation in Upper Silesia of a Polish labor-union type organization, now endorsed by *Katolik*, the Society for Mutual Aid of Christian Workers in Upper Silesia (Związek Wzajemnej Pomocy Chrześcijańskich Robotników Górno-śląskich), a group which in 1908 merged with other groups in Germany into the Polish Professional Union (Zjednoczenie Zawodowe Polskie).

In the strikes of 1889 and the 1890s the striking miners presented demands that in the main are reminiscent of highly industrialized states:[34] they wanted higher pay, shorter working hours, and improved fringe benefits. On the other hand, unrest in 1889 was also traceable to the workers' complaints that they did not know what the work rules were. More particularly, they protested that when paid by the shift and not by piecework, some of their shifts were not recorded if the demanded "normal production" was not delivered. Even more resented were the practices of forced overtime and of imposing fines in the form of demotion to poorly paid work. Finally, fringe benefits like free coal and cheap food were being undercut by the delivery of shoddy goods.

This second set of nonmonetary complaints reflects a situation not of worker reluctance to adopt the discipline demanded by modern industrial enterprise, but of management unwillingness to abandon the paternalism and high-handed ways commonly found in the early years of industrialization. Contrary to the assumption commonly made by students of modernizing situations, entrepreneurs and corporate leaders do not always formulate policies appropriate to their own economic needs, sometimes even preferring to function on the basis of social prejudices.[35] For example, the much vaunted labor shortage may have been due to extraordinarily low wages; and worker grievances were not always simply due to a distaste for work, as employers would have it. Other recorded reactions to these labor stoppages of the 1890s illustrate even more sharply this false contrast between the modernizing entrepreneur and the backward peasant turned industrial worker. For instance, the directors of the government mines run by the Berginspektion Königshütte commented that workers, particularly unskilled ones, complained of inadequate wages not because wages were too low, but because they squandered their money—thus the workers' "laziness" and "disorderly life." The mine directors also took the local working population to task for its "luxuriousness in clothing" and its "irresponsibly contracted marriages." Such pseudo-paternalism came out clearly in the threat of Friedrich Bernhardi, general director of the Giesche mining conglomerate, to evict striking miners from company housing at the Wildsteinsegen mine in 1890.[36] Employers may have been serving their own interests with such comments, but there is no reason for the observer to judge workers' actions by the same standards.

One must not go so far in the other direction as to say that workers were ready to be efficient and disciplined industrial employees had only the employers dealt with them differently. Absenteeism remained a significant problem down to 1914; even the promise of bonuses for regular attendance was insufficient to curb this practice. Rapid turnover of workers also was common. (See chapter 8.) These practices are sometimes assumed to be reflections of a pre-industrial mentality, when extra income is traded for leisure at a relatively low level, but these patterns of behavior also seemed to express discontent with working conditions at a time when trade unions were not available to express such dissatisfaction.

Rising demand for coal from the late 1880s on and a vigorous expansion of all the local heavy industries starting in the late 1890s led workers to expect higher wages, but such demands can best be placed in context by understanding them as part of a whole series of differences over conditions of work. The fourteen strikes in the core mining and smelting region (Beuthen county) in the 1890s were all extremely short-lived, usually lasting one to two days, indicating a burst of anger over particular working conditions, not a long-term movement for higher wages. So at the Deutschland mine in Schwientochlowitz in 1893 the police and army intervened to end a walkout over forced Sunday work, a lengthened workday, and threatened dismissals for malingering or destroying material. Elsewhere, at the Jakub mine of the giant Kattowitzer AG für Bergbau und Eisenhüttenbetrieb, the local government administrator reported that one of the major elements in a strike of 1897 was resentment at the new manager, who was proving to be much more energetic than his predecessor, presumably through efforts to increase profits by undoing the prevailing indulgency pattern. Short strikes also broke out over raised production norms, such as at the Charlotte mine in Rybnik in 1903, but it is hard to know if such tightening can be described as restricting lax management or merely as a general desire to increase profits.[37]

Modern students of labor strife tend to look for wage demands and organized groups pressing such demands. True, workers cared about wages—the major grievance in the Wolfgang mine strike in 1897—but such a concern must be seen as part of a package of attempts by workers to maintain or improve their status in many ways. It is only with the large-scale strike movement of 1905-1907, the most significant such period since the great strike of 1889, that an integrated set of demands appeared, one that seems in part to have been prompted by labor union planning: higher wages, shorter working hours, improved working conditions, and union recognition. (Union recognition was nowhere achieved in German heavy industry until 1919.) Yet the sources for these years also indicate a series of often isolated, uncoordinated outbreaks, perhaps encouraged in part by union organizing, but more likely the result of miners' taking advantage in an unorganized way of the heightened labor shortage brought on by a brisk demand for coal and zinc. Even though the government was allowing the immigration of Polish and Ruthenian seasonal workers in record numbers, management was too hard pressed to wait out strikes or even to try to impose blacklists of workers, as was ordinarily the practice. In the Rybnik region, where the first strikes of 1905 took place, 500 discharged workers found almost immediate reemployment in the very same area, while most of the workers dismissed for striking at the König mine were rehired very quickly by the same mine.[38]

When all is said and done, however, the student of industrial relations in the last 100 years still expects to find some traces of labor union organization in areas of large concentrations of industrial workers. Why did it prove so difficult for a long-lived large union to emerge in Upper Silesia? Why did high rates of absenteeism and turnover continue well into the twentieth century as the major form of refusal to work? Such questions are hard to answer. After all, as hard as it is to show why men do certain things, it is even harder to show why they do not do other things. Certainly the act of joining a union usually indicates a worker divorced from a primarily agricultural existence and one who in some form or another accepts the bureaucratic relationships implicit in the establishment of a bargaining unit. The existence of large-scale unions even provides *prima facie* evidence of worker acceptance of bureaucratic order in industry —thus the Ruhr region. Employers, of course, have to learn about the new order too; in Germany their recognition of unions as contractual adversaries did not occur until the Stinnes-Legien agreement of 1919.[39]

The usual answer to the puzzle of "retrograde" trade union development[40] is couched in terms of a hodgepodge of causes—Poles versus Germans, including nationalistic German Social Democrats; Catholics versus socialists; lack of effective union leadership; the debilitating effect of foreign workers as potential strike breakers; the peasant composition of the work force; lack of alternative industrial employment; state and employer surveillance of worker activity. All these are very much to the point, but they must be sorted out into hierarchical groupings to make some sense of social action in this area.

First of all, the entire economic framework of Germany was shifting in the second half of the nineteenth century; and with that change, state officials increasingly intervened in the factory order. The exhaustion of unlimited supplies of labor by 1890 had removed an easily available source of strikebreakers, but the labor force itself continued to grow rapidly enough to hinder any consolidation of group feeling, a condition aggravated by the high rates of turnover. On the other hand, the increasingly bureaucratic nature of the mining and smelting industries induced the Prussian state to become more and more involved in labor relations. At first, there was the consolidation of the mining brotherhoods into a large welfare organization and then the social welfare legislation of the 1880s; there followed the Kaiser's intervention in the strike of 1889 and an official investigation of the causes of the strike.[41] In the 1890s came the compulsory publication of a printed set of work rules and the extension of competence of the factory and mine inspectors. After 1900 came works councils for plants with over 100 men, the outlawing of arbitrary fines in the form of not counting so-called improperly filled coal wagons, safety control men, and labor courts. Not all of these proved effective, but gradually new conditions of contract underwritten by the state replaced some of the former employer capriciousness and encouraged a more organized response to changing working conditions. Thus long-run general socioeconomic relationships proved more hospitable to union-type organizations than had been the case earlier.

These developments characterized all of Prussia; the specifics of Upper Silesia are needed for full understanding of the situation. A shortage of workers often encourages independent worker action; local employers tried to remedy the shortage with women, children, and foreign seasonal laborers, but to no avail. The evolving labor market continued to aid workers who changed jobs frequently; it eventually boosted union organization.

Nor is it helpful to refer to the peasant composition of the labor force as an element blocking collective action, a situation evident in Russia at this time. It has been shown above that although large numbers of Upper Silesian mining and smelting workers were indeed fresh off the farm, many others had already acculturated to the industrial life style. The Ruhr experienced a similar influx of workers of rural origin after 1870, but they obviously did not prevent union organization.

On the other hand, certain bitter conflicts within the work force itself slowed any move to organized work groups. The most obvious dichotomy in the local labor force lay in its ethnic composition, German and Polish, the latter being of local provenance and speaking an Upper Silesian dialect. There is no way of determining the nationality or mother tongue of a particular worker from lists of names, but circumstantial evidence adduced throughout this study indicates that most miners below the supervisory level were Polish speaking; smelting employed many from both groups; metal finishing was heavily German. Moreover, each group tended to concentrate in certain areas within the Upper Silesian industrial region. On the western edge near the German-speaking farm districts across the Oder River, Germans predominated, as at the Gleiwitz rolling mill investigated by Friedrich Syrup. Plants further east, surrounded by areas inhabited by Polish-speaking peasants—Rybnik, Pless, Lublinitz, Tarnowitz—tended to have a large proportion of Poles on the payroll.[42] The cities showed a growing German population, but many of these engaged in non-industrial vocations like shopkeeping and white-collar pursuits; the factory hands chatted in Polish. The agglomeration around Zabrze was heavily Polish; perhaps for this reason the German authorities denied it the right of incorporation as a city until 1915, when the settlement was rechristened "Hindenburg."

Existing records show no cases of overt clashes between the two groups, but everything known about their organizations shows that there was very little mixing. As early as 1871 the Higher Mining Office forbade the hiring of supervisors who spoke only Polish, a clear indication that such had been the practice in the past. In the same year some workers at Königshütte complained to the central government about the rising cost of living, too intensive work, low wages, and the privileged position of Protestants. Living in the area were 16,000 Catholics—obviously Poles—and 2,000 Protestants—obviously Germans—but the latter dominated local government and received more funding for their schools. In an age when labor grievances centered on nonmoney working conditions, it is not hard to believe the undocumented account of a demonstration of miners near Beuthen in 1880 where the mine inspector was greeted with cries of "We want to hear Polish, not German."[43] The Polish Society for Mutual Aid was challenged by the Ruhr-based Union of German Miners (German socialist), but the latter, in contrast to the locals in the Ruhr, was not salvaged by strong leadership. The German-speaking, church-oriented Organization of Catholic Unions (based in Berlin) lay in wait, unwilling to cooperate with anyone else; it was in essence a yellow union because it renounced the right to strike. Besides, though more men enrolled in these locals than in socialist ones, most members worked in handicrafts or in small manufacturing shops— witness the small number of members resident in the inner industrial region (measured by the membership of Polish locals—see Table 24). In addition, all these organizations appealed more to miners than to smelting workers and metalworkers, who remained impervious to any union blandishments during the entire prewar period.[44]

In general, only loose ties connected political activity with worker demonstrations, but ethnic differentiation was apparent to all. Even the socialists, theoretically internationalist in outlook, could find little meeting ground because of nationalist divergences. The Prussian branch of the Polish Socialist Party (PPS), with headquarters first in Berlin and later in Kattowitz, moved in and out of the ranks of the German Social Democrats (SPD), who saw little reason to pander to Poles who appeared to place patriotism above the proletarian revolution, German style.[45] Regardless of how well the two got along, the local workers displayed scant interest. The SPD was pictured as both German and atheist. The Polish socialists did little better, even though their publications in the 1890s illustrated an understanding of the attachment of the local worker to the church (or to church forms) with such articles as "The Worker's Catechism" and the "Ten Commandments for Workers." The religious overtones declined after 1900, but no rise in popularity matched this shift, despite the complaints by factory inspectors of "provocative and insulting articles" in the Polish journals.[46]

During the Prussian state struggle with the Catholic church in the 1870s (*Kulturkampf*), the Polish mining and smelting workers were sometimes denounced as a "tool of the clergy and other agents of Rome." Things changed after the political settlement of the early 1880s, and business and government officials had little to complain of regarding the church. Its identification with Germanizing forces—personified in Bishop Kopp of Breslau—and its alliance with the local industrial magnates—such as Count Franz von Ballestrem, Center Party president of the *Reichstag* in the early twentieth century—made it a formidable foe of union organization. Local parish priests did their part by proclaiming socially conservative doctrine, like the preacher in Schwientochlowitz who in 1908 on the occasion of St. Barbara's Day, patron saint of miners, claimed that workers should not murmur against their employers; even though the work was hard, it was their Christian duty to bear it uncomplainingly.[47] However, by the early 1890s the Polish nationalist movement had gained sufficient respectability for it to be supported by a church group, *Katolik* and the Society for Mutual Aid; increasingly, there was a German church and a Polish church, just as there were German socialists and Polish socialists and German trade unions and Polish trade unions.

During the stormy strike years of 1905-1907, rival unions engaged in some common action, but no long-term cooperative effort developed. Membership in labor organizations, summarized in Table 24, reflected the latent and manifest conflict between the Poles and Germans. The Social Democratic mining union, the "Alter Verband," grew slowly, from fewer than 1,000 to about 2,600 in 1913, and membership in 1913 included only about 500 people in Polish-speaking locals. Occasionally it was credited with adding to worker unrest, but that was all. On the other hand, the Polish-speaking, church-oriented Society for Mutual Aid did enroll quite a few members, growing from 5,000 members in 1896 to about 14,000 in 1900, only to subside soon after. After the strike years of 1905-1907, the society went into temporary decline, dropping to under 4,000 members in 1908; but that date marked a turning point in unionization. The Society for Mutual Aid merged with Polish trade unions in the Ruhr and Posen to form the Polish Professional Organization (ZZP), and from then on membership in the Upper Silesian mining group climbed rapidly, albeit sporadically.[48]

Before the defeat of the great strike of 1913 caused a depletion in the ranks, about 10 percent of the entire local labor force in heavy

TABLE 24

Membership in Unions of Miners in the Upper Silesian
Industrial Region,
1902–1913

Union of German Miners (Verband Deutscher Bergarbeiter–Social Democratic)	
Year	Number of members
1902	925
1903	800
1904	1939
1906	1937
1907	2288
1908	2371
1913	2625
1913 (Polish only)	480

	Organization of Catholic Unions (Berlin wing)	
Year	Total number of members	Members of Polish groups
1905	10,117	?
1906	17,546	1065
1907	19,471	2128
1908	25,742	2728
1913	?	4129
1913 (all of administrative Upper Silesia)	?	7078

	Polish Professional Organization (ZZP)	
Year	Number of members	
1910	10,574	(miners)
1911	4,523	(smelter workers)
1913	20,451	
1913 (all of administrative Upper Silesia)	20,712	

SOURCE: Compiled from yearbooks of the Verband Deutscher Bergarbeiter and
scattered archival sources in Opole, Katowice, and Wroclaw by Felicja Figowa, *Związki
Robotników Polskich w byłej Rejencji Opolskiej w przededniu Pierwszej Wojny Światowej*
[Polish labor unions in the former regency of Oppeln on the eve of the First World
War] (Opole: Instytut Śląski, 1966): Union of German miners—pp. 14, 17, 19, 51;
Organization of Catholic Unions—pp. 29, 48–50; ZZP—pp. 12, 43–48.

industry enrolled in the union.[49] Significantly, only a minute proportion of members worked outside heavy industry—in 1913, fewer than
300 of a total of 20,700.

It is now perhaps clearer how large-scale unions came into being in Upper Silesia only in the few years before 1914, even though the labor force had in part reached a bureaucratic, "modern" phase some two decades earlier. From the standpoint of German and Prussian developments, one sees changing market conditions and a changing role for government intervention in industrial relations as crucial for establishing a context conducive to formal worker organization. Moving from the general to the particular, one must note that ethnic conflicts within the work force further delayed joint action; this obstacle was eventually circumvented by creating all-German or all-Polish groups. Finally, effective church opposition declined because a church-oriented group reappraised the demands of its backers and itself turned to labor organization. The alliance of activist Poles with a clerical organization had proved too much for the entrenched Catholic hierarchy and its allies in politics and business, a trend also apparent in the growth of Polish nationalist groups in Upper Silesia around 1900.

The emergence of "modern" group action in Upper Silesia became eminently clear in the great mining strike of 1913. Strikes in Germany seem to have moved in waves, occurring in the Ruhr, the Saar, and Upper Silesia at approximately the same time, almost always during a period of business prosperity and near full employment, and commonly in the wake of rising food prices. This coincidence was obvious in 1889 and 1905-1907; 1912 was an even clearer case of mutual encouragement by miners, as strikes broke out in England, France, the Ruhr, and in the Dąbrowa basin of Russian Poland (bordering on Upper Silesia). Upper Silesia followed in 1913.

The 1913 strike of Upper Silesian coal, zinc, and lead miners was unusual in several ways. First of all, it was a union-organized strike—by the ZZP, the Social Democratic Union of German Miners, and the minuscule Hirsch-Duncker unions—and as such was the first coordinated labor protest in the industrial history of Upper Silesia. Although only about 15 percent to 20 percent of all Upper Silesian miners were organized (at least 20,000 men in a mining force of about 120,000), at one point in May, 1913, some 55 percent of all crews were striking.[50]

The change in the character of worker grievances was truly evident in the major demands, centering on a pay raise and the introduction of an eight-hour day and mentioning little about work rules. It is also noteworthy that for the first time the strikers were essentially the skilled hewers, while the younger workers and semi-skilled and unskilled haulers tended to report to work; in previous large-scale strike actions the social alignment had been the reverse.[51]

All of these points—the coordinated union activity, the essentially economic demands, and the leadership of the more established workers—point to the changing nature of labor protest. Miners were now set in their occupations and had adjusted to employer-employee relationships which they had earlier been reluctant to accept. Certainly wage cuts and the extension of hours would not have been tolerated quietly, but this new kind of protest indicates that the definition of the everyday routine of mining seems gradually to have declined as a source of tension. Industrial labor discipline in large measure had been accepted; conflict now arose within a supposedly common pattern of rules, at least from the side of labor.

On the other hand, management still functioned under the assumptions of an earlier age. Mining and smelting employers in pre-1914 Germany were known for their bitter opposition to union activity and any displays of worker independence. In contrast to the usual picture of new industrial workers refusing to adopt the requirements of factory labor, in the 1913 strike in Upper Silesia management again showed itself unready or unwilling to accept labor as a valid source of input to the process of framing the structure of the workplace. That employers should defeat a strike is nothing novel, but their propaganda was quite absurd. In addition to mouthing the usual slogans about adequate wages, decent hours, and superb working conditions, industrial managers drew on the German-Polish difficulties of Prussia and Germany to support the case that the chief purpose of the strike was "... the weakening of Germandom in Upper Silesia." So went the general judgement on such political demands as the eight-hour day! Significantly, the mine inspectors' reports of the strikes did not even mention Polish nationalism as having any influence in this case.[52] Even though some corporation directors may truly have believed in an immediate threat from Polish nationalism, it is hard to picture this charge as anything more than a red herring designed to undercut any potential public support for a strike led by a Polish union and as a sign of absolute unwillingness to consider a changing role for workers, despite the numerous legal changes in working conditions after 1900. It seems that managers needed to be "modernized" fully as much as workers did.

A look backwards over the whole era of rapid industrialization reveals a clear coincidence of years of heightened worker protest with the five "boom" periods noted in the German economy of 1870 to 1913: 1870-1872, 1889, 1896-1899, 1903-1906, and 1910-1912.[53] Although there may have been at times short lags between Upper Silesian conditions and the German average, the general periodization is the same. Data on worker protest indicate an upsurge of activity precisely in these years, though not so vehement in the late 1890s as in the other years; in each case unrest abated when faced with a downturn in business, the lessening of the labor shortage, and the threat of unemployment. Most interesting is the way these worker demands changed. The conflicts in the early 1870s were in large measure the result of changes in work rules intended to make the labor force more productive; these changes were resented because they clearly curtailed the privileges hitherto enjoyed by workers. The year 1889 witnessed the same clash over work rules, but many of the old patterns of indulgence had been muted and now the question of wages became important. Perquisites of mining jobs were still valued highly, but arrangements for free or cheap coal or reduced-price food had now been regularized as a condition of work, not as a sort of right over which workers exercised ulimate control. In the late 1890s and in 1905-1907 worker complaints turned more and more to wages, hours, and other working conditions bearing on pay (like the measurement of coal produced); finally, in the 1913 strike wages stood out as the key demand.

Boom periods, of course, did not cause such activity; they merely presented the opportunity for workers to press their desires. Were one to focus on recession periods, in all probability the same conflicts would emerge but with management better able to determine the changing rules of the workplace. The long-term trend, however, was one in which workers came to recognize the right of owners and management to set and control the general conditions of work and in which the workers came increasingly to focus their grievances on issues directly affecting the amount of pay they received and the number of hours they worked. The emphasis here on periods of prosperity shows how grievances began to be frequently expressed through mass actions, sometimes organized by trade unions, or by individual activity such as frequent absenteeism and high job turn-over. This development accompanied worker acquiescence in a labor discipline thought necessary to run large-scale mining and smelting industries in the industrial age; in short, there emerged what from a later perspective one would call a "modern" industrial labor force.

10

Conclusion

Many areas of German history have surfaced in this study, a number of them suggestive of hypotheses for comparative history—rural-urban migration as influenced by extra-economic factors such as housing, the reputation of an area, and the prevailing folk culture; ethnic differentiation outweighing class differentiation, even among groups without a heightened national consciousness; industrial entrepreneurs as a cultural and social entity, endowed with their own world views and peculiar ways of acting in society. But most of all I have been interested in noting how industrial workers and their bosses accommodated themselves to new economic and social relations at the workplace.

To comprehend the social and economic evolution of the industrial labor force in Upper Silesia, it would not have been sufficient merely to list the oppressive working and living conditions endured by the mining and smelting workers in Upper Silesia. This approach has been undertaken in the customary context of the impeachment of capitalism for its merciless treatment of new industrial workers.[1] I do not want to go so far in the opposite direction as to justify the existence of a social system built in part on the social inequities stemming from industrial capitalism. However, by describing the process by which men become committed industrial workers, I have attempted to show what kinds of conflict mark modern industrial society in general and in particular those that took shape in Imperial Germany and its successors, the Weimar Republic and resuscitated Poland.

The ideological importance and high visibility of trade unions and Marxist or worker-oriented political parties have prompted some labor historians to dwell on these developments practically to the exclusion of other aspects of social change connected with the growth of a significant stratum of industrial workers. Yet the proliferation of such modern political stances can take place only on the basis of a sizable core of workers familiar with the notion of a particular industrial job to which they will report more or less regularly, and in fact the existence of worker organizations may give evidence of the prior existence of a group of workers of this sort. I have therefore thought it worthwhile to delve one step further back in time in order to see how the formation of a modern industrial labor force came about in the context of Upper Silesia before 1914.

To understand the worker one must also understand his boss. The conventional view of the entrepreneur sees him as providing capital and raw material, supplying the necessary techniques, administering production and distribution, and selling the products of the firm.[2] One must add here the formation of a modern labor force as another role assigned to the industrial entrepreneur. Though a subset of the category of "administering production," this one task is so important to society and to the firm itself that it must be explicitly stated and discussed. Radical economists dealing with the origins and functions of hierarchy in capitalist production may overstate their case by saying that the function of the boss in industrial production is solely to exploit the workers. However, evidence certainly exists that top managers are often more successful in extracting economic surplus from the workers than they are in some of the tasks conventionally assigned to management. For example, case studies show that one should not automatically assume managerial input to be the source of technological change.[3] So too with the labor force—changing technology did not suffice to create the worker discipline, docility, and reliability desired by Upper Silesian owners and managers, whose personal efforts in this area were often misdirected. Obvious cases in point lie in their handling of recruitment efforts in parts of Germany outside Upper Silesia and in their ineffectiveness in dealing with the agricultural ties of new industrial workers.

The entrepreneur also functions in an economic and technological world beyond his control. Economies of scale and demand for large inputs of capital result from much modern technology, "compel[ling] the concentration of production in factories."[4] In Upper Silesia the process was apparent in the smelting branches of the iron, zinc, and lead industries. Even charcoal-fueled blast furnaces in the eighteenth century and nineteenth century puddling of iron (in use in Upper Silesia until the twentieth century) had required significant capital investment. When the Bessemer and then the Siemens-Martin processes for making steel were introduced into Upper Silesia in the second half of the nineteenth century, there could be no doubt that the new firms demanded larger, more disciplined labor forces. On the other hand, owners and managers could hardly overlook an organization of labor which would permit them more efficiently to extract an economic surplus at the expense of the workers. In fact, discipline, not machine technology, often lies at the core of factory organization.

The mining industries, so hoary in their traditions and yet so important in the emergence of industrial economies, suggest that exploitation and the demands of technology are not the only way to view the modernizing of the labor force; this third way emphasizes economies of scale *in the labor market* as the key ingredient. In earlier times, feudal relationships like regalian rights and the legal status of the miners as a separate estate had combined with primitive technology to hinder development of factory labor relations. In the Upper Silesian coal and zinc mining industries the essentially cottage and craft nature of the production process remained unchanged despite technological advances after 1850, but the labor force nonetheless became modernized. The same striking course of events occurred in the Russian gold fields, where foreign entrepreneurs in the 1890s had to withdraw some of the advanced techniques they had imported because workers could not handle them; yet after 1904 management essentially had its modern labor force.[5] Economies of scale in production were of course important, but in these cases the explanation seems to be that as industrial employment increases, the alternatives available to owner and worker alike tend to become standardized; out of this context grow the end of paternalism, the rise of a conventional wage system, a labor recruitment system, bureaucratization of the workplace, and trade unions. Ethnicity too played a role in Upper Silesia, first as a hindrance to and later as a catalyst of the process.

The picture as drawn here suggests a synthesis of earlier views. One may be correct in dethroning the technology of production from its sacrosanct determining role, but enrepreneurial drive to greater profit does not always provide an adequate explanation of what happened in Upper Silesia and elsewhere. One must return to multiple causation, with technology and exploitation seen as varying in impact from one industry to another and from one society to another. Most important, the size of the labor market must be considered as more important than previous appraisals have allowed. In smelting and in the production of semifinished iron and steel and zinc products, technology as well as managerial desire for control demanded an organized hierarchical system of production. Miners, on the other hand, became modernized because the sheer size of the labor force required some organizational direction beyond the mining partnerships of the Renaissance and even beyond the rudimentary corporations which lasted till the nineteenth century. Hierarchy may not always be so purely rapacious nor even so purely capitalist as he claims; modernization of the labor force is not always equivalent to more efficient exploitation of workers by the bosses.[6]

Transition to a new way of life proved to be relatively easy for workers, despite what one might suspect in a situation of unlimited supplies of labor; and a student of economic development looking for the most significant block to industrialization certainly would not find it in the supply of labor. However, growth of output is not the only area of concern to the historian of industrializing areas; the analysis of social change should not be confined merely to categories deemed important by economic planners. The experience of Upper Silesia illustrates a changing world view of new industrial workers, an outlook of which a primary component lay in a vision of evolving economic relationships. Workers were less powerful than their bosses, but their behavior in the late nineteenth and early twentieth centuries suggests that they did not constitute a passive body nor a mere recalcitrant force being dragged forcibly into a new society. At least in part mining and smelting workers knew what they were about, and whenever feasible they attempted to shape institutions to their own liking. That they often failed is no reason to ignore their attempts.

A reasonable way to integrate employers and employees into an historical whole would be to test the notion of learning by employers and workers expounded in chapter 9. To do this, one would need to compare the behavior of the two groups just before the beginning of the First World War with their behavior at an earlier time, say in 1875 and 1895, to see what each really did learn. However, such a comparison would only be valid were all other things held equal, that is, excluding the concentration of capital, absolute growth of the local industries, changes in technology, and the like.

The fundamental position of most owners and managers changed so drastically in this period that it is hard to leave all other things equal. Still, one well-known mining firm, that of the Prince of Pless, did not incorporate and hardly expanded in these decades; and it is clear from the evidence cited in several places in this study that the policies of this firm did indeed show development toward a new kind of labor relations—change from extensive payment in kind to payment in cash, institution of works councils, posting of work rules, and so on. However, this firm also stood out as a very unusual organization, constantly on the lookout for new ways of establishing harmony at its mines and understanding "paternalism" as more than a subterfuge for controlling the lives of employees—witness the voluntary works councils of 1893. Other decision makers, those who determined the fortunes of heavy industry in Upper Silesia, stand in marked contrast to the Pless people. Constant conflicts over how to measure wagons of coal (resolved in the mining law of 1905), efforts by the Upper Silesian Mine and Smelter Owner Association to block pay raises and to use payments in kind in inflationary periods, extreme recalcitrance to admit worker grievances, and the branding of Polish nationalism as the true enemy during the strike of 1913 all suggest that managers had only reluctantly surrendered their so-called paternalistic policies of earlier years; they learned only slowly and hardly can be classified as pioneers of modernization. In fact, the small Pless works aside, entrepreneurs and managers changed their views but little on labor-management relations; they merely moved along with labor and commodity markets. Given the opportunity, they seem to have been eager to restore earlier patterns of authority. Moreover, their policies were often incapable of delivering the desired results. Managers wanted a docile, reliable, and efficient work force, but they did not seem to learn how to alter their policies of recruitment, wages and hours, and working conditions to achieve their goals.

Workers may have been more facile pupils. True, job opportunities expanded and living standards in general rose, albeit slowly after 1900, but changes in mining technology were significant enough to alter the individualized character of mining work. Yet mining and smelting workers seem to have forsaken their agricultural background, to have adopted more regular standards of work attendance, and to have recognized the managers as the responsible arbiters of a large range of decisions which earlier had been in dispute. Workers contended less and less over questions of rule-making and lines of authority; increasingly they acted within the evolving rules of the game by turning to so-called bread and butter issues. Surely these developments suggest a learning of a new kind of behavior thought characteristic of modern labor forces. Workers changed not only under the impact of shifts in the demand for labor but also as a result of acquiring new ways of regarding their position at work. In this sense they were certainly more "modern" than their employers.

The danger exists of presenting too stereotyped a picture of modern employers, of expecting far too much from even the most advanced entrepreneurs. Yet I am measuring them against their own professed goals, not against some ideal economic state. Perhaps the picture of bureaucratization as it emerges here is one that relates primarily to large firms, like those that constituted the Upper Silesian mining and smelting industries; industries run along the lines of small workshops, like metal finishing, may have exhibited different patterns of worker-manager relations. Pending such an investigation, one may say that in Europe and North America modernization of the labor force has tended to take the form of what I have labeled bureaucratization—formal work rules, clear-cut lines of authority, impersonal but more or less impartial relations between workers and bosses, all dominated by management. Where employers have updated their paternalistic policies (control over the extramural activities of workers), bargaining has remained in the main on the individual level; where employers have been less paternal but still recalcitrant in ceding any of their traditional rule-making power, labor strife and trade unions have emerged; and where employers have combined with governments in order to fight against any compromise with workers, revolutionary parties usually have appeared. Other patterns have at times emerged in the industrial societies of the West; there is no clear-cut situation defining modernity. Paternalism, for example, is far from being simply a transitional state on the road to Weberian rationality. On the whole, however, the trends of bureaucratization sketched here seem faithful to the general paths followed by labor forces in capitalistic industrial societies, a process accompanied by the gradual shedding of paternalism in industry. Not that workers are necessarily satisfied with these arrangements, nor is it inevitable that industry with a punishment-centered bureaucracy (one with the work rules and conditions handed down from on high) will triumph everywhere. This notion can accommodate other hierarchies of authority in industry—perhaps one with a stronger political bent, or perhaps one with worker control of production, or one with the return to or restructuring of paternalistic forms. Certainly all of these have their precedents—the political aspect of industrial development in the Soviet Union; various forms of worker control in Yugoslavia and elsewhere, including *Mitbestimmung* in Germany; paternalism in Japanese industry. All of these deviate from the employer-dominated bureaucratic trend, though they do not invalidate it as one possible avenue to modernity. Upper Silesia shows that this particular formation was not granted without struggle, and recurring demands in the contemporary world for "industrial democracy" suggest that the battle is not over.

Appendix

ALTERNATIVE PLACE-NAMES

The place-names found in this study are those in use in the period 1870-1914; however, many of these have since been changed because of the numerous boundary changes after each of the world wars. The list below contains those names mentioned in this book, and it is based on the following sources: Konstanty Prus, *Spis miejscowości polskiego Sląska Górnego* [A list of the localities in Polish Upper Silesia] (Bytom: Komisarjat Plebiscytowy dla Górnego Sląska, 1920); and the more modern and more comprehensive Stanislaw Rospond, *Slownik nazw geograficznych Polski Zachodniej i Pólnocnej* [A dictionary of geographical names of western and northern Poland] (Wroclaw: Polskie Towarzystwo Geograficzne, 1951).

German	Polish	Other
Bendzin	Będzin	
Beuthen	Bytom	
Breslau	Wroclaw	
Brünn		Brno (Czech)
Cosel	Koźle	
Czeladz	Czeladź	
Dombrowa	Dąbrówa	
Gleiwitz	Gliwice	
Gross Strehlitz	Strzelce opolskie	
Kattowitz	Katowice	
Klein Dombrowka	Dąbrówka Mala	
Klodnitz (canal)	Klodnica	
Königshütte	Królewska Huta; Chorzów	
Lemberg	Lwów	Lviv (Ukrainian)
Liegnitz	Legnica	
Lublinitz	Lubliniec	
Mährisch Ostrau	Morawska Ostrawa	Moravská Ostrava (Czech)
Malapane	Malapanew	
Myslowitz	Myslowice	
Oberschlesien	Górny Sląsk	Upper Silesia (English)
Oder (river)	Odra	
Oppeln	Opole	
Ozimek	Ozimek	
Pless	Pszczyna	

German	*Polish*	*Other*
Posen	Poznań	
Przemsa (river)	Przemsa	
Ratibor	Racibórz	
Rosdzin	Rosdzin	
Rybnik	Rybnik	
Schlesien	Sląsk	Silesia (English)
Schoppinitz	Szopienice	
Tarnowitz	Tarnowskie Góry	
Tost	Toszek	
Weichsel (river)	Wisla	Vistula (English)
Zabrze (1915-1945: Hindenburg)	Zabrze	

Bibliography

1. Archival Materials

The basic directory for the use of Polish archives is Irena Pietrzak-Pawlowska, ed., *Informator o zespolach archiwalnych zawierających materialy do historii przemyslu w latach 1815-1945* [Directory of archival collections containing materials on the history of industry, 1815-1945]. Warsaw: Naczelna dyrekcja archiwów państwowych, 1967. The following, arranged by archive, were the most valuable of the archival collections which I consulted; titles are those in use in the archive concerned.

Bytom, county archive (PAP Bytom)
Berginspektion Königshütte (BIKH)
Bergrevier Beuthen Nord
Bergrevier Beuthen Süd
Bergwerks- und Hüttendirektion des F. v. Donnersmarcks, Schwientochlowitz
Hohenzollerngrube

Hüttenverwaltung Laurahütte
Julienhütte Bobrek
Maxgrube Michalkowitz
Vereinigte Königs- und Laurahütte: Hüttenverwaltung Königshütte, Hüttenverwaltung Laurahütte

Katowice, provincial archive (WAP Katowice)
Cleophasgrube
Friedrichshütte
The Henckel von Donnersmarck-Beuthen Estates Limited
Hohenlohe-Welnowiec
Huta Batory (Bismarckhütte)
Kopalnia Eminencja (Eminenzgrube)

Kopalnia Myslowice (Myslowitzgrube)

Kopalnia Polska (Deutschlandsgrube)
Kopalnia Sląsk (Schlesiengrube)
Landratsamt Kattowitz
Landratsamt Pless
Landratsamt Rybnik
Landratsamt Tarnowitz

Gliwice, provincial archive branch (OT Gliwice)
Bergwerksdirektion Zabrze
Borsig-Kokswerke AG
Gewerkschaft Castellengo Abwehr

Gleiwitzer Grube
Hüttenamt Gleiwitz
Vereinigte Oberschlesische Hüttenwerke AG

Wroclaw, provincial archive (WAP Wroclaw)
Bergwerkgesellschaft Georg von Giesches Erben
Oberbergamt zu Breslau (OBB)
Rejencja opolska (Regierung Oppeln), Wydzial I (section 1) (RO)
Rejencja opolska, Prezydialne Biuro (Präsidialbüro)

2. *Published Sources*

Adelmann, Gerhard. *Quellensammlung zur Geschichte der sozialen Betriebsverfassung. Ruhrindustrie unter besonderer Berücksichtigung des Industrie- und Handelskammerbezirks Essen.* Vol. I: *Ueberbetriebliche Einwirkung auf die soziale Betriebsverfassung der Ruhrindustrie.* Bonn: Peter Hanstein, 1960.

Gąsiorowska-Grabowska, Natalia, ed. *Zródla do dziejów klasy robotniczej na ziemiach polskich.* Vol. II: *Sląsk, Wielkopolska, Pomorze, Warmia, Mazury, Zachodnia Galicja, 1850-1900* [Sources on the History of the Working Class in the Polish Lands. Vol. II: Silesia, Great Poland, Pomerania, Warmland, Mazuria, Western Galicia, 1850-1900]. Warsaw: Państwowe Wydawnictwo Naukowe, 1962.

3. *Contemporary Periodical Publications Cited Without Attribution to a Specific Author*

Gazeta robotnicza. Vol. 1, 1891. (Organ of the Polish Socialist Party in Prussia.)

Jahresberichte der königlichen Regierungs- und Gewerberäte und Bergbehörden. Vol. 1, 1888. (JRGB)

Katolik. Vol. 1, 1868. (Organ of the Związek Wzajemnej Pomocy [Society for Mutual Aid].)

Praca. Vol. 1, 1890. (Supplement to *Katolik.*)

Preussische Statistik.

Reichsarbeitsblatt. Vol. 1, 1903.

Statistisches Jahrbuch für den preussischen Staat.

Statistik des Deutschen Reiches.

Vierteljahrshefte zur Statistik des Deutschen Reiches.

Zeitschrift des oberschlesischen Berg- und Hüttenmännischen Vereins. Vol. 1, 1862. (ZOBH)

Zeitschrift für das Berg-, Hütten- und Salinenwesen. Vol. 1, 1853. (ZBHS). (Official publication of the Prussian state.)

4. *Books and Articles Cited in the Footnotes*

Adelmann, Gerhard. "Die Beziehungen zwischen Arbeitgeber und Arbeitnehmer in der Ruhrindustrie vor 1914." *Jahrbücher für Nationalökonomie und Statistik* 175 (1963); 412-427.

———. *Die soziale Betriebsverfassung des Ruhrbergbaus vom Anfang des 19. Jahrhunderts bis zum Ersten Weltkrieg unter besonderer Berücksichtigung des Industrie- und Handelskammerbezirks Essen.* Bonn: Ludwig Röhrschied, 1962.

Barger, Harold, and Sam H. Schurr. *The Mining Industries, 1899-1939.* New York: National Bureau of Economic Research, 1944.

Baumont, Maurice. *La Grosse industrie allemande et le charbon.* Paris: Gaston Boin, 1928.

Beck, Ludwig. *Die Geschichte des Eisens in technischer und kulturgeschichtlicher Beziehung,* Vol. V. Braunschweig: Friedrich Vieweg u. Sohn, 1895-1903.

Becker, Walter. "Die Bedeutung der nichtagrarischen Wanderungen für die Herausbildung des industriellen Proletariats in Deutschland, unter besonderer Berücksichtigung Preussens von 1850 bis 1870." In *Studien zur Geschichte der Industriellen Revolution in Deutschland,* edited by Hans Mottek *et al.,* pp. 209-240. Berlin: Akademie, 1960.

Bendix, Reinhard. *Work and Authority in Industry. Ideologies of Management in the Course of Industrialization.* New York: Harper and Row,

1963.
Bendix, Reinhard, and Seymour Lipset. *Social Mobility in Industrial Society*. Berkeley and Los Angeles: University of California Press, 1959.
Berg, Elliot J. "Backward-Sloping Labor Supply Functions in Dual Economies—the Africa Case." *Quarterly Journal of Economics* 75 (1961); 468-492.
Bernhard, Ludwig. *Die Polenfrage. Das polnische Gemeinwesen im preussischen Staat*. Leipzig: Duncker and Humblot, 1910.
Bernhardi, Friedrich. *Gesammelte Schriften*. Kattowitz: OBHV, 1908.
———. "Ueber die Ackerkultur und Gartenpflege bei den oberschlesischen und speziell den von der Bergwerksgesellschaft Georg von Giesches Erben beschäftigten Montanarbeitern." In his *Gesammelte Schriften*, 478-488. Kattowitz: OBHV, 1908.
Bernstein, Marvin P. *The Mexican Mining Industry, 1890-1905*. Albany: State University of New York, 1964.
Bialy, Franciszek. *Górnośląski związek przemyslowców górniczo-hutniczych, 1854-1914*. (OBHV, 1854-1914). Katowice: Śląsk, 1963.
Bismarckhütte, 1872-1922. Berlin: Eckstein, 1923.
Bleiber, Helmut. *Zwischen Reform und Revolution*. Berlin: Akademie, 1966.
Blumer, Herbert. "Early Industrialization and the Laboring Class," *Sociological Quarterly* 1 (1960); 5-14.
Boda-Krężel, Zofia, and Kazimiera Wicińska. "Nieszczęśliwe wypadki w górnictwie węgla i rud w okręgu Wyzszego Urzędu Górniczego we Wroclawiu (Oberbergamt zu Breslau) w II. pol. XIX w." [Accidents in coal and ore mining in the territory of the Higher Mining Office in Breslau in the second half of the nineteenth century]. *Studia i Materialy z Dziejów Śląska* 1 (1957): 299-343.
Bonikowsky, Hugo. "Die wirtschaftlichen Verhältnisse der oberschlesischen Montanindustrie." In *Handbuch des oberschlesischen Industriebezirks*, 239-460. Kattowitz: OBHV, 1913.
Born, Karl E. *Staat und Sozialpolitik seit Bismarcks Sturz*. Wiesbaden: Franz Steiner, 1957.
Braun, Rudolf. *Sozialer und kultureller Wandel in einem ländlichen Industriegebiet (Zürcher Oberland) unter Einwirkung des Maschinen- und Fabrikwesens im 19. und 20. Jahrhundert*. Zurich and Stuttgart: Eugen Rentsch, 1965.
Brepohl, Wilhelm. *Der Aufbau des Ruhrvolkes im Zuge der Ost-West-Wanderung*. Recklinghausen: Verlag Bitter and Co., 1948.
———. *Industrievolk im Wandel von der agraren zur industriellen Daseinform dargestellt am Ruhrgebiet*. Tubingen: J.C.B. Mohr (Paul Siebeck), 1957.
Brody, David. *Steelworkers in America: The Nonunion Era*. Cambridge: Harvard, 1960.
Broesicke, Max. "Die Binnenwanderungen im preussischen Staate." *Zeitschrift des Königlichen Preussischen Statistischen Landesamts* 47 (1907); 1-62.
———. "Die oberschlesischen Polen, 1905." *Zeitschrift des Königlichen Preussischen Statistischen Landesamts* 49 (1909): 25-62.
———. "Rückblick auf die Entwicklung der preussischen Bevölkerung von 1875 bis 1900." *Preussische Statistik* 188 (1904).
Brozek, Andrzej. "Imigracja ludności z Galicji i Kongresówki do przemyslu na Górnym Śląsku przed rokiem 1885" [Immigration from Galicia and the Congress Kingdom to Upper Silesian industry before 1885]. *Sobótka* 18 (1963); 159-185.
———. *Ostflucht na Śląsku* [Ostflucht in Silesia] Katowice: Śląsk, 1966.

———. "Robotnicy Górnośląscy wobec migracji robotniczej z Galicji i Kongresówki" [Upper Silesian workers and the worker migration from Galicia and the Congress Kingdom]. *Zaranie Śląskie* 24 (1961); 775-786.

———. *Robotnicy spoza zaboru pruskiego w przemyśle na Górnym Śląsku (1870-1914)* [Workers from beyond the Prussian partition area in Upper Silesian industry, 1870-1914]. Wroclaw: Ossolineum, 1966.

———. "Robotnicy ukraińscy w przemyśle górnośląskim przed I Wojną Swiatową" [Ukrainian workers in Upper Silesian industry before World War I]. Polish manuscript of "Ukrainski robotnike v promyslovosti Verchnoi Silezii pered pershoi svitovoiu vijnoiu," *Ukrainskii istorichnij zhurnal* 7 (1965).

———. "W sprawie imigracji ludności slowiańskiej na Górny Śląsk przed Pierwszą Wojną Swiatową" [On Slavic migration to Upper Silesia before World War I]. Polish manuscript of "K otázce imigrace slovanskeho obyvatelstva do Horniho Slezska před prvni světovou válkou,"*Slezsky Sbornik* 59 (1961): 491-511.

———. *Wysiedlenia Polaków z Górnego Śląska przez Bismarcka (1885-1887)* [The expulsion of Poles from Upper Silesia by Bismarck, 1885-1887]. Katowice: Śląsk, 1963.

———. "Ze studiów nad malym ruchem granicznym między Górnym Śląskiem a Zaglębiem Dąbrowskim na przelomie XIX i XX wieku" [Studies on a small border movement between Upper Silesia and the Dabrowski basin at the turn of the twentieth century]. *Sobótka* 13 (1958); 603-640.

Bry, Gerhard. *Wages in Germany, 1871-1945*. Princeton: Princeton Univ., 1960.

Büchsel, Hans-Wilhelm. *Rechts- und Sozialgeschichte des oberschlesischen Berg- und Hüttenwesens 1740 bis 1806*. Breslau and Kattowitz: Schlesien, 1941.

Burgdörfer, B. "Migration Across the Frontiers of Germany." In *International Migrations*, edited by Walter F. Willcox. Vol. II, pp. 313-389. New York: National Bureau of Economic Research, 1931.

Chaplin, David. *The Peruvian Industrial Labor Force*. Princeton: Princeton University, 1967.

Conrad, J. "Agrarische Untersuchungen: V. Der Grossgrundbesitz in Schlesien." *Jahrbücher für Nationalökonomie und Statistik* 3rd ser., 15 (1898); 705-729.

Davis, Lance, Richard Easterlin, and William Parker, eds. *American Economic Growth*. New York: Harper and Row, 1972.

"Denkschrift über die Untersuchung der Arbeiter- und Betriebsverhältnisse in den Steinkohlen-Bezirken," ZOBH 19 (1890):57-132.

Desai, Ashok V. *Real Wages in Germany, 1871-1913*. London: Oxford, 1968.

Dlugoborski, Waclaw. "Ekonomika Górnośląskiego hutnictwa w XVIII wiekuu" [The economics of Upper Silesian smelting in the eighteenth century]. *Zeszyty naukowe Wyzszej Szkoly Ekonomicznej w Katowicach* 19 (1963); 3-80.

———. "Geneza industrializcji Górnego Sląska." [The beginning of the industrialization of Upper Silesia]. *Zaranie Śląskie* 23 (1960); 163-173.

———. "Początki kszaltowanie się klasy robotniczej na Górnym Śląsku" [The beginnings of the formation of the working class in Upper Silesia]. *Kwartalnik historyczny* 61 (1954); 150-177.

———. "Polityka germanizacyjna i postawa ludności polskiej" [Germanification policy and the position of the Polish population]. In *Historia Śląska*, edited by Waclaw Dlugoborski. Vol. II, part 1, pp. 388-431. Wroclaw: Ossolineum, 1966.

———. "Przemysl i górnictwo" [Industry and mining and smelting]. In *Historia Sląska*, edited by Waclaw Dlugoborski. Vol. II, part 1, pp. 153-227. Wroclaw: Ossolineum, 1966.

———. "Rekrutacja górników w Zaglębiu Górno-Sląskim w okresie przed zniesieniem poddaństwa. Na przykladzie państwowej kopalni rud olowianych 'Friedrichsgrube' w Tarnowskich Górach" [The recruitment of miners in the Upper Silesian basin in the period before the abolition of serfdom. On the example of the government lead mine "Friedrichsgrube" in Tarnowitz]. *Przegląd Zachodni* 1950, no. 7/8; 49-88.

———. *Więź ekonomiczna między Zaglębiami Górnośląskim i Dąbrowskim w epoce kapitalizmu (do 1877 roku)* [The economic tie between the Upper Silesian and Dąbrowa basins in the epoch of capitalism up to 1877]. Katowice: Sląski Instytut Naukowy, 1973.

———. "Wstęp" [Introduction]. In *Historia Sląska*, edited by Waclaw Dlugoborski. Vol. II, part 1, pp. 6-19. Wroclaw: Ossolineum, 1966.

Dlugoborski, Waclaw, and Kazimierz Popiolek. "A Study on the Growth of Industry and the History of the Working Classes in Silesia." *Annales Silesiae* 1 (1960); 82-112.

Dobbers (Dobers?), Max. *Die königliche Friedrichshütte bei Tarnowitz in Oberschlesien. Festschrift zur Feier ihres hundertjährigen Bestehens von 1786-1886.* Berlin: Ernst & Korn, 1886.

Donnersmarckhütte. Oberschlesische Eisen- und Kohlenwerke Actien-Gesellschaft, Zabrze O/S, zu Anfang des Jahres 1900. N.p., n.d.

Dzieje Zjednoczenia Zawodowego Polskiego 1889-1939 [History of the Polish Professional Union, 1889-1939]. N.p.: Kartel ZZP na Sląsku, 1939.

Ehrenberg, Richard. "Schwäche und Stärkung neuzeitlicher Arbeitsgemeinschaften." *Archiv für exakte Wirtschaftsforschung* 3 (1909-1911); 401-458.

Fechner, Hermann. "Geschichte des Schlesischen Berg- und Hüttenwesens in der Zeit Friedrich's des Grossen, Friedrich Wilhelm's II. und Friedrich Wilhelm's III. 1741-1806." ZBHS 48 (1900); 49 (1901); 50 (1902).

Feldman, Gerald D. "German Business Between War and Revolution: The Origins of the Stinnes-Legien Agreement." In *Entstehung und Wandel der modernen Gesellschaft (Festschrift für Hans Rosenberg)*, edited by Gerhard A. Ritter, pp. 312-341. Berlin: Walter de Gruyter & Co., 1970.

Figowa, Felicja. *Związki robotników polskich w bylej rejencji opolskiej w przededniu pierwszej wojny światowej* [Polish labor unions in the former regency of Oppeln on the eve of the First World War]. Opole: Instytut śląski, 1966.

Fischer, Wolfram. *Der Staat und die Anfänge der Industrialisierung in Baden, 1800-1850. I: Die staatliche Gewerbepolitik.* Berlin: Duncker & Humblot, 1962.

———. "Die Stellung der preussischen Bergrechtsreform von 1861-1865 in der Wirtschafts- und Sozialverfassung des 19. Jahrhunderts." *Zeitschrift für die gesamte Staatswissenschaft* 117 (1961); 521-534.

Franzke, Karl. *Die oberschlesischen Industriearbeiter von 1740-1886.* Breslau: Verlag Priebatsch's Buchhandlung, 1936.

Fuchs, Konrad. "Die Bismarckhütte in Oberschlesien." *Tradition* 5 (1970); 255-272.

———. *Vom Dirigismus zum Liberalismus. Die Entwicklung Oberschlesiens als preussisches Berg- und Hüttenrevier.* Wiesbaden: Franz Steiner, 1970.

———. "Wirtschaftliche Führungskräfte in Schlesien 1850-1914." *Zeitschrift für Ostforschung* 21 (1972); 264-288.

"Die für die Arbeiter der staatlichen Berg-, Hütten- und Salzwerke Preussens bestehenden Wohlfahrtseinrichtungen." ZBHS 54 (1906); B-1-182.

Gothein, Eberhard. "Bergbau und Hüttenwesen." *Grundriss der Sozialö-konomik* 2nd rev. ed. Tübingen: J. C. B. Mohr (Paul Siebeck), 1923.

Galos, Adam. "Rugi pruskie na Górnym Śląsku (1885-1890)" [The Prussian expulsions in Upper Silesia, 1885-1890]. *Sobótka* 9 (1954); 56-107.

———. "Społeczeństwo polskie w zaborze pruskim w latach 1864-1885" [Polish society in the Prussian partition area, 1864-1885]. In *Historia Polski*, III:1, pp. 230-295. Warsaw: Państwowe Wydawnictwo Naukowe, 1963.

———. "Walka Kapitalistów górnośląskich o robotnika galicyjskiego (1904-1914)" [The struggle of Upper Silesian capitalists for the Galician worker, 1904-1914]. *Sobótka* 4 (1949); 160-186.

Galos, Adam, Felix H. Gentzen, and Witold Jakóbczyk. *Dzieje Hakaty* [History of the H-K-T Society]. Poznań: Instytut Zachodni, 1966.

Geisenheimer, L. *Festschrift zur fünfzigjährigen Jubelfeier der oberschlesi-schen Bergschule.* Tarnowitz: A. Sauer, 1889.

Gerschenkron, Alexander. "Some Aspects of Industrialization in Bulgaria, 1878-1939." In his *Economic Backwardness in Historical Perspective*, pp. 198-234. Cambridge: Harvard, 1962.

Glass, David V., and E. E. Grebenik. "World Population, 1800-1950." In *The Cambridge Economic History of Europe*, edited by M. M. Postan and H. J. Habakkuk, VI, pp. 56-138. Cambridge: At the University Press, 1965.

Goltz, Theodor von der. *Die ländliche Arbeiterfrage und ihre Lösung.* Danzig: A. W. Kafemann, 1874.

Gouldner, Alvin. *Patterns of Industrial Bureaucracy.* New York: Free Press, 1954.

Grosche. *Der staatliche Steinkohlenbergbau in Oberschlesien.* Zabrze: Kön-igliche Bergwerksdirektion, 1913.

Grumbach, Franz, and Heinz König. "Beschäftigung und Löhne der deut-schen Industriewirtschaft, 1888-1954." *Weltwirtschaftliches Archiv* 79/2 (1957); 125-155.

Grünberg, Karol, and C. Kozlowksi. *Historia polskiego ruchu robotniczego, 1864-1918* [History of the Polish workers' movement, 1864-1918]. Warsaw: Książka i Wiedza, 1962.

Günther, Adolph. "Die Wohlfahrtseinrichtungen der Arbeitgeber in Deutschland." *Schriften des Vereins für Sozialpolitik* 145 (1905); 1-94.

Haines, Michael. *Economic-Demographic Interrelationships in Developing Agricultural Regions: A Case Study of Prussian Upper Silesia, 1840-1914.* Diss. University of Pennsylvania, 1971.

Hall, R. Dawson. "Have Mining Engineers Accepted All That Developments in Machinery for Handling Coal Imply?" *Coal Age* 20 (July 7, 1921); 13-15.

Handbuch des oberschlesischen Industriebezirks. Kattowitz: OBHV, 1913. Der Bergbau im Osten des Königreichs Preussen, II, issued as Festschrift zum XII. allgemeinen Deutschen Bergmannstage in Breslau, 1913.

Harbison, Frederick, and Charles A. Myers. *Management in the Industrial World.* New York: McGraw-Hill, 1959.

Harbison, Frederick, and Ibrahim A. Ibrahim. "Some Labor Problems of Industrialization in Egypt." *Annals of the American Academy of Political and Social Science* 305 (1956); 114-124.

"Hard Core, Hard Profits," *Newsweek*, 30 December 1968, p. 45.

Haushofer, Heinz. *Die deutsche Landwirtschaft im technischen Zeitalter.* Stuttgart: Eugen Ulmer, 1963.

Henderson, William O. *The State and the Industrial Revolution in Prussia, 1740-1870*. Liverpool: Liverpool University, 1958.

Heymann, Hans G. "Die gemischten Werke im deutschen Grosseisengewerbe. Ein Beitrag zur Frage der Konzentration der Industrie." *Münchener volkswirtschaftliche Studien* 65 (1904).

Hinze, Kurt. *Die Arbeiterfrage zu Beginn des modernen Kapitalismus in Brandenburg-Preussen 1685-1806*. Berlin: Walter de Gruyter, 1963.

Hobsbawm, Eric J. "Custom, Wages, and Work-Load in Nineteenth-Century Industry." In his *Labouring Men*, pp. 405-435. Garden City, N.Y.: Anchor, 1967.

———. "The Machine-Breakers." In his *Labouring Men*, pp. 7-26. Garden City, N.Y.: Anchor, 1967.

Hoffmann, Walther G. "The Take-Off in Germany." In *The Economics of Take-Off Into Sustained Growth*, edited by Walt Rostow, pp. 95-118. London: Macmillan, 1963.

Hoffmann, Walther G., assisted by Franz Grumbach and Helmut Hesse. *Das Wachstum der deutschen Wirtschaft seit der Mitte des 19. Jahrhunderts*. Berlin: Springer, 1965.

Hollander, Samuel. *The Sources of Increased Efficiency: A Study of DuPont Rayon Plants*. Cambridge: MIT, 1965.

Hoselitz, Bert. "Non-Economic Barriers to Economic Development." *Economic Development and Cultural Change* 1 (1952); 8-21.

Hue, Otto. "Der preussische Staat als Bergwerksbesitzer." *Neue Zeit* 20:1 (1902); 788-793.

Imbusch, H. *Arbeitsverhältnisse und Arbeiterorganisationen im deutschen Bergbau*. Essen: Verlag des Gewerkvereins christlichen Bergarbeiter, n.d.

Die Industrie- und Handelskammer für die Provinz Oberschlesien. 1882-1932. Beuthen: Kirsch und Müller, 1932.

Inkeles, Alex. "Making Men Modern: On the Causes and Consequences of Individual Change in Six Developing Countries." *American Journal of Sociology* 75 (1969); 208-225.

Jaeger, Hans. *Unternehmer in der deutschen Politik (1890-1918)*. Bonn: Ludwig Röhrschied, 1967.

Jaros, Jerzy. *Historia górnictwa węglowego w Zagłębiu Górnośląskim do 1914 roku* [A history of coal mining in the Upper Silesian basin to 1914]. Wroclaw: Ossolineum, 1965.

———. *Historia kopalni Król w Chorzowie (1791-1945)* [History of the König mine in Königshütte, 1791-1945]. Katowice: Śląski instytut naukowy, 1962.

———. "Rozwój techniczny kopalni 'Król' od polowy XIX w. do roku 1918" [The technological development of the König mine from the middle of the 19th century to 1918]. *Kwartalnik Historii Kultury Materialnej* 3 (1955); 58-79.

Jonca, Karol. "Imigracja robotników polskich na Śląsk w końcu XIX i w początkach XX wieku" [The immigration of Polish workers into Silesia at the end of the nineteenth century and the beginning of the twentieth century]. *Studia Śląskie* 1 (1958); 139-158.

———. "Ochrona pracy kobiet i robotników młodocianych w przemyśle górniczo-hutniczym na Górnym Śląsku w latach 1878-1914" [The protection of women and minors in the mining and smelting industry in Upper Silesia, 1878-1914]. *Studia Śląskie* 2 (1959); 61-86.

———. *Polityka socjalna Niemiec w przemyśle ciężkim Górnego Śląska (1871-1914)* [The social welfare policy of Germany in the heavy industry of Upper Silesia, 1871-1914]. Katowice: Śląsk, 1966.

————. *Polozenie robotników w przemyśle górniczo-hutniczym na Śląsku 1889-1914* [The position of the workers in the mining and smelting industry in Silesia, 1889-1914]. Wroclaw: Ossolineum, 1960.

————. "Rozwój przemyslu górniczo-hutniczego w Bytomiu i w regionie bytomskim (od polowy XIX wieku do 1917 roku)" [The development of the mining and smelting industry in Bytom and in the Bytom region from the middle of the nineteenth century to 1917]. In *Dziewięc wieków Bytomia,* edited by Franciszek Ryszka, pp. 233-273. Katowice: Śląsk, 1956.

————. "Strajk na Górnym Śląsku w roku 1889" [The strike in Upper Silesia in 1889]. *Przegląd Zachodni* 8 (1952), special issue: *Studia Śląskie,* pp. 369-402.

————. "Z problemów stosowania ustawodawstwa socjalnego w śląskim hutnictwie cynku przed I Wojną Swiatową" [On the problems of applying social-welfare legislation in Silesian zinc smelting before World War I], *Studia Śląskie* 7 (1963): 7-37.

Jończyk, Jan. "O niektórych formach uzaleznienia robotników od przedsiębiorcy na Górnym Śląsku" [On several forms of making workers dependent on entrepreneurs in Upper Silesia]. *Czasopismo prawno-historyczne* 8 (1955); 203-256.

————. "Strajk górników w 1871 r. w Królewskiej Hucie na tle sytuacji klasy robotniczej na Górnym Śląsku (1869-1878)" [The miners' strike in 1871 in Königshütte on the background of the situation of the working class in Upper Silesia, 1869-1878]. *Przegląd Zachodni* 7 (1952), special issue: *Studia Śląskie,* pp. 310-368.

Junghann, O. *1802-1902. Die Gründung und Weiterentwicklung der Königshütte (Oberschlesien). Festschrift zur 100-jährigen Jubelfeier ihres Betriebes.* N.p., n.d.

Kaczyńska, Elzbieta, and Stefania Kowalska. "Struktura spoleczna robotników Zachodniego Okręgo Górniczego w latach 1840-1870" [The social structure of workers in the Western Mining Region, 1840-1870]. *Zaranie Śląskie* 27 (1964); 180-205.

Kerr, Clark. "Labor Markets: Their Character and Consequences." *American Economic Review* 40 (1950); 278-291.

Kerr, Clark, John T. Dunlop, Frederick H. Harbison, and Charles A. Myers. *Industrialism and Industrial Man.* Cambridge: Harvard, 1960.

Kessel-Zeutsch, Friedrich. *Bergwerksgesellschaft Georg von Giesche's Erben. Abriss zur 200-Jahrfeier 1904 für die Mitglieder geschriebenen Geschichte der Gesellschaft.* Breslau, 1934.

Kindleberger, Charles P. *Europe's Postwar Growth. The Role of Labor Supply.* Cambridge: Harvard, 1967.

————. "Technical Education and the French Entrepreneur." Forthcoming in *Enterprise and Entrepreneurs in Nineteenth and Twentieth Century France.* Edited by E. C. Carter II, R. Foster, and J. N. Moody. Baltimore: Johns Hopkins.

Kirchoff, Hans Georg. *Die staatliche Sozialpolitik im Ruhrbergbau 1871-1914.* Cologne and Opladen: Westdeutscher Verlag, 1958.

Knochenhauer, Bruno. *Die oberschlesische Montanindustrie.* Gotha: Flamberg, 1927.

Koch, Max Jürgen. *Die Bergarbeiterbewegung im Ruhrgebiet zur Zeit Wilhelms II. (1889-1914).* Düsseldorf: Droste, 1954.

Kocka, Jürgen. *Unternehmensverwaltung und Angestelltenschaft am Beispiel Siemens 1847-1914.* Stuttgart: Ernst Klett, 1969.

Köllmann, Wolfgang. "Grundzüge der Bevölkerungsgeschichte Deutschlands im 19. und 20. Jahrhundert." *Studium Generale* 12 (1959): 381-392.

————. "Industrialisierung, Binnenwanderung, und 'Soziale Frage' (Zur Entstehungsgeschichte der deutschen Industriegrossstadt im 19. Jahrhundert)." *Vierteljahrschrift für Sozial- und Wirtschaftsgeschichte* 46 (1959): 45-70.

Kornaczewski, R., ed. *Arbeiterfreund. Kalendar für den oberschlesischen Berg- und Hüttermann.* Kattowitz: Gebrüder Böhm, 1911.

Krantz, Fr. *Die Entwicklung der oberschlesischen Zinkindustrie in technischer, wirtschaftlicher und gesundheitlicher Hinsicht.* Kattowitz: Gebrüder Böhm, 1911.

Krüger, Horst. *Zur Geschichte der Manufakturen und der Manufakturarbeiter in Preussen. Die mittleren Provinzen in der zweiten Hälfte des 18. Jahrhunderts.* Berlin: Rütten & Loening, 1958.

Küster, R. *Kulturelle Wohlfahrtspflege in Oberschlesien.* 2nd ed. Kattowitz: Gebrüder Böhm, 1907.

Kuhn, Walter. *Siedlungsgeschichte Oberschlesiens.* Würzburg: Oberschlesischer Heimatsverlag, 1954.

Kuhna. *Die Ernährungsverhältnisse der industriellen Arbeiterbevölkerung in Oberschlesien. (In amtlichen Auftrage ausgearbeitet im Winter 1891/ 92).* Leipzig: Duncker & Humblot, 1894.

Kula, Witold. *Kszaltowanie się kapitalizmu w Polsce* [The formation of capitalism in Poland]. Warsaw: Państwowe Wydawnictwo Naukowe, 1955.

Ladomirska, Joanna. "Z dziejów śląskiej emigracji do Ameryki pólnocnej" [On the history of Silesian emigration to North America]. *Studia Sląskie* 10 (1966); 271-280.

Landes, David S. *The Unbound Prometheus.* Cambridge: At the University Press, 1969.

Lazinka, Józef. "Wychodźstwo polskie w Westfalii i Nadrenii 1890-1923" [The Polish emigrant community in Westphalia and the Rhineland 1890-1923]. *Sobótka* 4 (1949); 138-159.

Lebergott, Stanley. *Manpower in Economic Growth: The American Record Since 1800.* New York: McGraw-Hill, 1964.

Lebovics, Herman. " 'Agrarians' versus 'Industrializers.' Social Conservative Resistance to Industrialism and Capitalism in Late Nineteenth Century Germany." *International Review of Social History* 12 (1967); 31-65.

Lewis, W. Arthur. "Economic Development with Unlimited Supplies of Labour." *The Manchester School* 22 (1954). Reprinted in *The Economics of Underdevelopment,* edited by A. N. Agarwala and S. P. Singh, pp. 400-449. New York: Oxford, 1963.

Ligęza, Józef. "Kultura grupy górniczej. Próba charakterystyki" [The culture of a mining group. An attempt at characterization]. *Zaranie Sląskie* 22 (1959); 83-92.

Ligęza, Józef, and Maria Zywirska. *Zarys kultury górniczej: Górny Sląsk, Zaglębie Dąbrowskie* [Outline of a mining culture: Upper Silesia, the Dabrowa basin]. Katowice: Sląsk, 1964.

Mai, Joachim. *Die preussisch-deutsche Polenpolitik 1885/87. Eine Studie zur Herausbildung des Imperialismus in Deutschland.* Berlin: Rütten & Loening, 1962.

Marglin, Stephen A. "What Do Bosses Do? The Origins and Functions of Hierarchy in Capitalist Production." Unpublished paper. August, 1971.

Matschoss, Conrad. *Donnersmarckhütte, 1872-1922.* N.p., 1923.

Mazumdar, Dipak. "Underemployment in Agriculture and the Industrial Wage Rate." *Economica* N.S., 26 (1959); 328-340.

McKay, John P. *Pioneers for Profit. Foreign Entrepreneurship and Russian Industrialization, 1885-1913.* Chicago: University of Chicago, 1970.

Molt, Peter. *Der Reichstag vor der improvisierten Revolution.* Cologne and Opladen: Westdeutscher Verlag, 1963.

Moore, Wilbert E. *Industrialization and Labor.* Ithaca: Cornell, 1951.

———. "Labor Attitudes Toward Industrialization in Underdeveloped Countries." *American Economic Review* 45 (1955); 156-165.

Moore, Wilbert E., and Arnold S. Feldman, eds. *Labor Commitment and Social Change in Developing Areas.* New York: Social Science Research Council, 1960.

Morris, Morris D. *The Emergence of an Industrial Labor Force in India.* Berkeley and Los Angeles: University of California, 1965.

———. "Labor Discipline, Trade-Unions, and the State in India." *Journal of Political Economy* 63 (1955); 293-308.

Nalepa-Orlowska, Irma. "Fryderycjańskie osadnictwo hutnicze na Opolszczyźnie (1754-1803)" [Frederician smelting settlements in the Oppeln region, 1754-1803]. *Studia i Materialy z Dziejów Śląska* 5 (1963); 97-161.

———. "Typy robotniczego osadnictwa górniczo-hutniczego na Górnym Śląsku" [Types of mining and smelting worker settlements in Upper Silesia]. In *Górny Śląsk: Prace i Materialy Geograficzne,* edited by Antoni Wrzosek, pp. 345-380. Cracow: Wydawnictwo literackie, 1955.

Nef, John U. "Mining and Metallurgy in Medieval Civilization." *The Cambridge Economic History of Europe,* II, pp. 429-492. Cambridge; At the University Press, 1952.

Neff, Walter S. *Work and Human Behavior.* New York: Atherton Press, 1968.

Neubach, Helmut. *Die Ausweisungen von Polen und Juden aus Preussen 1885/86.* Wiesbaden: Otto Harrassowitz, 1967.

Nichtweiss, Johannes. *Die ausländischen Saisonarbeiter in der Landwirtschaft der östlichen und mittleren Gebiete des Deutschen Reiches.* Berlin: Rütten & Loening, 1959.

Orzechowski, Kazimierz. *Chlopskie posiadanie ziemi na Górnym Śląsku u schylku epoki feudalnej* [Peasant possession of land in Upper Silesia at the end of the feudal era]. Opole: Ossolineum, 1959.

Orzechowski, Marian. *Narodowa Demokracja na Górnym Śląsku (do 1918 roku)* [National Democracy in Upper Silesia to 1918]. Wroclaw: Ossolineum, 1965.

Orsagh, Thomas J. "Löhne in Deutschland 1871-1913: Neuere Literatur und weitere Ergebnisse." *Zeitschrift für die gesamte Staatswissenschaft* 125 (1969); 476-483.

Osthold, Paul. *Die Geschichte des Zechenverbandes, 1908-1933.* Berlin: Otto Elsner, 1934.

Pater, Mieczyslaw. *Centrum a ruch polski na Górnym Śląsku (1879-1893)* [The Center and the Polish national movement in Upper Silesia, 1879-1893]. Katowice: Śląsk, 1971.

———. *Ruch polski na Górnym Śląsku w latach 1879-1893* [The Polish national movement in Upper Silesia, 1879-1893]. Wroclaw: Wroclawskie Towarzystwo Naukowe, 1969.

Perlick, Alfons. *Biographische Studien zur schlesischen Heimatforschung.* Dortmund: Ostdeutsche Forschungsstelle, 1962.

———. *Landeskunde des oberschlesischen Industriegebietes.* Breslau: Schlesien, n.d.

———. *Oberschlesische Berg- und Hüttenleute.* Kitzingen/Main: Holzner, 1953.

Piernikarczyk, Józef. *Historia górnictwa i hutnictwa na Górnym Śląsku*

[A history of mining and smelting in Upper Silesia]. 2 vols. Katowice: Sląski Związek Akademicki, 1933 and 1936.

Piotrowski, J. "Attitudes Toward Work by Women." *International Social Science Journal* 14 (1962); 80-91.

Pollard, Sidney. "Factory Discipline in the Industrial Revolution." *Economic History Review* 2nd ser., 16 (1963); 254-271.

———. *The Genesis of Modern Management*. Cambridge: Harvard, 1965.

Polomski, Franciszek. "Ze wspomnień starego 'Westfaloka'—A. Podeszwy" [From the reminiscences of an old emigrant to Westphalia—A. Podeszwa]. *Studia Sląskie* 1 (1958); 253-264.

Polonsky, Antony. *Politics in Independent Poland, 1921-1939*. London: Oxford, 1972.

Popiolek, Kazimierz. *Górnośląski przemysl górniczo-hutniczy w drugiej polowie XIX wieku* [The Upper Silesian mining and smelting industry in the second half of the nineteenth century]. Katowice: Sląski Instytut Naukowy, 1965.

Popkiewicz, Józef, and Franciszek Ryszka. *Przemysl ciężki Górnego Sląska w gospodarce Polski międzywojennej (1922-1939)* [Heavy industry of Upper Silesia in the economy of interwar Poland, 1922-1939]. Opole: Ossolineum, 1959.

Pounds, Norman J. G. *The Upper Silesian Industrial Region*. Bloomington, Indiana: Indiana University, 1958.

Pounds, Norman J. G. and William N. Parker. *Coal and Steel in Western Europe: The Influence of Resources and Techniques on Production*. Bloomington, Indiana: Indiana University, 1957.

Quante, Peter. *Die Flucht aus der Landwirtschaft*. Berlin: Kurt Vowinckel, 1933.

Raba, Joel. *Robotnicy Sląscy, 1850-1870* [Silesian workers, 1850-1870]. London: Odnowa, 1970.

Raba, Julian. "Walka o jedność organizacyjną w górno-śląskim ruchu robotniczym na przelomie XIX i XX wieku" [The struggle for organizational unity in the Upper Silesian workers' movement at the turn of the twentieth century]. *Sobótka* 10 (1955); 382-432.

Raefler, Friedrich. *Das Schlafhauswesen im oberschlesischen Industriebezirk*. Diss., Breslau, 1915.

Redford, Arthur. *Labour Migration in England, 1800-1850*. Manchester: Manchester University, 1926.

Reichling, Gerhard. "Der Uebergang vom Bauern zum Arbeiter beim Aufbau des oberschlesischen Industriegebietes. Gezeigt am Beispiele von Rosdzin-Schoppinitz, Kr. Kattowitz." *Schlesische Blätter für Volkskunde* 3 (January, 1941); 1-29.

Reynolds, Lloyd G. "Some Aspects of Labor Market Structure." In *Readings in Labor Economics*, edited by Gordon F. Bloom, Herbert R. Northrup, and Richard L. Rowan, pp. 513-537. Homewood, Ill.: Richard D. Irwin, 1963.

Rimlinger, Gaston V. "International Differences in the Strike Propensity of Coal Miners: Industrial and Labor Experience in Four Countries." *Industrial and Labor Relations Review* 12 (1959); 389-405.

Ringer, Fritz K. "Higher Education in Germany in the Nineteenth Century." *Journal of Contemporary History* 2 (1967); 123-138.

Ritter, Gerhard A. *Die Arbeiterbewegung im Wilhelminischen Reich. Die sozialdemokratische Partei und die freien Gewerkschaften 1890-1900*. Berlin: Colloquium, 1959.

Rogmann, Heinz. *Die Bevölkerungsentwicklung im preussischen Osten in den letzten hundert Jahren.* Berlin: Volk und Reich, 1937.

Rose, William John. *The Drama of Upper Silesia.* London: Williams & Norgate, 1936.

Rosenberg, Hans. "The Economic Impact of Imperial Germany: Agricultural Policy." *Journal of Economic History* 3, suppl. (1943); 101-107.

———. "Die Pseudodemokratisierung der Rittergutsbesitzerklasse." In *Moderne deutsche Sozialgeschichte*, edited by Hans-Ulrich Wehler, pp. 287-308. Cologne: Kiepenheuer & Witsch, 1966.

Rospond, Stanislaw. *Dzieje polszczyzny śląskiej* [A History of the Polish language in Silesia]. Katowice: Sląsk, 1959.

Rottenberg, Simon. "Income and Leisure in an Underdeveloped Economy." *Journal of Political Economy* 60 (1952); 95-101.

Rybicki, Pawel. "Rozwój ludności Górnego Sląska od początku XIX wieku do Pierwszej Wojny Swiatowej" [The development of the population of Upper Silesia from the beginning of the twentieth century to the First World War]. In *Górny Sląsk, Prace i Materialy Geograficzne*, edited by Antoni Wrzosek, pp. 247-304. Cracow: Wydawnictwo literackie, 1955.

Sattig. "Uber die Arbeiterwohnungsverhältnisse im oberschlesischen Industriebezirk." ZOBH 31 (1892); 1-50.

Scott, Joan W. *The Glassworkers of Carmaux. French Craftsmen and Political Action in a Nineteenth-Century City.* Cambridge: Harvard, 1974.

Schneider, Lothar. *Die Arbeiterhaushalt im 18. und 19. Jahrhundert.* Berlin: Duncker & Humblot, 1967.

Schultz, Theodore. *Transforming Traditional Agriculture.* New Haven: Yale, 1964.

Schulze, Franz. *Die polnische Zuwanderung im Ruhrrevier und ihre Wirkungen.* Diss. Munich, n.d.

Schwenger, Rudolf. "Die betriebliche sozialpolitik im Ruhrkohlenbergbau." *Schriften des Vereins für Sozialpolitik* 186 (1932).

Seidl, Helmut. *Streikkämpfe der mittel- und ostdeutschen Braunkohlenbergarbeiter von 1890 bis 1914.* Leipzig: VEB Deutscher Verlag für Grundstoffindustrie, 1964.

Seidl, Kurt. "Die Arbeiterverhältnisse des oberschlesischen Industriebezirks." In *Handbuch des oberschlesischen Industriebezirks*, pp. 131-212. Kattowitz: OBHV, 1913.

———. *Das Arbeiterwohnungswesen im oberschlesischen Montanindustrie.* Kattowitz: OBHV, 1913.

Sering, Max. "Arbeiter-Ausschüsse in der deutschen Industrie." *Schriften des Vereins für Sozialpolitik* 46 (1890).

———. *Die Verteilung des Grundbesitzes und die Abwanderung vom Lande.* Berlin: Paul Parey, 1910.

Silcock, H. "The Phenomenon of Labour Turnover." *Journal of the Royal Statistical Society*, ser. A, 117, part 4 (1954); 429-440.

Slotkin, James Sydney. *From Field to Factory. New Industrial Employees.* Glencoe, Ill.: Free Press, 1960.

Smelser, Neil J. *Social Change in the Industrial Revolution.* Chicago: University of Chicago, 1959.

Spencer, Elaine Glowka. *West German Coal, Iron and Steel Industrialists as Employers, 1896-1914.* Diss. University of California, Berkeley, 1969.

Spiethoff, Arthur. *Die wirtschaftlichen Wechsellagen.* 2 vols. Tübingen: J. C. B. Mohr (Paul Siebeck), 1955.

Stasiak, Andrzej. *Przemiany stosunków mieszkaniowych w Zagłębiu Sląsko-Dąbrowskim na tle procesu uprzemyslowienia (lata 1870-1960)* [Changes in living conditions in the Silesian-Dabrowa basin on the background of the process of industrialization, 1870-1960]. Warsaw: Ministerstwo Budownictwa i Przemyslu Materialów Budowlanych, n.d.

————. "Stosunki mieszkaniowe w Królewskiej Hucie (Chorzów) w latach 1870-1914" [Living conditions in Königshütte 1870-1914]. *Zaranie Śląskie* 24 (1961); 613-631.

Staszków, Antonina. "Walka robotników Bytomia o wyzwolenie narodowe i spoleczne (od lat 70-ych XIX wieku do 1914 roku)" [The struggle of the workers of Beuthen for national and social liberation, from the 1870s to 1914]. In *Dziewięć wieków Bytomia*, edited by Franciszek Ryszka, pp. 275-311. Katowice: Śląsk, 1956.

Von Stojentin. "Der Vertragsbruch der landwirtschaftlichen Arbeiter in Pommern." *Zeitschrift für Agrarpolitik* 7 (1909); 181-194.

Stearns, Peter N. "Adaptation to Industrialization: German Workers as a Test Case." *Central European History* 3 (1970); 303-331.

Strauss, Rudolf. *Die Lage und die Bewegung der chemnitzer Arbeiter in der ersten Hälfte des 19. Jahrhunderts.* Berlin: Akademie, 1960.

Surman, Zdzislaw. "Z dziejów walki robotnika górno-śląskiego w r. 1905" [From the history of the struggle of the Upper Silesian worker in 1905]. *Sobótka* 10 (1955); 367-381.

Syrup, Friedrich. "Die soziale Lage der sesshaften Arbeiterschaft eines oberschlesischen Walzwerkes," *Schriften des Vereins für Sozialpolitik* 153 (1915); 131-218.

Szerer, Barbara. "Klasowe związki zawodowe na Śląsku w przededniu Pierwszej Wojny Swiatowej" [Class trade unions in Silesia on the eve of the First World War]. *Studia i Materialy z Dziejów Śląska* 9 (1968); 7-56.

————. "Ruch robotniczy na Śląsku w latach 1905-1907" [The workers' movement in Silesia, 1905-1907]. In *Studia i Materialy z Dziejów Śląska*, edited by Kazimierz Popiolek. Vol. I, pp. 223-297. Wroclaw: Polska Akademia Nauk, Zaklad Historii Śląska, 1957.

————."Wielki strajk górników w 1913 r. na Górnym Śląsku" [The great miners' strike of 1913 in Upper Silesia]. *Studia i Materialy z Dziejów Śląska* 8 (1967); 387-462.

Teuteberg, Hans. *Geschichte der industriellen Mitbestimmung in Deutschland.* Tubingen: J. C. B. Mohr (Paul Siebeck), 1961.

Thernstrom, Stephen. *Poverty and Progress: Social Mobility in a Nineteenth Century City.* Cambridge: Harvard, 1964.

Thomas, William, and Florian Znaniecki. *The Polish Peasant in Europe and America.* 2nd ed. New York: Dover, 1958.

Thompson, Edward P. *The Making of the English Working Class.* London: Victor Gollancz, 1963.

————. "Time, Work-Discipline, and Industrial Capitalism." *Past and Present* no. 38 (1967); 56-97.

Tims, R. W. *Germanizing Prussian Poland.* New York: Columbia, 1941.

Tittler. *Arbeiterverhältnisse und Arbeiterwohlfahrtseinrichtungen im oberschlesischen Industriebezirk.* Breslau: Königliches Oberbergamt, 1904.

Trempé, Rolande. *Les Mineurs de Carmaux, 1848-1914.* 2 vols. Paris: Editions Ouvrières, 1970.

Trist, E. L., and K. W. Bamforth. "Some Social and Psychological Consequences of the Long-Wall Method of Coal Getting." *Human Relations* 4 (1951); 3-38.

"21,706 Jobless Hired by G.M. in 8 Months." *New York Times,* 7 January

1969, p. 1, continued on p. 23.

Tyszka, Carl von. "Löhne und Lebenskosten in Westeuropa im 19. Jahrhundert." *Schriften des Vereins für Sozialpolitik* 145:3 (1914).

U.S. Bureau of the Census. *Historical Abstract of the United States. Colonial Times to 1957.* Washington: U.S. Bureau of the Census, 1960.

U.S. Department of Labor. *Employment and Earning Statistics for the United States, 1908-1968.* Washington: U.S. Government Printing Office, 1968.

Verein für Sozialpolitik. "Auslese und Anpassung der Arbeiterschaft." *Schriften des Vereins für Sozialpolitik* 133ff. (1910-1915).

Vereinigte Königs- und Laurahütte. Königshütte, 1897.

Vereinigte Königs- und Laurahütte, 1871-1921. N.p., 1921.

Vroom, Victor. *Work and Motivation.* New York: John Wiley and Sons, 1964.

Wächtler, Eberhard. *Bergarbeit zur Kaiserzeit. Die Geschichte der Lage der Bergarbeiter im sächsischen Steinkohlenrevier Lugau-Oelsnitz in den Jahren von 1889 bis 1914.* Berlin: Tribüne, 1962.

Walker, Mack. *Germany and the Emigration, 1816-1885.* Cambridge: Harvard, 1964.

Weber, Paul. *Die Polen in Oberschlesien.* Berlin: Julius Springer, 1914.

Weber, Max. *The Theory of Social and Economic Organization.* Trans. A.M. Henderson and Talcott Parsons. Glencoe, Ill.: Free Press, 1964.

———. "Die Verhältnisse der Landarbeiter im ostelbischen Deutschland." *Schriften des Vereins für Sozialpolitik* 55 (1892).

Wehler, Hans-Ulrich. "Die Polen im Ruhrgebiet bis 1918." *Vierteljahrsschrift für Sozial- und Wirtschaftsgeschichte* 48 (1961); 203-235.

———. *Sozialdemokratie und Nationalstaat.* Würzburg: Holzner, 1962.

Więcek, Józef. *Struktura zatrudnienia a płynność robotników w przemyśle węglowym w latach 1949-1959* [The structure of employment and turnover of workers in the coal industry 1949-1959]. Katowice: Śląsk, 1965.

Wojtun, Bronislaw S. *Demographic Transition in West Poland, 1816-1914.* Diss. University of Pennsylvania, 1968.

Work in America. Report of a Special Task Force to the Secretary of Health, Education, and Welfare. Cambridge: MIT, 1973.

Wutke, Konrad. *Aus der Vergangenheit des schlesischen Berg- und Hüttenlebens.* Festschrift zum XII. allgemeinen deutschen Bergmannstage in Breslau, 1913, vol. V. Breslau, 1913.

Wyslouch, Seweryn. "Kapitalistyczna przebudowa rolnictwa śląskiego i jej skutki w latach 1850-1880" [The capitalistic restructuring of Silesian agriculture and its effects, 1850-1880]. *Przegląd Zachodni* 8 (1952). Special issue: *Studia Śląskie*, pp. 1-119.

———. "Przebieg koncentracji w rolnictwie śląskim w latach 1850-1907" [The course of concentration in Silesian agriculture, 1850-1907]. In *Konferencja Śląska Instytutu Historii Polskiej Akademii Nauk,* pp. 390-407. Wroclaw: Ossolineum, 1954.

———. *Studia nad koncentracją w rolnictwie śląskim w latach 1850-1914* [Studies on concentration in Silesian agriculture, 1850-1914]. Wroclaw: Ossolineum, 1956.

Zelnik, Reginald. *Labor and Society in Tsarist Russia: The Factory Workers of St. Petersburg.* Stanford: Stanford University, 1971.

———. "The Peasant and the Factory." In *The Peasant in Nineteenth-Century Russia,* edited by Wayne Vucinich, pp. 158-190. Stanford: Stanford University, 1968.

Ziekursch, Johannes. *Hundert Jahre schlesischer Agrargeschichte. Vom Hubertus-Frieden bis zum Abschluss der Bauernbefreiung.* Breslau: Ferdinand Hirt, 1915.

Zur Feier des 50-jährigen Bestehens der Schlesischen Aktiengesellschaft für Bergbau und Zinkhüttenbetrieb zu Lipine: 1853-1903. N.p., n.d.

Zywirska, Maria, ed. *Zyciorysy górników* [Sketches of miners' lives]. Katowice: Związek Zawodowy Górników w Polsce, 1949.

Notes

CHAPTER 1

[1] For an old-fashioned, pro-Polish, but still useful historical survey in English, see William J. Rose, *The Drama of Upper Silesia* (London, 1936).

[2] E. P. Thompson, "Time, Work-Discipline, and Industrial Capitalism," *Past and Present* 38 (1967): 56-97.

[3] Rudolf Braun, *Sozialer und kultureller Wandel in einem ländlichen Industriegebiet (Zürcher Oberland)* (Zurich and Stuttgart, 1965). For a general statement: Bert Hoselitz, "Non-Economic Barriers to Economic Development," *Economic Development and Cultural Change*, I (1952): 8-21; Wilbert E. Moore and Arnold S. Feldman, eds., *Labor Commitment and Social Change in Developing Areas* (New York, 1960).

[4] E. P. Thompson, *The Making of the English Working Class* (London, 1963). A recent attempt to break the old mold, though still hampered by an emphasis on bureaucratic policy makers: Reginald Zelnik, *Labor and Society in Tsarist Russia: The Factory Workers of St. Petersburg* (Stanford, 1971).

[5] Review by Andrzej Brozek in *Zaranie Śląskie*, 23 (1960): 473, of Karol Jonca, *Polozenie robotników w przemyśle górniczo-hutniczym na Śląsku, 1889-1914* [The position of the workers in the mining and smelting industry in Silesia, 1889-1914] (Wroclaw, 1960). Diffuse and ill conceived, with no notion of an economic region and minimal conceptualization: Joel Raba, *Robotnicy Śląscy, 1850-1870* [Silesian Workers, 1850-1870] (London, 1970). On Germany: Gerhard A. Ritter, *Die Arbeiterbewegung im Wilhelminischen Reich* (Berlin, 1959). On Poland: Karol Grünberg and Cz. Kozlowski, *Historia polskiego ruchu robotniczego, 1864-1918* [History of the Polish workers' movement, 1864-1918] (Warsaw, 1962).

[6] A more balanced approach: Lance Davis, Richard Easterlin, and William Parker, eds., *American Economic Growth* (New York, 1972), chapter 6.

[7] Eric J. Hobsbawm, "The Machine Breakers" and "Custom, Wages, and Work-Load in Nineteenth-Century," in his *Labouring Men* (Garden City, N. Y., 1967), 7-26 and 405-435. In regard to patterns of protest, my work has been informed by Neil J. Smelser, *Social Change in the Industrial Revolution* (Chicago, 1959), and Alvin Gouldner, *Patterns of Industrial Bureaucracy* (New York, 1954). Cf. also David Chaplin, *The Peruvian Industrial Labor Force* (Princeton, 1967). See also the exciting study by Joan W. Scott, *The Glassworkers of Carmaux* (Cambridge, 1974), an account of the interplay of changing technology, the evolving labor market, shifting class consciousness, and declining artisan trades.

[8] Sidney Pollard, *The Genesis of Modern Management* (Cambridge, 1965).

[9] Frederick Harbison and Charles A. Myers, *Management in the Industrial World* (New York, 1959).

[10] Frederick Harbison and Ibrahim A. Ibrahim, "Some Labor Problems of Industrialization in Egypt," *Annals of the American Academy of Political and Social Science* 305 (1956): 114-124; Morris D. Morris, *The Emergence of an Industrial Labor Force in India* (Berkeley and Los Angeles, 1965).

CHAPTER 2

[1] Clark Kerr, "Labor Markets: Their Character and Consequences," *American Economic Review* 40 (1950): 278.

[2] Lloyd G. Reynolds, "Some Aspects of Labor Market Structure," in *Readings in Labor Economics*, ed. Gordon F. Bloom, Herbert R. Northrup, and Richard L. Rowan (Homewood, Ill., 1963), p. 516.

[3] Norman J. G. Pounds, *The Upper Silesian Industrial Region* (Bloomington,

Ind., 1958), 70-71. Pounds surveys the changing technology in Upper Silesia and the changing markets for local products.
⁴ Cf. the chart of coal distribution from Upper Silesia in 1910 in Pounds, p. 76. For a more optimistic appraisal of Upper Silesian industry, see Konrad Fuchs, "Die Bismarckhütte in Oberschlesien," *Tradition* 5 (1970); 255-272. For a sophisticated presentation of economic growth and development (including the labor market) in Upper Silesia up to the time of protective tariffs in the late 1870s, see Waclaw Dlugoborski, *Więź ekonomiczna między Zaglębiami Górnośląskim i Dąbrowskim w epoce kapitalizmu (do 1877 roku)* [The economic tie between the Upper Silesian and Dąbrowa basins in the epoch of capitalism up to 1877] (Katowice, 1973).
⁵ Maurice Baumont, *La Grosse industrie allemande et le charbon* (Paris, 1928), p. 451.
⁶ Special rates: Baumont, p. 423. National producers: Pounds, p. 73. Citation on north-south line: *ibid.* p. 75. Cf. also the chart of comparative prices of Ruhr and Upper Silesian coal, 1850-1910, *ibid.*, p. 75. English coal: Cf. the complaints of the OBHV executive committee, ZOBH 53 (1914); 282.
⁷ PAP Bytom, Bergrevier Beuthen Süd 74; 261, 18 October 1912.
⁸ Percentage of output: Hugo Bonikowsky, "Die wirtschaftlichen Verhältnisse der oberschlesischen Montanindustrie," *Handbuch des oberschlesischen Industriebezirks* (Kattowitz, 1913): 407. Total output: Baumont, p. 351.
⁹ A good summary of changes in coal mining technology is provided by Jerzy Jaros, *Historia górnictwa węglowego w Zaglębiu Górnośląskim do 1914 r.* [A history of coal mining in the Upper Silesian basin before 1914] (Wroclaw, 1965), 118-119.
¹⁰ ZBHS and ZOBH statistics, compiled and for 1870 converted to metric tons by Kazimierz Popiolek, *Górnośląski przemysl górniczo-hutniczy w drugiej polowie XIX wieku* [The Upper Silesian Mining and Smelting Industry in the Second Half of the Nineteenth Century] (Katowice, 1965), pp. 205-206.
¹¹ König mine: V. Meitzen, "Ueber den schachbrettförmigen Abbau auf Königsgrube," ZBHS 9 (1861); PAP Bytom, Königlich Bergwerksdirektion zu Zabrze, Akten betr. geschichtliche Entwicklung der Königsgrube, 1910-1922, both cited in Jerzy Jaros, "Rozwój techniczny kopalni 'Krol' od polowy XIX w. do roku 1918" [The technological development of the König mine from the middle of the nineteenth century to 1918]. *Kwartalnik Historii Kultury Materialnej* 3 (1955) 77. 1880-1913: Calculated on the basis of the statistics published annually in the ZBHS and the ZOBH, as compiled by Popiolek, 207-208. Early boring machines: ZOBH 47 (1908): 465-488. Spread of borers: Karol Jonca, "Rozwój przemyslu górniczo-hutniczego w Bytomiu i w regionie bytomskim (od polowy XIX wieku do 1914 roku)" [The development of the mining and smelting industry in Bytom and in the Bytom region from the middle of the nineteenth century to 1914], in *Dziewięć wieków Bytomia* [Nine centuries of Bytom] ed. Franciszek Ryszka (Katowice, 1956), p. 242.
¹² WAP Wroclaw, OBB 41; 190 (1911), 208 (1912).
¹³ Harold Barger and Sam H. Schurr, *The Mining Industries, 1899-1939* (New York, 1944), p. 171. Cf. also E. L. Trist and K. W. Bamforth, "Some Social and Psychological Consequences of the Long-Wall Method of Coal Getting," *Human Relations* 4 (1951): 3-38.
¹⁴ Gleiwitz: OT Gliwice, Hüttenamt Gleiwitz 2, reviews the first 100 years of this royal foundry in preparation for a centenary celebration. Ruhr Steel: Norman J. G. Pounds and William N. Parker, *Coal and Steel in Western Europe: The Influence of Resources and Techniques on Production* (Bloomington, Ind., 1957), p. 240. Siemens-Martin furnaces: Ludwig Beck, *Die Geschichte des Eisens in technischer und kulturgeschichtlicher Beziehung* (Braunschweig, 1895-1903), 5, p. 1004. Total furnaces: *Die Industrie- und Handelskammer für die Provinz Oberschlesien, 1882-1932* (Beuthen, 1932), 275-276.
¹⁵ To 1878, based on ZBHS, annual statistics; 1879-1914, based on the annual statistics of the OBHV, as compiled in Popiolek, *Górnośląski przemysl*, coal, pp. 205-206; pig iron, pp. 212-213; zinc, pp. 214-215.
¹⁶ 1806: Waclaw Dlugoborski, "Przemysl i górnictwo" [Industry and mining and smelting], in *Historia Sląska* [History of Silesia] ed. Waclaw Dlugoborski, Vol. 2, part 1 (Wroclaw, 1966), p.210. 1850s-1913: figures from ZBHS and ZOBH cited from Popiolek, pp. 205-215, with slight corrections to Popiolek.
¹⁷ These categories and the numbers in

the next paragraph come from ZOBH 1877-1914; statistics were published in a separate volume starting 1904. Data on employment in metal industries are generally not available for the years before 1877.

[18] Józef Popkiewicz and Franciszek Ryszka, *Przemysł ciężki Górnego Śląska w gospodarce Polski międzywojennej (1922-1939)* [Heavy industry of Upper Silesia in the economy of interwar Poland, (1922-1939)] (Opole, 1959), p. 3.

[19] Kurt Seidl, "Die Arbeiterverhältnisse des oberschlesischen Industriebezirks," in *Handbuch des oberschlesischen Industriebezirks* (Kattowitz, 1913), p. 133.

[20] The ZOBH from the 1870s to 1914 carried at least one article almost every year on the shortage of railway wagons. Labor shortage becomes prominent in the pages of this journal from the late 1880s on.

[21] ZBHS to 1878 and ZOBH from 1879, cited in Popiolek, pp. 206-207.

[22] ZOBH 46 (1907): 250.

[23] ZOBH 47 (1908): 236-237.

[24] Cleophas: WAP Katowice, Cleophasgrube 649, 14 December 1906, report to Revieramt Süd-Kattowitz; Cleophasgrube 647, 6 December 1907, letter to Landrat. Rybnik: WAP Katowice, Landratsamt Rybnik 703; 32-33, 11 June 1910, letter from Amtsvorsteher des Amtsbezirks Ellguth XIII to Landrat in Rybnik.

[25] WAP Wroclaw, OBB 40: 143, 19 April 1900, quarterly report of the Oberbergamt. ZBHS 48 (1900): B-537, report on 1899: "... der fast das ganze Jahr andauernde Mangel an Arbeiter...." WAP Katowice, Landratsamt Tarnowitz 525: 319-320, 13 October 1899; and 299, 22 October 1897.

[26] I did not run across any references to a definite labor shortage in this early period in ZOBH, ZBHS, or in the records of the various firms which I examined.

[27] Cf. Johannes Nichtweiss, *Die ausländischen Saisonarbeiter in der Landwirtschaft der östlichen und mittleren Gebiete des Deutschen Reiches* (Berlin, 1959), pp. 43-50.

[28] WAP Katowice, Cleophasgrube 647: 27-29.

[29] *Ibid.*, pp. 16-17.

[30] Hohenlohe: WAP Katowice, Hohenlohe 2354: 62. Complaints: ZBHS 52 (1904): B-605, 606.

[31] These remarks on the technical qualifications of the various grades of mine workers are based on Jaros, *Historia górnictwa*, pp. 209-214.

[32] WAP Katowice, Landratsamt Rybnik 469, 24 May 1905, letter to Landrat in Rybnik.

[33] Unskilled workers: Kurt Hinze, *Die Arbeiterfrage zu Beginn des modernen Kapitalismus in Brandenburg-Preussen 1685-1806*, (Berlin, 1963), pp. 50-56. Ruhr: Gerhard Adelmann, *Die soziale Betriebsverfassung des Ruhrbergbaus vom Anfang des 19. Jahrhunderts bis zum Ersten Weltkrieg unter besonderer Berücksichtigung des Industrie- und Handelskammerbezirks Essen* (Bonn, 1962), p. 154.

[34] One example of this gap in the records: the *Statistisches Jahrbuch für den Preussischen Staat* 11 (1914), gives extensive figures on employment in mining, but the steel industry is treated only under the general heading "Bergbau, Hütten- und Salinenwesen, Torfgräberei." The records of firms in the metal industries which I examined are of little help on this point because most of these records center on the post-1919 period.

[35] W. Arthur Lewis, "Economic Development with Unlimited Supplies of Labour," *The Manchester School*, 22 (1954), reprinted in A. N. Agarwala and S. P. Singh, *The Economics of Underdevelopment* (New York, 1963), p. 402. For objections to zero or negative returns for additional labor in agriculture, see Theodore Schultz, *Transforming Traditional Agriculture* (New Haven, 1964), chapter 4.

[36] Hans Rosenberg, "The Economic Impact of Imperial Germany: Agricultural Policy," *Journal of Economic History* 3, suppl. (December, 1943): 101-107.

[37] One such revision is given by Dipak Mazumdar, "Underemployment in Agriculture and the Industrial Wage Rate," *Economica*, N.S. 26 (1959): 328-340. Lewis notes that the "supply of labour is therefore 'unlimited' so long as the supply of labour at this price [subsistence level wages plus a small amount] exceeds the demand." Lewis in Agarwala and Singh, p. 403. For a full-scale application of Lewis's model, see Charles Kindleberger, *Europe's Postwar Growth. The Role of Labor Supply* (Cambridge, Mass., 1967). Kindleberger too has to admit that the model does not exactly fit everywhere.

[38] Heinz Rogmann, *Die Bevölkerungsentwicklung im preussischen Osten in den letzten hundert Jahren* (Berlin, 1937), table of death rates, pp. 218-221, table of birth rates, pp. 212-215. Both of these tables were compiled from a large number

of sources,mainly the *Statistik des Deutschen Reiches* and the *Preussische Statistik* but also including a number of other official publications. Further references to births and deaths will be from these same tables. Demographic data of the nineteenth century are of course not so accurate as one would hope, but for present purposes this margin of error is probably not crucial. It can be said in general that these statistics tend to corroborate non-statistical evidence about nineteenth-century population growth in Germany and are in line with data from other western European countries in the indstrial period and from other modernizing countries in the twentieth century. Another important source of demographic information for Upper Silesia is Bronislaw S. Wojtun, *Demographic Transition in West Poland, 1816-1914* (diss., University of Pennsylvania, 1968). Wojtun critically evaluates all the available statistical information on Oppeln regency (and other areas), though he tends to underrate Rogmann's contribution (p. 6). Cf. also D. V. Glass and E. Grebenik, "World Population, 1800-1950," in *The Cambridge Economic History of Europe*, Vol. 6 (Cambridge, 1965), pp. 56-138.

[39] Death rates for the German Reich were slightly higher than those of Prussia; Reich birth rates, slightly lower.

[40] Mack Walker, *Germany and the Emigration, 1816-1885* (Cambridge, Mass., 1964), p. 175.

[41] Max Broesicke, "Rückblick auf die Entwicklung der preussischen Bevölkerung von 1875 bis 1900," *Preussische Statistik* 188 (1904): 18-19.

[42] Entailed estates: Theodor von der Goltz, *Die ländliche Arbeiterfrage und ihre Lösung* (Danzig, 1874); Max Sering, "Die innere Kolonisation im östlichen Deutschlands," *Schriften des Vereins für Sozialpolitik* 56 (1893). Agriculture to industry: Max Broesicke, "Die Binnenwanderungen im preussischen Staate," *Zeitschrift des königlichen preussischen statistischen Landesamts* 47 (1907): 15, 23-25, rejects the first hypothesis without proposing the second. More definite stands for the flight from agriculture are taken by Peter Quante, *Die Flucht aus der Landwirtschaft* (Berlin, 1933), pp. 277ff., and Rogmann, pp. 175-189. Both Quante and Rogmann offer extensive summaries of the literature on this problem.

[43] Johannes Ziekursch, *Hundert Jahre schlesischer Agrargeschichte.* (Breslau, 1915), pp. 75ff.

[44] Walker, *passim*; Rogmann, pp. 236-239, and the large number of sources cited there.

[45] First Poles: Joanna Ladomirska, "Z dziejów śląskiej emigracji do Ameryki pólnocnej" [On the history of Silesian emigration to North America], *Studia Śląskie* 10 (1966): 271-280. Business cycle: B. Burgdörfer, "Migration Across the Frontiers of Germany," in *International Migrations*, ed. Walter F. Willcox, vol. 2 (New York, 1931), pp. 313-389.

[46] East-west migration: Cf. Wilhelm Brepohl's studies for a general description of the process. The Poles who participated in this migration are treated in Hans-Ulrich Wehler, "Die Polen im Ruhrgebiet," *Vierteljahrsschrift für Sozial- und Wirtschaftsgeschichte* 48 (1961): 203-235. East Prussia: Rogmann, pp. 234-235, based on *Statistik des Deutschen Reiches* 231:1 (1935): 66. Eastern counties: Rogmann, *ibid.* pp. 250-260, and the sources cited there. Rogmann lists each county separately.

[47] Pawel Rybicki, "Rozwój ludności Górnego Śląska od początku XIX wieku do Pierwszej Wojny Swiatowej" [The development of the population of Upper Silesia from the beginning of the nineteenth century to the First World War], in *Górny Śląsk: Prace i Materialy geograficzne* [Upper Silesia: Geographical studies and materials] ed. Antoni Wrzosek (Cracow, 1955), pp. 260-262. Rogmann, pp. 234-235, 260, and the sources cited there. Cf. Andrzej Brozek, *Ostflucht na Śląsku* [Ostflucht in Silesia] (Katowice, 1966), pp. 48-60.

[48] High rate of natural increase: Rogmann, pp. 258-259, 230. Emigration: Max Sering, *Die Verteilung des Grundbesitzes und die Abwanderung vom Lande* (Berlin, 1910), statistical annex, pp. 34-36. Industrialized counties: Sering, pp. 34-36. Rogmann, p. 258, present a similar table, probably based on Sering, but he omits Kattowitz, Rybnik, and Pless because in this table his is dealing with boundaries of 1936, not of pre-World War I Prussia. This approach illustrates one of the problems encountered in using the historical literature on Upper Silesia, although the major tendency is for historians to annex lost territories, not to let them go. Location of industry: maps in Pounds—coal mines, pp. 64-68 (based on ZOBH); lead and zinc mines, pp. 87 and 91 (based on ZOBH); iron and steel plants, pp. 109-110 (based on *Handbuch des oberschlesischen Industriebezirks)*. Population gain:

Preussische Statistik 206:1 (census of
1905); 382-285; 234:1 (census of 1910): 301-
305.

⁴⁹ Ziekursch; Seweryn Wyslouch,
"Kapitalistyczna przebudowa rolnictwa
śląskiego i jej skutki w latach 1850-1880"
[The capitalistic restructuring of Silesian
agriculture and its effects, 1850-1880],
Przegląd Zachodni 8 (1952), special issue:
Studia Sląskie, pp. 1-119; *Studia nad kon-
centracją w rolnictwie śląskim w latach
1850-1914* [Studies on the concentration
of Silesian agriculture, 1850-1914] (Wro-
claw: Ossolineum, 1956). Cf. also Michael
Haines, *Economic-Demographic Interre-
lationships in Developing Agricultural
Regions: A Case Study of Prussian Upper
Silesia, 1840-1914* (Diss., University of
Pennsylvania, 1971).

⁵⁰ Average income: Wyslouch, *Studia*,
pp. 76-77. The large tracts of uncultivated
woods in the area lowered the average
income, but in turn these forests indicated
poor agricultural land. Quasi-proletariat:
pp. 221-223.

⁵¹ Rybicki, p. 277. I have located the first
figure in *Preussische Statistik* 177 part
2:26; but I have not been able to determine the source of the second figure.
Other circumstances indicate that Rybicki's figure is plausible.

⁵² Broesicke, "Binnenwanderungen,"
pp. 5-6.

⁵³ Rybicki, p. 284, presumably based on
the occupational census. Cf. Walter Kuhn,
Siedlungsgeschichte Oberschlesiens
(Würzburg, 1954), pp. 260-262.

⁵⁴ Large estates: This is one of the major
themes running through Wyslouch's
works. Ziekursch, pp. 75ff., notes the beginnings of this rural proletariat even in
the eighteenth century. To other parts of
Germany: Rogmann, pp. 232-235, and the
sources cited there.

⁵⁵ This problem of foreign contract labor
in Upper Silesian industry interested
scholars long before 1945, but except for
Nichtweiss, the most extensive studies
have been done by Polish scholars: Karol
Jonca, "Imigracja robotników polskich na
Sląsk w końcu XIX i w początkach XX
wieku" [Immigration of Polish workers
into Silesia at the end of the nineteenth
and the beginning of the twentieth cen-
turies] *Studie Sląskie*, 1 (1958): 139-158;
Jonca, *Polozenie*, pp. 73-90; Adam Galos,
"Rugi pruskie na Górnym Sląsku (1885-
1890)" [The Prussian expulsions in Upper
Silesia, 1885-1890], *Sobótka* 9 (1954): 56-
107; Adam Galos, "Walka kapitalistów
górnośląskich o robotnika galicyjskiego

(1904-1914)" [The struggle of Upper Silesian capitalists for the Galician worker,
1904-1914], *Sobótka* 4 (1949): 160-186; and
a long series of articles and books by
Andrzej Brozek, of which the most general
is *Robotnicy spoza zaboru pruskiego w
przemyśle na Górnym Sląsku (1870-1914)*
[Workers from beyond the Prussian partition area in Upper Silesian industry, 1870-
1914] (Wroclaw, 1966).

⁵⁶ DZA Merseburg, Rep. 77, Tit. 1176,
Nr. 2a, Vol. 5, p. 40, cited by Andrzej
Brozek, "Imigracja ludności z Galicji i
Kongresówki do przemyslu na Górnym
Sląsku przed rokiem 1885" [Immigration
from Galicia and the Congress Kingdom
to Upper Silesian industry before 1885],
Sobótka 18 (1963): 173.

⁵⁷ The problem of the expulsions as they
affected Silesia is dealt with thoroughly
by Brozek, *Wysiedlenia Polaków z Górnego Sląska przez Bismarcka (1885-1887)*
[The expulsions of Poles from Upper Silesia by Bismarck, 1885-1887] (Katowice,
1963), and by Galos, "Rugi pruskie." Little
insight is added by Joachim Mai, *Die
preussisch-deutsche Polenpolitik, 1885-
1887: Eine Studie zur Herausbildung des
Imperialismus in Deutschland* (Berlin,
1962). An important corrective approach
is supplied by Helmut Neubach, *Die Ausweisungen von Polen und Juden aus
Preussen 1885/86* (Wiesbaden, 1967), but
the author gets bogged down in reporting
newspaper reaction to the events of the
time.

⁵⁸ ZBHS and ZOBH, cited in Popiolek,
pp. 205-219.

⁵⁹ Commuters: Cf. the large number of
nonresident Poles listed in the work list
of Morgenstern mine in the 1870s—WAP
Katowice, Hohenlohe 2662, *passim*. Andrzej Brozek goes into this phenomenon
more thoroughly in "Ze studiów nad
malym ruchem granicznym między Górnym Sląskiem a Zaglębiem Dąbrowskim
na przelomie XIX i XX wieku" [Studies
on a small border movement between
Upper Silesia and the Dabrowski basin at
the turn of the twentieth century] *Sobótka* 13 (1958); 603-640. On pre-1885:
WAP Wroclaw, RO 1: 12504; 454, cited
in Brozek, "Ze studiów," pp. 603-607.
Down to 1914: WAP Wroclaw, RO 1:
11917, cited in Brozek, "Ze studiów," pp.
606-607.

⁶⁰ Expulsions: Calculated by Brozek,
Wysiedlenia, p. 44, on the basis of WAP
Wroclaw, RO 1: 12504; 452. Hinterland:
WAP Katowice, Landratsamt Pless 1091,
25 June 1905, statement of OBHV to the

Regierungspräsident in Oppeln.
[61] Broesicke, "Binnenwanderungen," p.
16. For a fascinating description of the life
style of these international migrants, see
the "Life-Record of an Immigrant," in
William Thomas and Florian Znaniecki,
*The Polish Peasant in Europe and Ameri-
ca*, 2nd ed. (New York, 1958), Vol. 2, pp.
1915-2226.
[62] E.g., request by Cleophas mine, WAP
Katowice, Cleophasgrube 647: 9, 23 November 1905, and the repeated requests of
the Heinitz and Florentine mines, PAP
Bytom, Bergrevier Beuthen Nord 158,
passim.
[63] Brozek, *Robotnicy spoza zaboru*, p. 48.
[64] Cf. the complaint of the Cleophas
mine in 1907, WAP Katowice, Cleophasgrube 647: 27-29, and the memo of the
OBHV to the minister of the interior in
1908, PAP Bytom, BIKH 531: 60-65.
[65] WAP Katowice, Landratsamt Kattowitz 45; 115-127.
[66] Nichtweiss, pp. 58-59.
[67] PAP Bytom, Bergrevier Beuthen
Nord 158: 14.
[68] Andrzej Brozek, "Robotnicy
ukraińscy w przemyśle górnośląskim
przed I Wojną Swiatową" [Ukrainian
workers in Upper Silesian industry before
World War I], original Polish manuscript
of an article published in abridged form:
"Ukrainski robitnike v promyslovosti
Verchnoi Silezii pered pershoi svitovoiu
vijnoiu," *Ukrainskii istorichnij zhurnal* 7
(1965). My thanks to Dr. Brozek for let-
ting me see this manuscript. Jonca, *Polozenie*, p. 82, gives figures for Poles and
Ukrainians in the entire Oppeln regency.
Brozek, "Robotnicy ukraińscy," pp. 43-45,
lists the foreign workers in Upper Silesia
by nationality and by type of employment.
[69] WAP Katowice, Cleophasgrube 647;
62-63.
[70] No Jews: PAP Bytom, BIKH 531, 21
January 1891, cited by Jonca, *Polozenie*,
p. 76. Other examples: WAP Katowice,
Friedrichshütte, T/133/1, apparently a
temporary catalogue number that no
longer exists, August 1912, and Friedrichshütte 925, Hauptverwaltungsbericht,
1912, both cited by Jonca, *Polozenie*, p.
85; WAP Katowice, Cleophasgrube 647:
68-69, 26 August 1912. Hiring: The Vereinigte Königs- und Laurahütte employed a
number of foreign Jews in 1912 and asked
permission to rehire them for the next
year. WAP Katowice, Landratsamt Kattowitz 46; 1. A 1908 form for registering

foreign workers included under its question of religion the heading "mosaisch."
WAP Katowice, Cleophasgrube 647: 53.
Labor office: *Jüdisches Volksblatt*, cited
in *Gazeta Robotnicza* [Polish Socialist
Party [PPS] organ published in Kat-
towitz] 22, 22 June 1912.
[71] 1890s: DZA Merseburg, Rep. 77, Tit.
1135, nr. 1, Adh. 1, vols. 1-3, *passim*, cited
by Brozek, *Robotnicy spoza zaboru*, p. 56.
Complaints: ZOBH 1890-1914, annual
reports of the board of directors, *passim*.
1900-1906: DZA Merseburg, Rep. 87B, 210,
pp. 147-148, and Walter Sroka, *Die Aus-
landsarbeiterfrage in der oberschlesischen Montanindustrie* (diss. Jena, 1922),
p. 22, both cited by Brozek, *Robotnicy
spoza zaboru*, p. 57. Prewar years: Brozek
calculated these on the basis of these
sources: WAP Wroclaw, RO I:12355: 55,
172; RO I:12356: 158; ZOBH 1910: 606;
1912: 41; 1913: 227, 485—Brozek, p. 57. Migrant jobs: Sroka, p. 24, based on ZOBH
and cited by Brozek, p. 68.
[72] WAP Katowice, Cleophasgrube 647
and 649, *passim*, and JRGB 1909: 540.
[73] Metal industry: Friedrich Syrup, "Die
soziale Lage der sesshaften Arbeiterschaft
eines oberschlesischen Walzwerkes,"
*Schriften des Vereins für Sozialpoli-
tik* 153 (1915); 136. Zinc: Brozek, *Robotnicy spoza zaboru*, p. 73. Few foreigners:
WAP Katowice, Friedrichshütte 1019, 29
August 1907.
[74] Stanley Lebergott, *Manpower in
Economic Growth: The American Record
Since 1800* (New York, 1964), p. 125. A
general survey of the position of women
and children in Upper Silesian heavy industry is given by Jonca, *Polozenie*, pp.
190-205, and *Polityka socjalna Niemiec w
przemyśle ciężkim Gornego Sląska* (1871-
1914) [The social-welfare policy of Germany in the heavy industry of Upper
Silesia (1871-1914) (Katowice, 1966), pp.
124-151.
[75] 1875-1889: Jonca, *Polityka socjalna*,
p. 136. Jonca cites JRGB for 1876, 1881,
1890, 1901, and 1911, but this periodical
was not published until 1888. He probably
means *Jahresberichte der Fabrikinspek-
toren* for 1876 and 1881. 1912: JRGB 1912:
633, cited in Jonca, *Polityka socjalna*, p.
85. This table, from JRGB, lists the number of women and children employed in
the mines under the jurisdiction of the
mining offices in Breslau and in Dortmund. The figures combine the Upper and
Lower Silesian coal fields; however, the
operations in the Waldenburg (Lower Si-

189

lesia) area were small and there was no metallurgical industry to speak of. Thus for present purposes these figures are not grossly distorted.

76 ZBHS for selected years, cited in Jonca, "Ochrona pracy kobiet i robotników mlodocianych w przemyśle górniczo-hutniczym na Górnym Sląsku w latach 1878-1914" [The protection of women and minors in the mining and smelting industry in Upper Silesia, 1878-1914], *Studia Sląskie* 2 (1959); 85. These proportions fluctuated from year to year—e.g., in 1907 the number employed in smelting declined considerably. ZOBH 47 (1908): 475.

77 New employees: JRGB 1907: 516. Total minors: JRGB 1912: 633, cited in Jonca, "Ochrona Pracy," p. 85. 1902: ZOBH, cited by Tittler, *Arbeiterverhältnisse und Arbeiterwohlfahrtseinrichtungen im oberschlesischen Industriebezirk* (Breslau, 1904), p. 7.

78 *Statistisches Jahrbuch für den preussischen Staat* 11 (1914): 156ff.

79 Cleophas: WAP Katowice, Cleophasgrube 642: 9-95. Castellengo: PAP Bytom, Bergrevier Beuthen Nord 474K. Neuhof: PAP Bytom, Bergrevier Beuthen Nord 1004: 75.

80 A brief survey of all such legislation is given by Jonca, *Polityka socjalna*, pp. 124-125.

81 Jonca, *Polozenie*, pp. 182-195 (cost of living indexes).

82 Schaffgotsch: PAP Bytom, Bergrevier Beuthen Süd 74: 285-286. Boring company: PAP Bytom, BIKH 215: 167-169. Total mining force: *Industrie- und Handelskammer*, p. 197.

83 A handy source of biographical information is Alfons Perlick, *Oberschlesische Berg- und Hüttenleute* (Kitzingen/Main, 1953). Unfortunately the big German dictionaries of biography until recently did not bother with industrial leaders. Konrad Fuchs, "Wirtschaftliche Führungskräfte in Schlesien 1850-1914," *Zeitschrift für Ostforschung* 21 (1972); 264-288, gives short biographies of people he considers representative leaders of the Silesian economy.

84 Waclaw Dlugoborski, "Ekonomika górnośląskiego hutnictwa w XVIII wieku" [The economics of Upper Silesian smelting in the eighteenth century], *Zeszyty Naukowe Wyzszej Szkoly Ekonomicznej w Katowicach* 19 (1963): 3-80. Landowning: J. Conrad, "Agrarische Untersuchungen: V. Der Grossgrundbesitz in Schlesien," *Jahrbücher für Nationalökonomie und*

Statistik, 3rd. ser. 15 (1898): 713. Coal mines: *Industrie und Handelskammer*, p. 196.

85 Production: tables from ZBHS and ZOBH compiled by Popiolek, pp. 206-230. Big firms and cartels: Popiolek, table p. 173, Popkiewicz and Ryszka, pp. 4-29, and Konrad Fuchs, *Vom Dirigismus zum Liberalismus. Die Entwicklung Oberschlesiens als preussisches Berg- und Hüttenrevier* (Wiesbaden, 1970), pp. 247-258. German historians have usually ignored these trends of ownership and infiltration of the big banks into Upper Silesia, but Polish writers since 1945 have been only too glad to pounce on clear evidence of finance capital in eastern Germany. Unfortunately, no one has written any high-grade analytic account of this chain of developments.

86 Popkiewicz and Ryszka, pp. 8-15.

CHAPTER 3

1 Ludwig Bernhard, *Die Polenfrage. Das polnische Gemeinwesen im preussischen Staat* (Leipzig, 1910). On the Eastern Marches Association see R. W. Tims, *Germanizing Prussian Poland* (New York, 1941), and Adam Galos, Felix H. Gentzen, and Witold Jakóbczyk, *Dzieje Hakaty* [History of the H-K-T Society] (Poznań, 1966).

2 Max Broesicke, "Die oberschlesischen Polen, 1905," *Zeitschrift des Kgl. preussischen statistischen Landesamts* 49 (1909): 25, based on official censuses.

3 Paul Weber, *Die Polen in Oberschlesien* (Berlin, 1914), p. 20.

4 Language: Von Fircks, cited by Broesicke, "Die oberschlesischen Polen," p. 25. Catholics: *Preussische Statistik*, volumes for censuses of 1871, 1875, and every fifth year thereafter to 1910.

5 German speakers: Broesicke, "Die oberschlesischen Polen," p. 25. Census bias: P. Weber, p. 27ff., emphasizes the German population growth. Ludwig Bernhard in the introduction to this very book points out the biases apparent in the censuses: Kuhn, p. 261. Kuhn refers generally to the increase of evangelical Protestants, whom he with good cause identifies with immigrating Germans. Official Prussian statistics bear out this claimed increase, but the percentage increase is no greater than that of Catholics.

6 L. Geisenheimer, *Festschrift zur fünfzigjährigen Jubelfeier der oberschlesischen Bergschule* (Tarnowitz, 1889), p. 73.

Cf. also the biographies of hundreds of applicants for supervisory positions with the Hohenlohe firm, WAP Katowice, Hohenlohe 1989-2582.

[7] Total population: *Preussische Statistik* 234:62-72. The number of Poles includes about 87,000 people counted as having German and Polish mother tongues; these certainly were locally born Upper Silesian Poles who were undergoing a process of Germanification. Cf. P. Weber, pp. 27-28; and Broesicke, "Die oberschlesischen Polen," pp. 29-30. German majority: Kuhn, p. 265, whose estimates are based on the statistics of the national censuses, in turn based on language questionnaires which became increasingly suspect after 1890 for their anti-Polish bias. Neither Paul Weber nor Broesicke makes this type of extreme statement; cf. Ludwig Bernhard's foreword to P. Weber.

[8] Broesicke, "Die oberschlesischen Polen," pp. 59-60, based on the occupational census of 1907.

[9] WAP Katowice, Landratsamt Rybnik 703: 32-33, 11 June 1910. Cf. also the implication of German foremen against Polish miners in the series of short miner autobiographies in Maria Zywirska, *Zyciorysy Górników* [Sketches of miners' lives] (Katowice, 1949).

[10] Based on statistics of ZOBH 1891-1914, cited by Jonca, *Polozenie*, p. 71 (total number of workers); and Popiolek, pp. 295-306 (coal miners).

[11] Local origins: Kurt Seidl, "Die Arbeiterverhältnisse," p. 131; Baumont, p. 537; Adam Galos and Kazimierz Popiolek, "Stosunki gospodarczo-spoleczne na ziemiach polskich zaboru pruskiego po uwlaszczeniu" [Economic and social relations in the Polish lands of the Prussian partition after the peasant emancipation], *Historia Polski* [History of Poland], vol. 3, part 1 (Warsaw: Państwowe Wydawnictwo Naukowe, 1963), p. 221. For archival material, see Gerhard Reichling, "Der Uebergang vom Bauern zum Arbeiter beim Aufbau des oberschlesischen Industriegebiets. Gezeigt am Beispiele von Rosdzin-Schoppinitz, Kr. Kattowitz," *Schlesische Blätter für Volkskunde* 3 (January 1941): 1-29, which is the only important study of this type concerning the permanent work force. Brozek is very much concerned with the geographical origins of foreign seasonal workers in *Robotnicy spoza zaboru*, pp. 79-98, and "Robotnicy ukraińscy," p. 12ff.

[12] Posen and Berlin: *Statistik des Deutschen Reiches*, 1st series, 57:202-221. Locally born and immigrants: *Ibid.* 151 (1900): 52-61. Industrial region: Broesicke, "Die Binnenwanderungen," p.35. Broesicke's industrial area is somewhat smaller than mine, omitting the partially industrialized counties of Pless, Rybnik, and Tost-Gleiwitz.

[13] Syrup, pp. 136, 142.

[14] Brozek, *Wysiedlenia*, p. 44.

[15] Commuters: E.g., the numerous commuters noted in WAP Katowice, Hohenlohe 2662 and 2663 (Morgensterngrube 1869-1876 and 1877-1885). Berlin: *Statistik des Deutschen Reiches*, new series, 68:65*-69*.

[16] WAP Katowice, Hohenlohe 2652 (worker lists, 1868-1881) (unpaginated). The groupings are to be found in the original lists.

[17] WAP Katowice, Hohenlohe 2653 (worker lists, 1879-1900) (unpaginated)—group of 89 from first third of the volume.

[18] *Ibid.*, numbers 139-203 in a list near the end of the volume. Other examples of mines: WAP Katowice, Kopalnia Myslowice (Myslowitz mine) 138 (1872-1890); Hohenlohe 2659-2660 (Georggrube, 1879-1891). Smelters: WAP Katowice, Friedrichshütte 698-704 (1895-1908).

[19] This paragraph is based on Reichling, pp. 1-5, who used a number of records no longer available. 1914 population: *Statistik des Deutschen Reiches* 240, Anhang, p. 11. Reichling, p. 1, gives the 1941 population as 25,000.

[20] WAP Katowice, Hohenlohe 2662 (Morgensterngrube—Arbeiterliste), *passim*.

[21] *Katolik* 28, 1 October 1895, ad by Saturn mine for miners.

[22] Recruiting elsewhere: Jerzy Jaros, *Historia kopalni Król w Chorzowie (1791-1945)* [History of the König mine in Königshütte, (1791-1945)] (Katowice, 1962), p. 43, probably based on Fechner, "Geschichte." Mining office recruiters: Dlugoborski. "Rekrutacja," p. 64, based on records of the Friedrichsgrube in WAP Katowice.

[23] Jonca, *Polozenie*, pp. 154-157; tables of annual wages based on ZBHS statistics, 1890-1914.

[24] Lower Silesia: PAP Bytom, BIKH 215: 142. Saxony: Helmut Seidl, *Streikkämpfe der mittel- und ostdeutschen Braunkohlenbergarbeiter von 1890 bis 1914* (Leipzig, 1964), *passim*.

[25] Gaston V. Rimlinger, "International

Differences in the Strike Propensity of Coal Miners: Industrial and Labor Experience in Four Countries," *Industrial and Labor Relations Review* 12 (1959): 394-398.

[26] JRGB 1912; 644.

[27] WAP Wroclaw, RO Prezydialne Biuro (Präsidial-Büro) 250; 7-11, 4 February 1909.

[28] This offer is discussed in a series of documents in PAP Bytom, BIKH 215: 81-89, November 1908-January 1909. The text of the OBHV reversal is given in WAP Katowice, Friedrichshütte 102; 8, indicating that all the firms of the area knew of the offer.

[29] Witold Kula, *Kszaltowanie się kapitalizmu w Polsce* [The formation of capitalism in Poland] (Warsaw, 1955), pp. 23-24, 89.

CHAPTER 4

[1] General: See Bert Hoselitz, "Non-Economic Barriers to Economic Development," *Economic Development and Cultural Change,* 1 (1952): 8-21, and the essays in Wilbert Moore and Arnold Feldman, eds., *Labor Commitment and Social Change in Developing Areas* (New York, 1960). Link with the land: Antony Polonsky, *Politics in Independent Poland, 1921-1939* (London, 1972), p. 6.

[2] Kerr *et al.,* pp. 145-148.

[3] Ziekursch, pp. 61-83, 349-350.

[4] Thompson, *Making,* p. 2 and *passim.,* and "Time, Work-Discipline and Industrial Capitalism," *Past and Present* 38 (December, 1967): 91-94.

[5] Morris, *Emergence,* pp. 6-7.

[6] Max Weber, *The Theory of Social and Economic Organization,* trans. A. W. Henderson and Talcott Parsons (Glencoe, Ill., 1964), p. 152. Cf. Morris D. Morris, "Labor Discipline, Trade-Unions, and the State in India," *Journal of Political Economy* 63 (1955); 293-294.

[7] Jan Jończyk, "O niektórych formach uzaleznienia robotników od przedsiębiorcy na Górnym Sląsku" [On several forms of making workers dependent on entrepreneurs in Upper Silesia], *Czasopismo prawno-historyczne* 8 (1955, no. 2): 219. A much more sophisticated version of this exploitation argument is given by Stephen Marglin, "What Do Bosses Do? The Origins and Functions of Hierarchy in Capitalist Production," (unpublished paper, August 1971).

[8] *Zycie Warszawy* (a Warsaw daily), 3 January 1968, p. 1.

[9] Refusal to change: Wilbert Moore, "Labor Attitudes Toward Industrialization in Underdeveloped Countries," *American Economic Review* 45 (1955): 158-159. West Africa: Elliot J. Berg, "Backward-Sloping Labor Supply Functions in Dual Economies—the Africa Case," *Quarterly Journal of Economics* 75 (1961): 468-492.

[10] Still the best work on the eighteenth and early nineteenth century Silesian peasantry is Ziekursch's study (for the legal stratification, pp. 158-168). However, his work has been extended and somewhat expanded by Helmut Bleiber, *Zwischen Reform und Revolution* (Berlin, 1966), and by Kazimierz Orzechowski in a lengthy series of publication—e.g., *Chlopskie posiadanie ziemi na Górnym Sląsku u schylku epoki feudalnej* [Peasant possession of land in Upper Silesia at the end of the feudal era] (Opole, 1959). For the later nineteenth century, the writings of Seweryn Wyslouch are useful though often tendentious, the most encompassing piece being *Studia nad koncentracją w rolnictwie śląskim w latach 1850-1914* [Studies on concentration in Silesian agriculture, 1850-1914] (Wroclaw, 1956). The interrelationship between technological change and rural overpopulation in Upper Silesia has been explored in Haines.

[11] Ruhr: Koch, p. 13. On the eighteenth century cf. Brepohl, *Aufbau,* pp. 39-41, 45-47. Saxony: Helmut Seidl, *Streikkämpfe,* p. 10. 1780s: Ziekursch, pp. 305-319. 1840s: Bleiber, pp. 74-75.

[12] Harvest: PAP Bytom, BIKH, Generalbefahrungsprotokolle 1791-1804, cited by Irma Nalepa-Orlowska, "Fryderycjańskie osadnictwo hutnicze na Opolszczyźnie (1754-1803)," [Frederician smelting settlements in Oppeln regency, (1754-1803)], *Studia i Materialy z Dziejów Sląska* 5 (1963): 101. Fishing: Kuhn, p. 244. Hauling: Franzke, pp. 47-48, in part based on Kurt Schroth, *Geschichte der Verkehrs- und Absatzverhältnisse beim oberschlesischen Steinkohlenbergbau in den ersten 100 Jahren seiner Entwicklung 1748-1845* (diss. Breslau, 1912).

[13] Pseudo-democratization of the Junkers: Hans Rosenberg, "Die Pseudodemokratisierung der Rittergutsbesitzerklasse," in *Moderne deutsche Sozialgeschichte* ed. Hans-Ulrich Wehler (Cologne and Berlin, 1966), pp. 287-308. Center party: Peter Molt, *Der Reichstag vor der*

improvisierten Revolution (Cologne and Opladen, 1963), pp. 81-96. Reichspartei: Hans Jaeger, *Unternehmer in der deutschen Politik (1890-1918)* (Bonn, 1967), p. 108; Molt, pp. 97-99. Richest men: survey by Adolf Martin, cited by Rose, p. 156.

[14] Agricultural technology: Heinz Haushofer, *Die deutsche Landwirtschaft im technischen Zeitalter* (Stuttgart, 1963), pp. 134-135; Haines, chap. 5. Population: Wojtun, pp. 344-346. On "push" and "pull" in relation to local agriculture, Haines, chaps. 5 and 6.

[15] E.g., JRGB 1893: 162-163.

[16] JRGB 1897: 573; *Katolik* (Polish newspaper in Upper Silesia) 46, 8 April 1913.

[17] WAP Katowice, Landratsamt Pless 1210, pp. 92-93. The figure of total employment at the Carlssegen mine (795 men) is taken from the list supplied by Barbara Szerer, "Wielki strajk górników w 1913 r. na Górnym Śląsku" [The great miners' strike of 1913 in Upper Silesia], *Studia i Materiały z Dziejów Śląska* 8 (1967): 426-429. The author gives no figures on total employment for the Neu Przemsa mine.

[18] *Preussische Statistik* 76:1 (occupational census of 1882): 313-316.

[19] "Mining and smelting" is here defined as including those workers listed in all three censuses under *Erzgewinnung, Hüttenbetrieb, Stein- und Braunkohle*, and *Eisengiesserei*. Not included are the auxiliary chemical industry (primarily sulphuric acid) and the small machine industry. Some of those listed as artisans (especially blacksmiths, locksmiths, plumbers) were surely also employed in the mines and foundries, but it is impossible to separate these out.

[20] Herman Lebovics, " 'Agrarians' versus 'Industrializers.' Social Conservative Resistance to Industrialism and Capitalism in Late Nineteenth Century Germany," *International Review of Social History* 12 (1967); 31-65.

[21] Principal: *Oberschlesien* 1 (1902): 465 Cows: Staatsarchiv Breslau, Rep. 207 (Landratsämte), Beuthen Acc. 11/19, both sources cited by Franzke, pp. 86-87.

[22] *Preussische Statistik* 76:3: 30-33, 131-133 (1882); 142:2: 209-213 (1895). *Statistik des Deutschen Reiches* 212:1: 40-43 (1907). Cf. the results for each of Wyslouch's nine regions in *Studia*, pp. 146-170.

[23] Eberhard Franke, *Das Ruhrgebiet und Ostpreussen* (diss. Marburg, 1934), cited in Wolfgang Köllmann, "Grundzüge der Bevölkerungsgeschichte Deutschlands

im 19. and 20. Jahrhundert," *Studium Generale* 12 (1959): 388.

[24] Comments on the pre-1890 period will be limited because of the scarcity of materials. Much of the comment made here is based on Franzke, pp. 46ff., and Reichling, pp. 5ff., both of whom had access to archival sources difficult or impossible to obtain today. Other useful studies are Kurt Seidl, *Das Arbeiterwohnungswesen im oberschlesischen Montanindustrie* (Kattowitz, 1913), and Friedrich Raefler, *Das Schlafhauswesen im oberschlesischen Industriebezirk* (diss. Breslau, 1915).

[25] Reichling, p.6.

[26] *Statistik des Deutschen Reiches*, new series, 4:1 (census of 1882): 90-91, 102-103, 120-121, 280-281. Mining and smelting as defined above for the three censuses.

[27] WAP Katowice, Hohenlohe 2664, entries 2450-2650.

[28] Complaints: JRGB 1891: 113. Tariff war: JRGB 1893: 163. Beet sugar: JRGB 1894: 592, and 1897: 513-514.

[29] Shorter work weeks: ZBHS 1890-1914, annual reports on the state of mining in Prussia. Good weather: WAP Wroclaw, OBB 41: 180. Rybnik and Pless: E.g., WAP Wroclaw, Schlesisches Oberpräsidium 2615, cited by Jonca, "Imigracja robotników," p.141.

[30] Brozek, "Robotnicy ukraińscy," pp. 12ff., discusses their geographical origin in detail. Mass switches: E.g., PAP Bytom, Berg- und Hüttendirektion des Fürsten von Donnermarck 380: 96, cited by Brozek, "Robotnicy ukraińscy," p.24. Industry to agriculture and back: WAP Katowice, Kopalnia Polska (Deutschlandsgrube) 436: 175-176, 6 August 1910.

[31] Polomski, "Ze wspomnień."

[32] A complete list for 1890 is found in Sattig, p. 23. For 1906: "Die für die Arbeiter der staatlichen Berg- und Hütten- und Salzwerke Preussens bestehenden Wohlfahrtseinrichtungen," ZBHS 54 (1906); 60-61.

[33] Friedrich Bernhardi, "Über die Ackerkultur und Gartenpflege bei den oberschlesischen und speziell den von der Bergwerksgesellschaft Georg von Giesches Erben beschäftigen Montanarbeitern," *Gesammelte Schriften* (Kattowitz, 1908), p. 478.

[34] Ruhr: Rudolf Schwenger, "Die betriebliche Sozialpolitik im Ruhrkohlenbergbau," *Schriften des Vereins für Sozialpolitik* 186:1 (1932): 211. Saxony: H. Seidl, *Streikkämpfe*, p.156.

[35] Based on censuses of 1882, 1895, and 1907 and assuming the borderline between viable and nonviable holdings to be about 5 hectares. See *Preussische Statistik* 76:3; 30-33, 131-133 (1882); 142:2: 209-213 (1895); *Statistik des Deutschen Reiches* 212:2; 40-43 (1907).

[36] *Statistik des Deutschen Reiches* 212:1: 34-43. No data are available by county.

[37] *Statistik des Deutschen Reiches* 212:2: appendix; 100, 112.

[38] For an excellent review of the status of the Russian peasant in the factory from the end of the eighteenth century to 1917 see Reginald Zelnik, "The Peasant and the Factory," in *The Peasant in Nineteenth-Century Russia*, ed. Wayne Vucinich (Stanford, 1968), pp. 158-190. As an example of non-European developments, see Simon Rottenberg, "Income and Leisure in an Underdeveloped Economy," *Journal of Political Economy* 60 (1952): 95-101, on Antigua.

[39] WAP Wroclaw, OBB 38: 34, document reproduced in *Zródla do dziejów klasy robotniczej na ziemiach polskich* [Sources on the history of the working class in the Polish lands], ed. Natalia Gąsiorowska-Grabowska, vol. 2 (Warsaw, 1962), pp. 52-53.

[40] WAP Katowice, Friedrichshütte 706, 29 September 1913.

[41] Commission report: "Denkschrift über die Untersuchung der Arbeiter- und Betriebs-Verhältnisse in den Steinkohlen-Bezirken," ZOBH 29 (1890): 70. Polish newspaper: complaint in *Katolik*, 24 January 1882. Mittel-Lazisk: WAP Katowice, Landratur Pless 1767: pp.3-3a, in Gąsiorowska-Grabowska, pp. 354-355. Potatoes and a pig: WAP Wroclaw, OBB 906: 237-242, in Gąsiorowska-Grabowska, p. 55.

[42] Results quoted in Sattig, pp. 21-24.

[43] "Denkschrift über die Untersuchung," p. 70.

[44] On the importance of cows as opposed to other farm animals for small-scale peasants in Prussia, cf. Max Weber, "Die Verhältnisse der Landarbeiter im ostelbischen Deutschland," *Schriften des Vereins für Sozialpolitik* 55 (1892): 14-15.

[45] "Peasant roots": Ligęza and Zywirska, pp. 78-79. Goats: Alfons Perlick, *Landeskunde des oberschlesischen Industriegebietes* (Breslau, n.d.), pp. 274-275. "Problem of tilling land": Ligęza and Zywirska, p. 70.

[46] Moore and Feldman, p. 1.

[47] For the Ruhr, DZA Merseburg, Rep. 120, Abt. B, Tit. IX, Sect. 6, no. 123, vol. 3, 6 September 1899, report on the situation of the workers in the Westphalian basin, cited by Jonca, *Polozenie*, p. 159.

[48] JRGB 1893: 163.

CHAPTER 5

[1] Foreign workers: Adelmann, *Die soziale Betriebsverfassung*, pp. 29, 48-66, 153-154. Locally born: Broesicke, "Die Binnenwanderungen," p. 47.

[2] Arthur Redford, *Labour Migration in England, 1800-1850* (Manchester, 1926), pp. 158-164. U.S.: David Brody, *Steelworkers in America* (Cambridge, Mass., 1960), pp. 96-111. India: Morris, *Emergence*, pp. 39-84, esp. pp. 62ff.

[3] Little work has been done on the pre-industrial working force in Silesia. With just a few exceptions, most of the older German works are of little use as interpretive studies; unfortunately, many Polish writers have continued the tradition of antiquarian studies. The Prussian school of historiography tended to glorify a few high bureaucrats as the keys to understanding Silesia—for example, Konrad Wutke, *Aus der Vergangenheit des schlesischen Berg- und Hüttenlebens* (Breslau, 1913)—or else to speak in institutional terms—for example, Hermann Fechner, "Geschichte des schlesischen Berg- und Hüttenwesens in der Zeit Friedrich's des Grossen, Friedrich Wilhelm's II. und Friedrich Wilhelm's III. 1741-1806," ZBHS 48, 49, 50 (1900-1902). This trend has been continued by W. O. Henderson, *The State and the Industrial Revolution in Prussia, 1740-1870* (Liverpool, 1958). Of more thoughtful works, Hinze, *Die Arbeiterfrage* and Horst Krüger, *Zur Geschichte der Manufakturen und der Manufakturarbeiter in Preussen* (Berlin, 1958), mention Upper Silesia only as an aside. Karl Franzke, *Die oberschlesischen Industriearbeiter von 1740-1886* (Breslau, 1936), bases his remarks about the pre-industrial period on rather flimsy evidence. Cf. the comments by Waclaw Dlugoborski, "Rekrutacja górników w Zagłębiu Górno-śląskim w okresie przed zniesieniem poddaństwa. Na przykladzie państwowej kopalni rud olowianych 'Friedrichsgrube' w Tarnowskich Górach" [The recruitment of miners in the Upper Silesian basin in the period before the abolition of serfdom. On the example of

the government lead mine Friedrichsgrube in Tarnowitz], *Przegląd Zachodni* 1950 (no. 7/8): 53-54. Hans-Wilhelm Büchsel, *Rechts- und Sozialgeschichte des oberschlesischen Berg- und Hüttenwesens 1740 bis 1806* (Breslau and Kattowitz, 1941), is a much more informative study based in part on archival materials which are difficult or impossible to obtain now. For a general historiographical survey, see Waclaw Dlugoborski's introduction to *Historia Sląska* [History of Silesia], ed. Waclaw Dlugoborski, vol. 2, part 1 (Wroclaw, 1966), pp. 6-19. Dlugoborski himself has done some extremely thoughtful and provocative studies in this area; besides his "Rekrutacja" mentioned above, there is his "Początki kszaltowania się klasy robotniczej na Górnym Sląsku" [The beginnings of the formation of the working class in Upper Silesia], *Kwartalnik historyczny* 61 (1954): 150-177. A useful summary for the non-Polish reading public is found in Waclaw Dlugoborski and Kazimierz Popiolek, "A Study on the Growth of Industry and the History of the Working Classes in Silesia," *Annales Silesiae* 1 (1960): 82-112. The latest German study, Konrad Fuchs, *Vom Dirigismus zum Liberalismus* (Wiesbaden, 1970), concentrates on markets, increases in production, and owners; it has little to say on the labor force.

⁴ Büchsel, pp. 45ff. on the *Bergordnung*, pp. 59ff. on iron production. For an excellent overview of the historical problem of iron manufacture in the eighteenth century, see Dlugoborski, "Ekonomika górno-śląskiego hutnictwa," 19 (1963): 3-80.

⁵ Allgemeines Landrecht, Tl. II, art. 16, no. 307, cited in Franzke, p. 50.

⁶ Wolfram Fischer, *Der Staat und die Anfänge der Industrialisierung in Baden, 1800-1850*, I: *Die staatliche Gewerbepolitik* (Berlin, 1962), pp. 338-339.

⁷ Dlugoborski, "Ekonomika," pp. 45-52.

⁸ Dlugoborski, "Rekrutcja," p. 80.

⁹ Seventeenth and eighteenth centuries: Hinze, pp. 48-56; Fechner, ZBHS 49 (1901); B-64-65.

¹⁰ Living quarters: Nalepa-Orlowska, "Frydercyjańskie osadnictwo," with a summary in English, p. 161. 1792: Fechner, ZBHS 50 (1902): B-206. Unruly behavior: Dlugoborski, "Rekrutacja," pp. 65-67.

¹¹ For evidence on the Polish and local character of the workers, see Max Dobbers (Dobers?), *Die königliche Friedrichshütte bei Tarnowitz in Oberschlesien* (Berlin, 1886), pp. 24-25; Waclaw Dlugoborski,

"Geneza industrializacji Górnego Sląska" [The beginning of the industrialization of Upper Silesia], *Zaranie Sląskie* 23 (1960, no. 2): 167-168.

¹² Some writers speak of "wasserpolnisch," the local dialect, as a separate language; this position is dubious. Cf. Stanislaw Rospond, *Dzieje polszczyzny śląskiej* [A History of the Polish Language in Silesia] (Katowice, 1959), pp. 359-446.

¹³ On *Steiger*, Franzke, p. 36; on Knappschaft elders, "Instructions wegen Verwaltung des Knappschafts-Instituts des schlesischen Ober-Berg-Amts District," (Berlin, 1811) par. 4, point 4, cited by Waclaw Dlugoborski, "Polityka germanizacyjna i postawa ludności polskiej" [Germanification policy and the position of the Polish population] in *Historia Sląska*, ed. Waclaw Dlugoborski, vol. 2, part 1, p. 412. Royal smelters: Dlugoborski, "Polityka," p. 412. German miners: Büchsel, pp. 123-132, emphasizes such cases.

¹⁴ Joseph Partsch, *Schlesien*, 2, p. 18, cited by Dlugoborski, "Rekrutacja," p. 60.

¹⁵ Prisoners: WAP Wroclaw, OBB 468: 48-49, 17 January 1855, in Gąsiorowska-Grabowska, pp. 28-29. Poles: WAP Wroclaw, OBB 468: 51, 19 May 1859, in Gąsiorowska-Grabowska, pp. 32-33.

¹⁶ Dlugoborski, "Geneza," pp. 167-168.

¹⁷ For "missed opportunities," cf. Alexander Gerschenkron, "Some Aspects of Industrialization in Bulgaria, 1878-1939," in his *Economic Backwardness in Historical Perspective* (Cambridge, Mass., 1962), pp. 198-234.

¹⁸ Walther G. Hoffmann, "The Take-Off in Germany," in *The Economics of Take-Off into Sustained Growth*, ed. Walt Rostow (London, 1963), pp. 95-118.

¹⁹ 1851—Miteigentümergesetz; 1854—Knappschaftsgesetz; 1860—Gesetz über die Beaufsichtigung des Bergbaus durch die Bergbehörden; 1865—Gesetz über die Kompetenz der Oberbergämter; 1865—Allgemeines Berggesetz für die preussischen Staaten. For a general discussion of the laws, see Wolfram Fischer, "Die Stellung der preussischen Bergrechtsreform von 1850-1865 in der Wirtschafts- und Sozialverfassung des 19. Jahrhunderts," *Zeitschrift für die gesamte Staatswissenschaft* 117 (1961): 521-534.

²⁰ WAP Wroclaw, Schlesisches Oberpräsidium 200, Acc. 54/16 2733: 60-61, in Gąsiorowska-Grabowska, pp. 172-173.

²¹ WAP Katowice, Hohenlohe 2655 (Stammrolle Alfred, for the years 1863-1899), *passim*; Hohenlohe 2654 (Hohen-

lohe Stammrolle, for the year 1868), *passim*.

[22] WAP Katowice, Friedrichshütte 699, 15 August 1899 (not paginated).

[23] Minors: WAP Katowice, ·Friedrichshütte 698, 26 February 1898: 2 April 1900 (not paginated). Smelting families: WAP Katowice, Friedrichshütte 698, 6 January 1898.

[24] Calculated from WAP Katowice, Friedrichshütte 698 (for the years 1895-1898), 699 (1899-1900), 700 (1901-1902), 701 (1903), 702 (1904), 703 (1905), 704 (1906-1908), job applications, *passim*.

[25] Syrup, pp. 205-206.

[26] Mining force: ZBHS 1852-1874. König mine: Jaros, *Historia kopalni 'Król,'* p. 103. Cf. Popiolek's compilation of statistics in *Górnośląski przemysl*, pp. 212-219. Smelting force: ZBHS, cited by Popiolek, pp. 212-219.

[27] Exhaustion of arable emphasized by Haines, chapter 5.

[28] In order: *Katolik* 25, 10 June 1892; 26, 18 July 1893; 30, 25 September 1897; 30, 25 December 1897. I perused all the volumes of *Katolik* from 1888 to 1914 and looked at many of the pre-1888 volumes. Publication started in the late 1860s, but the files of this newspaper in the Biblioteka śląska in Katowice were incomplete as of 1968. I also surveyed *Gazeta Robotnicza*, the organ of the Polish Socialist Party (PPS) in Prussia, published first in Berlin and then in Kattowitz. Naturally, this paper carried no advertisements by Upper Silesian employers. The *Kattowitzer Zeitung*, the leading German language newspaper in Upper Silesia, was not available to me in Wroclaw or Katowice. Various writers at times cite this German paper, but they may be relying on isolated clippings.

[29] PAP Bytom, BIKH 215: 35-36.

[30] There is very little information on this subject, but we do have the estimate of 7.5 million children in Germany (population 47 million) attending *Volksschulen* in 1885. Fritz K. Ringer, "Higher Education in Germany in the Nineteenth Century," *Journal of Contemporary History*, 2 (July 1967): 132.

[31] The advertisement and the original inquiry are given in PAP Bytom, BIKH 215: 44; telegrams announcing arrivals of workers during the next few months are found on pp. 53-65.

[32] PAP Bytom, BIKH 215: 69-80, contains offers from a number of labor purveyors.

[33] PAP Bytom, BIKH 215: 48.

[34] WAP Katowice, Hohenlohe 2654, *passim* (lists of workers at the Alfred mine).

[35] WAP Katowice, Cleophasgrube 647, 21 November 1908, letter to Landrat (not paginated).

[36] WAP Katowice, Landratsamt Tarnowitz 525: 299, 22 October 1897.

[37] WAP Katowice, Hohenlohe 321, second p. 190.

[38] WAP Katowice, Hohenlohe 318-322 (1892-1905), *passim*; Friedrichshütte 697-704, *passim*.

[39] PAP Bytom, BIKH 618: 229-298 (1868-1884).

[40] Nowitzki: PAP Bytom, BIKH 838, 6 December 1902. Five sons: WAP Katowice, Hohenlohe 2354: 80, 13 January 1896. Another example: Hohenlohe 2354: 83, 18 January 1896.

[41] Cf. the work lists in WAP Katowice, Hohenlohe 2652 (1868-1881), 2653 (1879-1900).

[42] WAP Katowice, Hohenlohe 320: 80,19 December 1899.

[43] Syrup, pp. 208-210; and Jozef Ligęza, "Kultura grupy górniczej. Próba charakterystyki" [The culture of a mining group. An attempt at characterization], *Zaranie Sląskie* 22 (1959), p. 88. On the feeling of disgrace, see JRGB 1899: 206. On the 1960s, see J. Piotrowski, "Attitudes Toward Work by Women," *International Social Science Journal* 14 (1962): 80-91.

[44] Perlick, *Landeskunde*, pp. 274-275, and Jozef Ligęza and Maria Zywirska, *Zarys kultury górniczej* [Outline of a mining culture] (Katowice, 1964), p. 88.

[45] WAP Katowice 2664, *passim*. This list of 3,500 men hired by the Fanny mine from 1864 to 1886 is marked by a number of such groupings.

[46] Austria: *Praca*, 26 July 1904, p. 1. Hungary: WAP Katowice, Cleophasgrube 649: 3. Germans abroad: Cf. the veto of the enthusiastic proposal by an employee of the Hohenlohe works in 1903—WAP Katowice, Hohenlohe 212: 201-203.

[47] On Czechs in Upper Silesia, cf. Andrzej Brozek, "W sprawie imigracji ludności slowiańskiej na Górny Sląsk przed Pierwszą Wojną Swiatową" [On Slavic migration to Upper Silesia before World War I] Polish manuscript of "K otázce imigrace slovanskeho obyvatelstva do Horniho Slezska před prvni světovou válkou," *Slezsky Sbornik* 59 (1961): 491-511.

[48] *Preussische Statistik* 234:1: 60-61.

[49] Neubach, pp. 31, 127-128.

[50] This recruiting mess is described by Nichtweiss, pp. 76ff. with some supplementary materials on Ruthenians in Brozek, "Robotnicy ukraińscy," *passim.* Nichtweiss, p. 76n., lists a large number of contemporary writers who described the abuses of the recruiting system.

[51] There are numerous reports on border controls in extant records, mainly from Pless county, which was the ordinary entry point from Galicia—for example, WAP Katowice, Landratsamt Pless 1088, 1091, and 1092, *passim.*

[52] PAP Bytom, BIKH 531: 21. Hanyckyj's work is touched on in Brozek, "Robotnicy ukraińscy," pp. 29ff., and in Nichtweiss, pp. 80-101.

[53] Nichtweiss, p. 99.

[54] There is not a great deal of literature on this subject. Brozek, *Ostflucht, passim,* presents much statistical material, but he emphasizes the 1930s. Józef Lazinka, "Wychodźstwo polskie w Westfalii i Nadrenii, 1890-1923" [The Polish emigrant community in Westphalia and the Rhineland, 1890-1923], *Sobótka* 4 (1949): 138-159, serves as an introduction to the question of emigration to Westphalia. The fascinating comments of an old emigrant are set down in Polomski, "Ze wspomnień." See also Wehler, "Die Polen."

[55] For a reasoned exposition of this view, cf. Moore, *Industrialization and Labor.*

[56] East Prussia: *Königshütter Volkszeitung* 2 April 1908. Dąbrowa basin: Brozek, "Ze studiów," pp. 615-616.

[57] 1850s: Adelmann, *Soziale Betriebsverfassung,* p. 66. Recruiters: Letter from Franz Haniel to Oberbergamt Dortmund, 30 September 1853, in Staatsarchiv Münster, Oberbergamt Dortmund B, Gruppe 119, no. 1, pp. 59-60, document reproduced in Gerhard Adelmann, *Quellensammlung zur Geschichte der sozialen Betriebsverfassung,* vol. 1 (Bonn, 1960), pp. 55-57. Silesians in the Ruhr: K. Gegen, *Die Herkunft der Arbeiter in den Industrien Rheinland-Westfalens bis zur Gründerzeit* (diss. Bonn, 1916), p. 15, cited in Walter Becker, "Die Bedeutung der nichtagrarischen Wanderungen für die Herausbildung des industriellen Proletariats in Deutschland, unter besonderer Berücksichtigung Preussens von 1850 bis 1870," in *Studien zur Geschichte der Industriellen Revolution in Deutschland* (Berlin, 1960), p. 223.

[58] Westphalian recruiters: *Dzieje kolonii polskiej na obczyźnie* [A history of the Polish colony abroad] (Bottrop, 1911), p.

7, cited in Lazinka, p. 142. Rybnik: WAP Wroclaw, RO Wydzial I (RO—section I), 10050; 45-46, in Gąsiorowska-Grabowska, pp. 143-144.

[59] Brepohl, *Aufbau,* pp. 74, 115.

[60] WAP Katowice, Landratsamt Tarnowitz 477: 9-9a, 15 August 1889, in Gąsiorowska-Grabowska, pp. 259-260.

[61] Jończyk, "Strajk Górników," pp. 349-353, mentions no post-strike emigration; I assume that Jończyk's ideological orientation would have decreed the use of such evidence if available.

[62] JRGB 1897; 513.

[63] Recruiters: *Katolik* 46, 8 April 1913. Emigration: ZBHS 62 (1914): B-404. Rehiring: WAP Katowice, Landratsamt Kattowitz 169: 104, 182-198, contains a *Reichstag* inquiry about alleged mass reprisals and administrative reports on the actual course of post-strike employment. Returning emigrants: ZBHS 62 (1914): B-398-399.

[64] Moore, *Industrialization,* pp. 15-20, dwells on this point as one sign of an underdeveloped society.

[65] Poles in the Ruhr: Franz Schulze, *Die polnische Zuwanderung im Ruhrrevier* (diss. Munich: n.d.), pp. 30-31. Newspapers: E.g., *Gazeta robotnicza* 17, 23 April 1907, p. 4; 21, 14 January 1911, p. 4; 22, 29 June 1912, p. 4; *Katolik* 43, 6 January 1910, supplementary page.

[66] König mine: PAP Bytom, BIKH 215: 25, 40. Beuthen area: *Górnoślązak,* 30 September 1906, cited by Brozek, *Robotnicy spoza zaboru,* p. 173. Employers' association: PAP Bytom, BIKH 215: 104. Labor shortage: *Reichsarbeitsblatt* 12 (1914); 6. Westphalian recruiters: e.g., WAP Katowice, Landratsamt Rybnik 469, 24 May 1905; ZOBH 45 (1906): 317; ZBHS 57 (1909): B-232; WAP Wroclaw, OBB 41: 227, report on third quarter of 1912. Rising emigration: PAP Bytom, BIKH 531; 25-30, 6 August 1906.

[67] Broesicke, "Die Binnenwanderungen," pp. 38-39.

[68] PAP Bytom, BIKH 215; 66, 28 September 1907, circular of OBHV.

[69] WAP Katowice, Cleophasgrube 647: 59-60, 8 November 1909.

[70] For a discussion of the various patterns of internal migration in Germany, see Köllmann, "Industrialisierung, Binnenwanderung und 'Soziale Frage,' " p. 52ff.

[71] ZBHS 53 (1905): B-543-544; 54 (1906): B-627-628.

[72] Adelmann, *Soziale Betriebsverfas-*

sung, pp. 153-154, on the Ruhr labor shortage.

CHAPTER 6

[1] WAP Katowice, Landratur Kattowitz 552; 42-43, in Gąsiorowska-Grabowska, pp. 36-38.

[2] WAP Katowice, Hohenlohe 321: second p. 190.

[3] Small plants: Dobbers, pp. 24-25. 1850s and 1860s: ZBHS, in Popiolek, p. 205.

[4] *Stammrolle*: WAP Katowice, Hohenlohe 2654 and 2655, "Stammrolle Alfred" (1868 and 1863-1899), and 2658 "Stammrolle Paulina" (18??-1902); WAP Katowice, Kopalnia Myslowice (Myslowitzgrube) 185, "Stammrolle," (1872-1890)—it is not positive that the last-named list belongs to the Myslowitz mine. *Arbeiterliste*: WAP Katowice, Hohenlohe 2652, "Arbeiterliste," plant name indeterminable (1868-1881); 2653, "Arbeiterliste," plant name indeterminable (1879-1900); 2659, 2660, 2661, "Arbeiterliste, Georggrube," (1879-1889, 1879-1891); 2662, 2663, "Arbeiterliste, Morgensterngrube," (1869-1876, 1877-1885); 2664, "Arbeiterliste, Fannygrube," (1864-1886).

[5] Friedrich Kessel-Zeutsch, *Bergwerkgesellschaft Georg von Giesche's Erben.* (Breslau, 1934), pp. 46-47.

[6] *Zur Feier des 50-jährigen Bestehens der Schlesischen AG für Bergbau und Zinkhüttenbetrieb zu Lipine, 1853-1903* (n.p., n.d.), p. 25. Rolling mill: Syrup, p. 136. Employers' goal: e.g., report of OBB in WAP Wroclaw, Schlesisches Oberpräsidium 2645, Hauptverwaltungsbericht, 1896, cited by Jonca, *Polozenie*, p. 246; ZBHS 50 (1902): B-863.

[7] Personnel lists: Syrup, p. 136. Pauline mine: WAP Katowice, Hohenlohe 2658, "Stammrolle Paulina" (18??-1902).

[8] Syrup, pp. 136, 143, 142, 211.

[9] *Zur Feier ... der Schlesischen AG*, p. 25.

[10] Reichling, p. 3.

[11] WAP Katowice, Hohenlohe 167:129 (1899); 2006, 17 April 1900 (not paginated).

[12] Moral duty: PAP Bytom, BIKH 838, 12 February and 25 February 1908 (not paginated), letters of OBHV to its members. Education: JRGB 1901: 352. Labor shortage: JRGB 1901: 355.

[13] Ruthenians: WAP Katowice, Kopalnia Polska (Deutschlandsgrube) 436: 131-133 (1909). Quitting: WAP Katowice, Cleophasgrube 647: 62-63 (1910), and 649:

41 (1911).

[14] There is a good deal of contemporary literature on housing in Upper Silesian industry, usually concerned with descriptions of various programs; these materials are excellent as sources for the present study. The most informative articles are "Die für die Arbeiter der staatlichen Berg-, Hütten- und Salzwerke Preussens bestehende Wohlfahrtseinrichtungen," ZBHS 54 (1906): B-1-182; Sattig, "Ueber die Arbeiterwohnungsverhältnisse im oberschlesischen Industriebezirk," ZOBH 31 (1892): 1-50. K. Seidl, *Arbeiterwohnungswesen.* Andrzej Stasiak has recently been very concerned with housing placed in the broader perspective of industrial growth: *Przemiany stosunków mieszkaniowych w Zaglębiu Sląsko-Dąbrowskim na tle procesu uprzemyslowienia (lata 1870-1960)* [Changes in living conditions in the Silesian-Dąbrowa basin on the background of the process of industrialization, 1870-1960] (Warsaw, n.d. [1968?]); and "Stosunki mieszkaniowe w Królewskiej Hucie (Chorzów) w latach 1870-1914" [Living conditions in Königshütte [Chorzów] 1870-1914], *Zaranie Sląskie* 24 (1961): 613-631. Also useful are two articles by Irma Nalepa-Orlowska: an exhaustive study of unpublished archival material, "Fryderycjańskie osadnictwo," and "Typy robotniczego osadnictwa górniczohutniczego na Górnym Sląsku" [Types of mining and smelting worker settlements in Upper Silesia], in *Górny Sląsk*, ed. Antoni Wrzosek (Cracow, 1955), pp. 345-380.

[15] WAP Wroclaw, Schlesisches Oberpräsidium 2645, Hauptverwaltungsbericht of OBB in 1896, cited by Jonca, *Polozenie*, p. 246.

[16] For the early period, cf. Fechner, "Geschichte" ZBHS 49: B-64-65, and Nalepa-Orlowska, "Typy."

[17] Kuhn, p. 246, and comment of the Silesian Oberpräsidium, cited by F. Krantz, *Die Entwicklung der oberschlesischen Zinkindustrie* (Kattowitz, 1911), pp. 63-64.

[18] Cited by Tittler, pp. 32-33.

[19] Wilhelmine smelter: Friedrich Bernhardi, *Gesammelte Schriften* (Kattowitz, 1908), p. 455, cited by Franzke, p. 57. Schlesische AG: Nalepa-Orlowska, "Typy," pp. 364-365.

[20] Haines, chap. 5.

[21] "Die für die Arbeiter," p. B-3. Italics in the original.

[22] The *Beihülfehäuser* are broken down

by company in Sattig, pp. 4-5.

[23] Government: ZBHS 21 (1873): B-153. 20 firms: Sattig, p. 23.

[24] PAP Bytom, BIKH, Arbeitseinstellungen und Arbeiterunruhen 1889-1890: pp. 175-200, 21 August 1889, in Gąsiorowska-Grabowska, p. 274.

[25] Company housing: JRGB 1889: 125-126. Cows: Reichling, p. 11. Smelter workers: Syrup, pp. 201-202.

[26] 1873 claim: ZBHS 21 (1873): B-152. Housing: K. Seidl, Arbeiterwohnungswesen, pp. 17-18.

[27] Details of various programs are scattered all through the records of various firms and in numerous jubilee publications. Here is a list referring to the programs of a number of the largest companies; much of what follows is based on these sources: PAP Bytom, BIKH 171 (1901); WAP Katowice, Cleophasgrube 719 (1902-1912): 231ff; WAP Katowice, Donnersmarck-Bytom 1974-1976 (1901-1904); WAP Katowice, Hohenlohe 184 (1894); WAP Katowice, Landratsamt Pless 1076 (1900); WAP Wroclaw, OBB 41 (1910): 161; OBB 1326 (1891): 234-239, in Gąsiorowska-Grabowska, pp. 315-318; OBB 1602 (1908). Bismarckhütte, 1872-1922 (Berlin, 1923); "Die für die Arbeiter"; JRGB 1888-1913, passim; O. Junghann, 1802-1901. Die Gründung und Weiterentwicklung der Königshütte (Oberschlesien) (n.p., n.d.); R. Kornaczewski, ed., Arbeiterfreund. Kalender für den oberschlesischen Berg- und Hüttenmann (Kattowitz, 1911 edition), pp. 72-76; 75 Jahre Borsigwerk (n.p., n.d.); Vereinigte Königs- und Laurahütte (Königshütte, 1897); Vereinigte Königs- und Laurahütte, 1871-1921 (n.p., 1921), pp. 4, 56ff.; Zur Feier der Schlesischen AG; Grosche, Der staatliche Steinkohlenbergbau in Oberschlesien (Zabrze, 1913), pp. 31-35. Jonca, Polozenie, pp. 241-254; Nalepa-Orlowska, "Typy," pp. 367ff.; K. Seidl, Arbeiterwohnungswesen; Syrup, pp. 197ff.

[28] JRGB 1889-1913, annual reports on the state of mining and smelting in Upper Silesia.

[29] "Die für die Arbeiter," pp. 60-61.

[30] E.g., WAP Wroclaw, Schlesisches Oberpräsidium 2645, Hauptverwaltungsbericht 1896, cited in Jonca, Polozenie, p. 246; ZBHS 61 (1913): B-61, report on 1912.

[31] The colony is described in R. Kornaczewski, ed., Arbeiterfreund: Kalendar, pp. 59-67; a plan of the settlement is found in Kuhn, p. 357. Tenant difficulties: Kuhn,

p. 247.

[32] Truck gardens: Syrup, pp. 200-201. Urbanization: Stasiak, "Stosunki mieszkaniowe," pp. 613-614.

[33] The best source of information on dormitories is Raefler, but his study (based on questionnaires returned by industrialists) is rendered difficult to use by a fascination for meaningless percentage relationships. Worker dormitories are discussed very often in contemporary sources. In addition to those sources on housing noted above, these proved useful: PAP Bytom, Donnersmarck 839 (1880s); WAP Katowice, Kopalnia Polska (Deutschlandsgrube) 436 and 437 (1908-1911); ZOBH 35 (1896): 377.

[34] A set of house rules from 1883 has been preserved in PAP Bytom, Donnersmarck 839:56.

[35] One in five in 1913: K. Seidl, Arbeiterwohnungswesen, pp. 24-25. Occupancy: Raefler, pp. 1-3. Housemaster: WAP Katowice, Kopalnia Polska (Deutschlandsgrube) 436: 222-224. Jail cell: Raefler, p. 29. Total spaces available; Raefler, pp. 1-3.

[36] A. Schaffrath, Die Wohlfahrtseinrichtungen in der oberschlesischen Montanindustrie (manuscript, 1919), p. 80, cited by Jaros, Historia górnictwa, p. 251. Computations based on Raefler's figures indicate that about 25 percent of single male workers lived in dormitories.

[37] Ruhr: Raefler, p. 20. Cf. also K. Seidl, Arbeiterwohnungswesen, pp. 24-25. Avoiding subtenancy: JRGB 1889: 128-129.

[38] Ligęza, "Kultura," p. 88. Mazumdar, p. 339, bases his objections to Lewis's propositions on unlimited supplies of labor on the fact that certain groups (including women) who are underemployed in the countryside tend to drop out of the labor force when the move to industry is made.

[39] Size of flat: housing census of 1918, cited by Stasiak, "Stosunki mieszkaniowe," p. 617. General remarks: cf. Nalepa-Orlowska, "Typy"; Stasiak, Przemiany stosunków and "Stosunki mieszkaniowe"; and Jonca, Polozenie, pp. 241-254.

[40] Raefler, p. 1. Statistics are confusing on this point. For 1913, Raefler lists 33,000 family dwellings and 28,600 beds in dormitories and a total working population of about 160,000. Other mining regions: Adolf Günther, "Die Wohlfahrtseinrichtungen der Arbeitgeber in Deutschland," Schriften des Vereins für Sozialpolitik 145 (1905): 121.

[41] Inspection: *Gazeta robotnicza*, 18 May 1901, cited by Bialy, *Górnośląski związek* ... *1854-1914*, p. 104. Eviction: Such a case is cited in *Gazeta robotnicza*, 6 June 1891. Cf. Günther, pp. 34-35. Two-week notice: Such a case is cited in *Praca*, 20 October 1891.

[42] Justizrat Milde as a representative of the Oberschlesischer Knappschaftsverein, cited by Perlick, *OS Berg- und Hüttenleute*, p. 63.

[43] Many of these were mentioned in note 27. Others of the type: JRGB 1888-1913, yearly reports on the mining and smelting industries; ZBHS 1870-1913; Bernhardi, *Gesammelte Schriften: Handbuch des oberschlesischen Industriebezirks*; Kessel-Zeutsch; R. Küster, *Kulturelle Wohlfahrtspflege in Oberschlesien*, 2nd ed. (Kattowitz, 1907); Kuhna, *Die Ernährungsverhältnisse der industriellen Arbeiterbevölkerung in Oberschlesien* (Leipzig, 1894); Conrad Matschoss, *Donnersmarckhütte, 1872-1922* (n.p., 1923). Cf. also Jonca, *Polozenie*, pp. 235-240, and his article "Z problemów stosowania ustawodawstwa socjalnego w śląskim hutnictwie cynku przed I Wojną Swiatową" [On the problems of applying social-welfare legislation in Silesian zinc smelting before World War I], *Studia Śląskie* 7 (1963): 7-37; Günther, pp. 1-194. There are numerous archival references to such programs—e.g., PAP Bytom, Donnersmarck 841; WAP Katowice, Friedrichshütte 649; and WAP Wroclaw, OBB 908: 625-627, this last document in Gąsiorowska-Grabowska, pp. 297-312.

[44] Government mines: "Die für die Arbeiter," p. 21. Low-priced food: e.g., OBB report on 1890, WAP Wroclaw, OBB 908: 625-627, in Gąsiorowska-Grabowska, pp. 207-308. Money grants: PAP Bytom, Donnersmarck 841: 85 (company pamphlet).

[45] Deductions: as reported in *Gazeta robotnicza*, 9 February 1901, p. 3. Cooperatives: *Praca*, 8 July 1895.

[46] OBB report on 1863, WAP Wroclaw, OBB 907: 237-242, in Gąsiorowska-Grabowska, p. 55.

[47] *Donnersmarckhütte*, 1900, and Matschoss, *Donnersmarckhütte*. Bathhouses: JRGB 1897: 188.

[48] Toilets: "Die für die Arbeiter," p. B-13. 1902 report: ZBHS 50 (1902): B-563.

[49] Jonca, *Polityka socjalna*, pp. 202-209, takes a completely negative approach to pension funds. On the restrictive nature of welfare funds, see Jonca, *Polityka soc-*

jalna, pp. 190-212, and Bialy, *Górnośląski związek* ... *1854-1914*, pp. 97-113.

[50] Refunds: JRGB 1897: 194 on Hohenlohe. On Donnersmarck, WAP Katowice, Donnersmarck 565, cited by Jonca, *Polityka socjalna*, p. 204. Transfer of funds: JRGB 1899: 205. No refund: JRGB 1897: 194. Cf. also WAP Wroclaw, RO I 8782, letter of Pensionskasse der Vereinigten Königs- und Laurahütte, 29 July 1910, and WAP Wroclaw, RO I 8743, protest letter of 400 workers of the Kattowitzer AG für Bergbau und Hüttenbetrieb, 6 February 1912, both cited in Jonca, "Z problemów," p. 19. Also *Praca*, 2 November 1908, complaint about the Huldschinsky and Caro-Hegenscheidt smelting works. Bankruptcies: *Praca* 13, 19 May 1903; 14, 16 February and 5 April 1904.

[51] JRGB 1902: 143.

[52] WAP Katowice, Friedrichshütte 659, Theodor Wyderek (not paginated).

[53] *Ibid.*, August Kupka.

[54] Apologist: Franzke, pp. 64-65. Upper Silesian worker: Bernhardi, *Gesammelte Schriften*, p. 459.

[55] The following records are replete with numerous applications for a variety of benefits: WAP Katowice, Hohenlohe 318-322 (zinc smelter); 2261-2263 (Maxgrube); 2354-2355 (Neue Helenegrube); Friedrichshütte, 658-659.

[56] Relatives: WAP Katowice, Hohenlohe 318: 86, 14 December 1893. Drink: WAP Katowice, Hohenlohe 318: 138, 28 September 1894.

[57] Army: WAP Katowice, Hohenlohe 212: 71, 1 June 1896 (being hired); Hohenlohe 2354: 77b, 8 December 1895 (not being hired). Voting: PAP Bytom, BIKH, Anlegung und Ablegung der Arbeiter 1870-1885: 42, in Gąsiorowska-Grabowska, pp. 191-192.

[58] Church organization: WAP Katowice, Hohenlohe 321: 1, 3 August 1901. Service awards: WAP Katowice, Kopalnia Polska (Deutschlandsgrube) 341, 15 October 1907.

[59] Germandom: *Handbuch des oberschlesischen Industriebezirks*, p. 245, cited from the Polish translation in Jonca, *Polozenie*, p. 254. Newspaper quotes: PAP Bytom, BIKH 785, 12 March 1904 (not paginated). Newspaper run: Bialy, *Górnośląski związek* ... *1854-1914*, p. 122.

[60] Patriotic Germans: Bylaws of group at Cleophasgrube—WAP Katowice, Cleophasgrube 617: 4. "Echo": WAP Katowice, Hohenlohe 319: 30 and 36, in Gąsiorowska-Grabowska, pp. 371-373.

"Lutnia": WAP Katowice, Hohenlohe 319: 75-78, in Gąsiorowska-Grabowska, pp. 376-377. Lower Silesians in the veterans' organizations: Barbara Szerer, "Klasowe związki zawodowe na Śląsku w przededniu Pierwszej Wojny Swiatowej" [Class trade unions in Silesia on the eve of the First World War], *Studia i Materiały z Dziejów Śląska* 9 (1968): 37.

[61] Myslowitz-Kattowitz: ZBHS 66 (1898): A-77. 1910 census report: WAP Katowice, Landratsamt Pless 1030.

[62] On the general course of social welfare in Germany, cf. Karl E. Born, *Staat und Sozialpolitik seit Bismarcks Sturz* (Wiesbaden, 1957). Details on Upper Silesia are given in Jonca, *Polityka socjalna*, pp. 190-222; Jonca, "Z problemów"; K. Seidl, *Arbeiterverhältnisse*, pp. 153ff.

[63] For the pre-1850 Knappschaft organization, see Büchsel, pp. 72-94, 160-179. A brief survey of Knappschaft activity both before and after 1854 is presented in Baumont, pp. 607-618.

[64] Approving elections: *Handbuch des oberschlesischen Industriebezirks*, p. 156, cited by Jonca, *Polityka socjalna*, p. 205. Board of directors: cf. the veto of a planned meeting of a board of directors of a Saar Knappschaft—Günther, pp. 116-117. Firing: *Praca* 19, 2 March 1909.

[65] WAP Wroclaw, RO I 9915: 260, memo of OBHV opposing the 1905 bill to amend the mining laws.

[66] JRGB 1888-1914, *passim*.

[67] Pless: Max Sering, "Arbeiter-Ausschüsse in der deutschen Industrie," *Schriften des Vereins für Sozialpolitik* 46 (1890); 5, 27ff. The tasks of the *Arbeiterausschüsse* are given by Adelmann, *Soziale Betriebsverfassung*, p. 136; more generally on these committees—Teuteberg, *Geschichte*, pp. 410-421. Hohenzollern mine: *Praca*, 30 August 1910, p. 1. Debate on wages: letter to OBB from minister of commerce and trade, PAP Bytom, Bergrevier Beuthen Nord, 20 December 1910. Neue Helene mine: report on 1907, PAP Bytom, Bergrevier Beuthen Nord, 10 February 1908, pp. 2-3. No business at meetings: e.g., WAP Katowice, Friedrichshütte 659, 7 and 11 June 1910 (not paginated). Report on councils: JRGB 1907; 526; also JRGB 1908-1913, annual reports on Regierungsbezirk Oppeln and Oberbergamtsbezirk Breslau.

[68] *Schlesische Zeitung*, 12 April 1912 (clipping in file of WAP Wroclaw, RO I 10051; 39-40).

[69] WAP Wroclaw, RO I 2952: 251.

CHAPTER 7

[1] For a sensitive and stimulating discussion of new workers in industry, see Peter Stearns, "Adaptation to Industrialization: German Workers as a Test Case," *Central European History* 3 (1970); 303-331. Helpful, but too little cognizant of the differences among societies—Alex Inkeles, "Making Men Modern: On the Causes and Consequences of Individual Change in Six Developing Countries," *American Journal of Sociology* 75 (1969); 208-225.

[2] ZBHS, statistical section; ZOBH, statistical section. ZBHS contains little on smelting by region; ZOBH contains more. For regional averages of wages in the German smelting centers, cf. Franz Grumbach and Heinz König, "Beschäftigung und Löhne der deutschen Industriewirtschaft, 1888-1954," *Weltwirtschaftliches Archiv* 79/2 (1957); 144. However, the source of these figures is not clear.

[3] For a discussion of various descriptions of the business cycle in Germany, see Gerhard Bry, *Wages in Germany, 1871-1945* (Princeton, 1960), pp. 475-480.

[4] Statistics from ZBHS and ZOBH, cited in Popiolek, pp. 207-210.

[5] JRGB 1905; 473.

[6] Data on wages come from ZBHS 1865-1914 (coal-mining), and ZOBH 1887-1914, with a separate volume for statistics from 1904 on (metal industries). I am extremely grateful to Prof. Waclaw Dlugoborski of Katowice for collecting the data from ZOBH.

[7] Grumbach and König, p. 144.

[8] ZBHS 1875-1914, statistical section. See Table 12.

[9] All-German wage: Walther Hoffmann *et al., Das Wachstum der deutschen Wirtschaft seit der Mitte des 19. Jahrhunderts* (Berlin, 1965), pp. 459-462. Shifts: ZBHS 1887-1914, statistical section. Cf. also the section on absenteeism in chapter 8.

[10] K. Seidl, "Arbeiterverhältnisse," p. 136.

[11] WAP Katowice, Friedrichshütte 658, 7 and 11 November 1905 (not paginated).

[12] "Hand to mouth": JRGB 1899: 217. A day off: Cf. the complaint of the smelter owners repeated in JRGB 1899; 203. Carousing: ZOBH 21 (1882): 223.

[13] Bry; Ashok V. Desai, *Real Wages in Germany, 1871-1913* (London, 1968); Grumbach and König; Thomas J. Orsagh, "Löhne in Deutschland, 1871-1913:

Neuere Literatur und weitere Ergebnisse," *Zeitschrift für die gesamte Staatswissenschaft* 125 (1969): 476-483; Spiethoff, vol. 2. Important information is also found in Hoffman *et al.*, *Das Wachstum.* Cf. also Jonca, *Polozenie*, pp. 150-194.

[14] Kuhna gives contemporary statistics, but his period (1892-1894) is much too narrow to render any meaningful conclusions.

[15] Rye: Jonca, *Polozenie*, pp. 186-188. The price of rye was derived from average prices in six Upper Silesian cities, as given in the *Amtsblatt der Kgl. Regierung zu Oppeln.* Other food products: Jonca depends heavily on Carl von Tyszka, "Löhne und Lebenskosten in Westeuropa im 19. Jahrhundert," *Schriften des Vereins für Sozialpolitik* 145:3 (1914), but this work is not completely trustworthy. Jonca also uses extensively tables presented in volume 2 of Spiethoff. Rents: e.g., Lothar Schneider, *Der Arbeiterhaushalt im 18. und 19. Jahrhundert* (Berlin, 1967), p. 137, gives an average of rents from Berlin, Hamburg, Breslau, Leipzig, and Dresden. Cf. Desai, pp. 73-96, and 123-125, who has a similar list, based on H. Lindemann, "Wohnungsstatistik," *Schriften des Vereins für Sozialpolitik* 94 (1901): 291.

[16] This index is presented by Desai, p. 117, and is based on a long series of sources (pp. 120-121, 123, 124). The rent figures are based on Lindemann (see note 15 above), meaning that no Upper Silesian cities are included in the average. Cf. Orsagh, p. 481, who gives a "corrected index," but without breaking down the cost-of-living into its component parts.

[17] Desai, pp. 97-105.

[18] Based on Spiethoff, vol. 2, table 15. Jonca uses this table to show that consumption of cereals and potatoes appreciably increased in the German Empire 1889-1915, but he disregards the editor's warning about not comparing pre-1893 with post-1893 figures. (Vol. 2, introduction, p. 18.)

[19] Costs and unrest: Cf. the speech by G. Williger, chairman of the OBHV in ZOBH 50 (1911): 275, cited by Bialy, *Górnośląski Związek . . . 1854-1914*, p. 73. Appeals to government: Bialy, *Górnośląski Zwiazek . . . 1854-1914*, pp. 71-73. Rebuke: WAP Katowice, Friedrichshütte 658, 7 and 11 November 1905.

[20] Much of the raw data on hours of work in mining has been collected by Jonca, *Polozenie*, pp. 116-149.

[21] "Denkschrift über die Untersuchung," p. 70.

[22] ZBHS 1890: 70.

[23] *Reichsarbeitsblatt*, 1 (1903): 456.

[24] PAP Bytom, Donnersmarck 840: 320.

[25] PAP Bytom, BIKH 143: 99-104, Arbeitsordnung, paragraph 11.

[26] Neue Fortuna: PAP Bytom, Bergrevier Beuthen Nord 484: 70-78, 81-90, 92-101. Work rules: *Ibid.*, p. 108.

[27] Swing shift: JRGB 1908: 498, report on Bergrevier Nord-Gleiwitz. Government mines: *Praca*, 7 January 1896, cited in "Gesamtüberblick über die polnische Tagesliteratur," 1895 and 1896, compiled in WAP Wroclaw, RO Prezydialne Biuro 14: 618. Donnersmarckhütte: JRGB 1908: 498-499.

[28] This paragraph is based on Pounds, *Upper Silesian Industrial Region*, pp. 112-115. Pounds's remarks are corroborated by the annual statistics published in ZBHS.

[29] 1861 rules: WAP Katowice, Friedrichshütte 694; 4, 89ff. Sunday work and swing shift: WAP Katowice, Friedrichshütte 101: 14-15. 8-hour shifts: WAP Katowice, Friedrichshütte 665, 28 April 1892.

[30] JRGB 1900: 136-137.

[31] Twelve-hour day and swing shifts: PAP Bytom, Donnersmarck, 840: 121, Arbeitsordnung of 1892, as amended 1899-1900; 13-hour day and women: p. 14.

[32] JRGB 1908: 181; 1909: 169.

[33] ZOBH 52 (1913): 274.

[34] 24-hour operations: Provisions of the Gewerbeordnung of 1891, section 105b, quoted in WAP Katowice, Friedrichshütte 101: 18-19. Sunday rest: JRGB 1900: 136. Strike: JRGB 1903: 160-161.

[35] Outlawing forced overtime: Cf. the offensive of the OBB against illegal forced overtime—PAP Bytom, Bergrevier Beuthen Nord 102, 16 Aug. 1906: 104, 30 June 1908 (not paginated). Rebellious workers: PAP Bytom, Donnersmarck 365, Bericht 1898, cited by Jonca, *Polozenie*, p. 130. 1908 warning: PAP Bytom, Bergrevier Beuthen Nord 104, 30 June 1908; similarly Bergrevier Beuthen Nord 104, 16 August 1906 (not paginated). 1913 complaints: PAP Bytom, Bergrevier Beuthen Nord 121: 218. 1910 overtime: JRGB 1910: 172-173.

[36] Samuels-Glück: PAP Bytom, Bergrevier Beuthen Nord 102, 16 August 1906 (not paginated). "High-living": JRGB 1910: 170-171. Shortage of skilled workers: JRGB 1910: 178.

[37] The all-German averages are based on

statistics gathered by Ruth Meinert, *Die Entwicklung der Arbeitszeit in der deutschen Industrie 1820-1936* (diss., Münster, 1958), as cited by Walther Hoffman *et al.*, *Das Wachstum*, pp. 213-214.

[38] 1912 data: ZBHS 61 (1913), statistical section.

[39] JRGB 1907-1914, annual reports on industry in Regierungsbezirk Oppeln and on mining in Oberbergamtsbezirk Breslau.

[40] Brandenburg mine: JRGB 1908; 505; 1909: 531. König mine: PAP Bytom, BIKH I-670, cited by Jonca, *Polozenie*, p. 148. Heinitz and Blei-Scharley mines: JRGB 1912: 649. Rest leaves and numerous holidays: e.g., JRGB 1908: 195.

[41] JRGB 1900: 135.

[42] ZBHS 1887-1914, statistical section, annual average number of shifts worked (not given in earlier volumes).

CHAPTER 8

[1] On the question of the disciplining of the labor force, cf. those studies mentioned in connection with the peasant-industrial worker. Cf. also Victor Vroom, *Work and Motivation* (New York, 1964), pp. 107-108, 178-192; Pollard, *Genesis*, pp. 161-173, and "Factory Discipline." For a more concrete definition of "modern," see Inkeles.

[2] This is the approach of Thompson, "Time, Work-Discipline."

[3] Walter S. Neff, *Work and Human Behavior* (New York, 1968), p. 135.

[4] ZOBH 27 (1888): 347-349.

[5] Not hiring recent quitters in the Oelsnitz-Lugau region of Saxony—Eberhard Wächtler, *Bergarbeit zur Kaiserzeit* (Berlin, 1962), pp. 91ff. Complaints: ZBHS 48 (1900): B-560; 50 (1902): B-861-862; 58 (1910): B-374.

[6] Recorded in JRGB, ZBHS, and ZOBH.

[7] Ruhr, 1860s: the Hibernia mine in Gelsenkirchen. Staatsarchiv Münster, Oberbergamt Dortmund B, Gr. 119, no. 5, vol. 2, cited in Adelmann, *Soziale Betriebsverfassung*, p. 66. Ruhr, 1907: Hans Georg Kirchoff, *Die staatliche Sozialpolitik im Ruhrbergbau 1871-1914* (Köln and Opladen, 1958), p. 161. Lugau-Oelsnitz: Wächtler, p. 91.

[8] Data for the Ruhr are much more complete than for Upper Silesia. Cf. Kirchoff, p. 161, and the table of those hired and leaving work in the Ruhr 1896-1925 in Adelmann, *Quellensammlung*, pp. 145-146.

[9] JRGB 1905: 162-163.

[10] *Ibid.*

[11] General Motors: "21,706 Jobless Hired by G.M. in Eight Months," *New York Times*, 7 January 1969, p. 23 (continued from p. 1). Electronics: "Hard Core, Hard Profits," *Newsweek*, 30 December 1968, p. 45. See also U.S. Department of Labor, *Employment and Earnings Statistics for the United States, 1909-68* (Washington: U.S. Government Printing Office, 1968), pp. 18, 146-159. U.S. Bureau of the Census, *Historical Abstracts of the United States. Colonial Times to 1957* (Washington: U.S. Bureau of the Census, 1960), p. 100, gives no figures for turnover in mining and smelting and for "manufacturing" goes back only to 1919. Upper Silesia today: Józef Więcek, *Struktura zatrudnienia a płynność robotników w przemyśle węglowym w latach 1949-1959* [The structure of employment and the turnover of workers in the coal industry 1949-1959] (Katowice, 1965), p. 78. West Germany: Reinhard Bendix and Seymour Lipset, *Social Mobility in Industrial Society* (Berkeley and Los Angeles, 1959), pp. 293-294. Further evidence on the ubiquity of the problem: H. Silcock, "The Phenomenon of Labour Turnover," *Journal of the Royal Statistical Society*, ser. A, 118, part 4 (1954): 429-431.

[12] Conscious of low wages: WAP Wroclaw, OBB 1550, Betriebsbericht for 1898 of the government's Gleiwitz smelter, cited in Jonca, *Polozenie*, p. 65. Decline in turnover: ZBHS 51 (1903): B-493, report on 1902; WAP Wroclaw, OBB 41: 131, report on first quarter, 1910. Westphalian recession: ZBHS 57 (1909): B-232.

[13] Compiled from WAP Katowice, Hohenlohe 2655 (1863-1899) and 2657 (1870s and 1880s).

[14] Hugo Solger, *Der Kreis Beuthen in Oberschlesien* (Breslau, 1860), cited in Franzke, p. 65; ZBHS 55 (1907): B-609; 56 (1908): B-574; 68 (1910): B-374.

[15] Bonuses: e.g., the examples listed in JRGB 1908; 524, cited by Jonca, *Polozenie*, p. 173. This phenomenon is noted in most volumes of JRGB. Housing: JRGB 1902: 426. Seasonal workers: WAP Wroclaw, OBB 41: 120, report on the fourth quarter, 1909.

[16] Salary lag: ZOBH 36 (1897): 249. Model work rules: PAP Bytom, Donnersmarck 840: 357.

[17] Jonca, *Polityka socjalna*, pp. 95-96. Jonca does not bother to mention contract-breaking by employees.

[18] Six smelters: JRGB 1902: 143. Ho-

henlohe, 1904: Those leaving without giving notice had to sign the work register (presumably to receive their back pay); these percentages are based on those signatures. WAP Katowice, Hohenlohe 321, second p. 234-second p. 242. Hohenlohe, 1905; WAP Katowice, Hohenlohe 322, 28 October 1905 (not paginated). Business downturn: JRGB 1902: 405. Ruhr: Paul Osthold, *Die Geschichte des Zechenverbandes, 1908-1933* (Berlin, 1934), p.68, gives the number of those leaving without notice on the basis of workers' identity cards (*Arbeitsnachweise*). The total turnover in the Ruhr is based on figures supplied in Adelmann, *Quellensammlung*, pp. 144-146. Ruhr metal industry: Richard Ehrenberg, "Schwäche und Stärkung neuzeitlicher Arbeitsgemeinschaften," *Archiv für exakte Wirtschaftsforschung* 3 (1909-1911): 479.

[19] Ruthenians, 1907: PAP Bytom, BIKH 531, 6 August 1906, cited by Brozek, "Robotnicy ukraińscy," p.23. On foreign workers cf. also PAP Bytom, Donnersmarck 380: 96, cited in *ibid.*, and WAP Katowice, Landratsamt Pless 1091, 16 November 1897 and *passim* (not paginated). Returning to jobs: e.g., PAP Bytom, Bergrevier Beuthen Nord 158: 51-53 (sometime between 1906 and 1913); PAP Bytom, BIKH 531: 68-69 (1909); WAP Katowice, Kopalnia Polska (Deutschlandsgrube) 436: 175-176 (1910). Agricultural workers: Von Stojentin, "Der Vertragsbruch der landwirtschaftlichen Arbeiter in Pommern," *Zeitschrift für Agrarpolitik* 7 (1909): 182.

[20] Blacklisting: Kirchoff, p. 161ff. Cf. the chapter "Tomasz Rybok" in Zywirska, *Zyciorysy*. For this identity-card system in the Ruhr, cf. Osthold, pp. 61ff.

[21] E.g., JRGB 1896: 150.

[22] Inefficiency: noted by the Higher Mining Office in WAP Wroclaw, OBB 41; 120, report on the fourth quarter 1909. Accidents: Zofia Boda-Kręzel and Kazimiera Wicińska, "Nieszczęsliwe wypadki w górnictwie węgla i rud w okręgu Wyzszego Urzędu Górniczego we Wroclawiu (Oberbergamt zu Breslau) w II. pol. XIX w." [Accidents in coal and ore mining in the territory of the Higher Mining Office in Breslau in the second half of the nineteenth century], *Studia i Materialy z Dziejów Śląska* 1 (1957): 299-343 (for 1862-1891); and Jonca, *Polozenie*, pp. 204-222 (for 1889-1914).

[23] Official report in the Oberbergamt Dortmund B, Group 119, no. 251, quoted by Elaine G. Spencer in her *West German Coal, Iron and Steel Industrialists as Employers, 1896-1914* (Diss. University of California, Berkeley, 1969), chapter 3.

[24] Profits: cf. the list of dividends of eleven great Upper Silesian firms in 1912, Popiolek, p. 230. Management and personnel: cf. Pollard, *Genesis*, pp. 2-4, 25ff., and on coal mining, 61ff; also his article "Factory Discipline." Rybnik mine: JRGB 1904: 547.

[25] R. Dawson Hall, "Have Mining Engineers Accepted All That Developments in Machinery for Handling Coal Imply?" *Coal Age* 20 (7 July 1921): 13.

[26] JRGB 1905: 160.

[27] Cf. Pollard, *Genesis*, pp. 181ff.; Thompson, "Time"; Marvin Bernstein, *The Mexican Mining Industry, 1890-1950* (Albany, 1964), p. 84.

[28] Solger, *Der Kreis*, quoted in Franzke, p. 65.

[29] ZOBH 46 (1907): 250, annual report of the board of directors.

[30] After paydays: e.g., WAP Wroclaw, OBB 41: 18 (first quarter 1907); WAP Katowice, Landratsamt Rybnik 703: 32-33 (1910): JRGB 1901; 349; ZOBH 46 (1907); 250; ZBHS 57 (1909); B-232; ZBHS 58 (1910); B-374. "Hand to mouth": JRGB 1899: 217. Low incomes: e.g., K. Seidl, *Arbeiterverhältnisse*, p. 138. 10 percent loss: ZOBH 53 (1913): 278. Mining regions: Baumont, p. 537.

[31] WAP Katowice, Hohenlohe 322, 11 July 1905 (not paginated).

[32] WAP Katowice, Hohenlohe 318: 24-25.

[33] König mine: PAP Bytom, BIKH 143: 52-60. Ruhr: ZBHS 60 (1912): B-352.

[34] This paragraph is based on ZBHS, statistical section, annual number of shifts worked, 1887-1914.

[35] Withholding advances: ZOBH 31 (1882): 223. Fines: e.g., the work rules of Hohenlohe smelters in WAP Katowice, Hohenlohe 57, 2 November 1899, cited by Jonca, *Polozenie*, p. 170, and the model work rules of the OBHV for 1898 and 1905, PAP Bytom, BIKH 143: 60-79 (1898), and 188ff. (1905). "Laziness": WAP Katowice, Hohenlohe 212: 47-48 (February 1894).

[36] Bibiella mine: JRGB 1903: 491 and 500, cited by Jonca, *Polozenie*, p. 172. Silesia mine: PAP Bytom, BIKH 215: 35-36 (1906). Other examples of bonuses: JRGB 1901: 349, 357; ZBHS 58 (1910): B-58. Rybnik mine: Raefler, p. 24.

[37] JRGB carried repeated complaints to this effect—e.g., 1899: 203, 217. For an

acute analysis of the limitations of a purely economic approach to a backward
bending supply curve of labor, see Rottenberg, "Income and Leisure," pp. 95-101.
[38] PAP Bytom, Bergrevier Beuthen
Nord 121, 8 March 1912.
[39] Absenteeism among the young: e.g.,
ZBHS 55 (1907): B-609. Decline of absenteeism in business downturn: ZBHS 51
(1903): B-493, report on 1902. 1906 complaints; ZOBH 66 (1907): 250.
[40] WAP Katowice, Landratsamt Rybnik
703: 32-33 (1910).
[41] Harbison and Ibrahim, p. 124.

CHAPTER 9

[1] Cf. the remarks on the changing work
situation in Thompson, "Time, Work-Discipline." For an extended sociological
treatment, see Alvin Gouldner, *Patterns
of Industrial Bureaucracy* (New York,
1954).
[2] A case study of bureaucracy in another
type of firm is Jürgen Kocka, *Unternehmensverwaltung und Angestelltenschaft
am Beispiel Siemens 1847-1914* (Stuttgart,
1969).
[3] For the structure of Upper Silesian
industry, see Pounds, chapters 4-6, and
Hans G. Heymann, "Die gemischten
Werke im deutschen Grosseisengewerbe.
Ein Beitrag zur Frage der Konzentration
der Industrie," *Münchener volkswirtschaftliche Studien* 65 (1904).
[4] Perlick, *Oberschlesische Berg- und
Hüttenleute*, pp. 206-207; cf. Bernhardi,
Gesammelte Schriften.
[5] Connections with banks: Popkiewicz
and Ryszka, pp. 8-15. General information
about top management: Perlick, *Oberschlesische Berg- und Hüttenleute, passim*; and Bruno Knochenhauer, *Die
oberschlesische Montanindustrie* (Gotha,
1927), pp. 110-145.
[6] 1885: ZOBH 24 (1885): 80-86. 1913:
ZOBH 52 (1913): 189-197.
[7] WAP Katowice, Hohenlohe 273, 15
April 1896, pp. 18-18a, in Gąsiorowska-
Grabowska, pp. 368-379.
[8] Dlugoborski, "Ekonomika . . . hutnictwa w XVIII wieku," for a general survey
of eighteenth-century smelting.
[9] Based on an interview with B. Buzek
conducted by Jerzy Jaros. Jaros, *Historia
Górnictwa*, p. 229.
[10] PAP Bytom, Donnersmarck 839: 56.
[11] For patterns of bureaucracy, see
Gouldner, pp. 140-150, 216-217.

[12] WAP Katowice, Hohenlohe 212: 47-
48.
[13] Jończyk, "Strajk górników w 1871 r.,"
p. 311.
[14] PAP Bytom, BIKH, *passim*; WAP
Katowice, Friedrichshütte, *passim*. On the
men who headed the OBB, see Alfons
Perlick, *Biographische Studien zur schlesischen Heimatforschung* (Dortmund,
1962), pp. 155-184.
[15] Wages at König mine: Jaros, "Rozwój
techniczny," p. 58. Safety equipment:
Jonca, *Polityka socjalna*, p. 118. Marketing policies: Otto Hue, "Der preussische
Staat als Bergwerksbesitzer," *Neue Zeit*
20:1 (1902): 788-793. Foreign workers:
WAP Wroclaw, OBB 41: 161, report on
the fourth quarter of 1910. Women and
children: cf. the rebuke by OBB of the
Berginspektion Königshütte in PAP
Bytom, BIKH 520: 20, 15 March 1890.
Working conditions: cf. the report of a
factory inspector on conditions at the
Gleiwitz smelter, WAP Wroclaw, OBB
1602, 6 September 1902 (not paginated).
Employers' association: cf. the list of delegates to OBHV meetings in ZOBH 48
(1904): 231, where the state representatives held the largest number of
votes, and WAP Katowice, Friedrichshütte 1020, meeting of 1911, where the
fiscus held the second largest number of
votes.
[16] On the transition to wages and hours,
see Stearns, "Adaptation." For the reemergence of working conditions in mature
economies, see *Work in America. Report
of a Special Task Force to the Secretary
of Health, Education, and Welfare* (Cambridge, Mass., 1973).
[17] WAP Katowice, Landratsamt Tarnowitz 528, "Straf-Reglement für die Grä-
flich Guido Henckel v. Donnersmarckschen
Berg- und Hüttenwerke."
[18] Prayer: Work rules from the 1880s,
WAP Katowice, Landratsamt Tarnowitz
525: 99. Funerals: PAP Bytom, BIKH,
"Arbeitseinstellungen und Arbeiterunruhen, 1889-1890," pp. 175-200, in Gąsiorowska-Grabowska, pp. 260-274.
[19] Insubordination: WAP Katowice,
Friedrichshütte 695, 16 February 1888 and
passim. Threatening supervisors: WAP
Katowice, Hohenlohe 2354: 199, 17 May
1899 and *passim* (1899-1902).
[20] Iron and steel workers: *Industrie- und
Handelskammer*, p. 309. Blue Monday:
WAP Katowice, Landratsamt Rybnik
703: 32-33, letter from *Amtsvorsteher* of

Amtsbezirk Ellguth XIII to the Landrat in Rybnik, 11 June 1910. Drinking on the job: WAP Katowice, Friedrichshütte 695, 18 November 1899 (not paginated). [21] Large bills: A. Klaussmann, *Oberschlesien vor 55 Jahren und wie ich es wiederfand* (Berlin, 1911), pp. 211-212; J. Piernikarczyk, *Historia górnictwa i hutnictwa na Górnym Śląsku* [A History of mining and smelting in Upper Silesia], vol. 2 (Katowice, 1936), p. 411, both cited by Jaros, *Historia górnictwa*, p. 232. Group payment: WAP Katowice, Landratsamt Rybnik 734, 28 January 1880; Landratsamt Tarnowitz 525: 342; and *Katolik* 12, 31 July 1879. Non-alcoholic drinks: JRGB 1904: 184. Seltzer machine: letters of inquiry in WAP Katowice, Friedrichshütte 649, *passim*. Closing the taverns: the system is praised in JRGB 1903: 176; further information is found in WAP Katowice, Hohenlohe 2364: 245-246. Forced compliance: WAP Katowice, Hohenlohe 2364: 245-246.

[22] WAP Katowice, Landratsamt Pless 1210, 2 May 1913 and *passim* (not paginated).

[23] Kessel-Zeutsch, pp. 46-47; ZOBH 16 (1877): 81; and the comments by Bialy, *Gornośląski Związek . . . 1854-1914*, p. 64.

[24] The term is Gouldner's, pp. 45ff.

[25] The details of many of these practices are presented in "Die für die Arbeiter." Taking coal: PAP Bytom, "Arbeitereinstellungen und Arbeiterunruhen, 1871-1875," pp. 158-178, in Gąsiorowska-Grabowska, p. 127.

[26] Information on 1871 strike from report of local mining officials: PAP Bytom, BIKH, "Arbeitereinstellungen und Arbeiterunruhen, 1871-1875," pp. 18-27, in Gąsiorowska-Grabowska, pp. 93-98.

[27] PAP Bytom, BIKH, "Arbeitseinstellungen und Arbeiterunruhen, 1871-1875," pp. 158-178, in Gąsiorowska-Grabowska, pp. 118-130.

[28] Data gathered by Haines, table III-39.

[29] Scharley mine: Antonina Staszków, "Walka robotników Bytomia o wyzwolenie narodowe i spoleczne (od lat 70-tych XIX wieku do 1914 roku)" [The struggle of the workers of Beuthen for national and social liberation from the 1870s to 1914], in *Dziewięc Wieków Bytomia*, ed. Franciszek Ryszka, (Katowice, 1956), pp. 282-283. Archival sources: research report by Kazimierz Popiolek in Gąsiorowska-Grabowska, pp. 153-154. Output and employment:

ZOBH 1868-1914, and ZBHS 1854-1914, compiled by Popiolek, pp. 205-230. Friedrich smelter: WAP Wroclaw, OBB 1280: 45-46, in Gąsiorowska-Grabowska, pp. 173-174.

[30] Katolik 4, 30 November 1871 *et seq.*; issues of 1870-1914, *passim*.

[31] Editor's notes, Gąsiorowska-Grabowska, pp. 207-211, based on WAP Katowice, Landratur Kattowitz 530: 3-5, and Landratur Kattowitz 228.

[32] Seven mines: JRGB 1909: 540. Migrants in 1890s: Brozek, *Robotnicy spoza zaboru*, pp. 55-57.

[33] OBB report on 1889, WAP Wroclaw, OBB 908, in Gąsiorowska-Grabowska, p. 277. General account of the strike: Karol Jonca, "Strajk na Górnym Śląsku w roku 1889" [The strike in Upper Silesia in 1889], *Przegląd Zachodni* 8 (1952), special issue: *Studia Śląskie*, pp. 369-402.

[34] See the extensive list of complaints in PAP Bytom, BIKH, "Arbeitseinstellungen und Unruhen, 1889-1890," pp. 175-200, in Gąsiorowska-Grabowska, pp. 260-268. For the 1890s, WAP Wroclaw, OBB 908: 625-657 (Königin-Luise mine 1890), in Gąsiorowska-Grabowska, p. 302; WAP Katowice, Landratur Tarnowitz 823: 23-24 (Mathilde mine, 1893), in Gąsiorowska-Grabowska, pp. 330-331; and JRGB 1897: 486 (Wolfgang mine, 1897).

[35] This assumption seems to underlie the reasoning present in one of the best introductions to questions of labor in industrializing situations—Kerr et al., esp. pp. 3-13 and 140-165 on the stages of commitment.

[36] Comments of mine directors: PAP Bytom, BIKH, "Arbeitseinstellungen und Arbeiterunruhen, 1889-1890," pp. 140-151, in Gąsiorowska-Grabowska, pp. 249-253. Bernhardi's threat: PAP Bytom, BIKH, "Arbeitseinstellungen und Arbeiterunruhen, 1890-1909," p. 72 in Gąsiorowska-Grabowska, p. 297.

[37] Beuthen walkouts: Staszków, p. 297, based on WAP Wroclaw, Rejencja opolska (Regierungsbezirk Oppeln), 4450, and Schlesisches Oberpräsidium, Rep. 200, Acc. 54/16, no. 2645. Deutschland mine: Staszków, pp. 297-298. Jakub mine: WAP Katowice, Landratur Kattowitz 127: 179-180, in Gąsiorowska-Grabowska, pp. 381-382. Charlotte mine: JRGB 1903: 507.

[38] Wolfgang mine: Julian Raba, "Walka o jedność organizacyjną w górno-śląskim ruchu robotniczym na przelomie XIX i XX wieku" [The struggle for organizational unity in the Upper Silesian workers'

movement at the turn of the twentieth century], *Sobótka* 10 (1955): 386. Strikes of 1905-1907: JRGB 1907: 526-527. See also JRGB 1905: 490-491; 1906, p. 565. Strikes in Rybnik: JRGB 1905: 490-491. Strike at König mine: PAP Bytom, BIKH a-182: 305ff.
    [39] Gerald D. Feldman, "German Business Between War and Revolution: The Origins of the Stinnes-Legien Agreement," in *Entstehung und Wandel der modernen Gesellschaft (Festschrift für Hans Rosenberg)*, ed. Gerhard A. Ritter (Berlin, 1970), pp. 312-341.
    [40] E.g., Grünberg-Kozlowski on Polish workers.
    [41] Report published in ZBHS 38 (1890).
    [42] Cf. the studies of Poles in Upper Silesia by P. Weber, Broesicke, and Kuhn.
    [43] Supervisors: PAP Bytom, BIKH, "Bergpolizeiliche Verordnungen 1846-1874," p. 60; in Gąsiorowska-Grabowska, pp. 89-90. Workers' complaint: PAP Bytom, Arbeitseinstellungen und Arbeiterunruhen 1871-75, pp. 55-57, in Gąsiorowska-Grabowska, pp. 90-92. 1880 demonstration: Staszków, p. 288.
    [44] The insignificance of the Upper Silesian locals of the metalworker unions emerges clearly in the listing of all local groups in the province of Silesia—Szerer, "Klasowe związki zawodowe," p. 26.
    [45] A basic survey is found in Hans-Ulrich Wehler, *Sozialdemokratie und Nationalstaat* (Würzburg, 1962).
    [46] Newspaper articles: *Gazeta robotnicza* (PPS newspaper), 11 February 1893; 12 August 1893. Factory inspectors' complaint: JRGB 1897: 185-186.
    [47] "Tool of the clergy": WAP Katowice, Landratsamt Tarnowitz, pp. 156-160, report of Beuthen Landrat office on union activity in the area, in Gąsiorowska-Grabowska, p. 159. Schwientochlowitz sermon: *Kurier Śląski*, 16 December 1908, quoted in WAP Wroclaw, RO, Prezydialne Biuro 64: 535. For a general introduction to the questions of Polish Catholicism and Polish nationalism in Upper Silesia, see Mieczyslaw Pater, *Centrum a ruch polski na Górnym Śląsku (1879-1893)* [The Center and the Polish national movement in Upper Silesia, 1879-1893], (Katowice, 1971); Mieczyslaw Pater, *Ruch polski na Górnym Śląsku w latach 1879-1893* [The Polish national movement in Upper Silesia, 1879-1893] (Wroclaw, 1969); and M. Orzechowski, *Narodowa Demokracja*. An older work, but still useful: Ludwig Bernhard, *Die*

Polenfrage (Leipzig, 1910).
    [48] Social Democratic mining union: Felicja Figowa, *Związki Robotników Polskich w bylej Rejencji Opolskiej w przededniu Pierwszej Wojny Swiatowej* [Polish labor unions in the former regency of Oppeln on the eve of the First World War] (Opole, 1966), in order of citation: pp. 17, 19, 14, 51—labeled as the "class-oriented miners' union." Adding to unrest: WAP Katowice, Landratur Kattowitz 127: 179-189, in Gąsiorowska-Grabowska, pp. 381-382. Membership in Society for Mutual Aid: for 1896, report of Beuthen border commissioner, WAP Wroclaw, Schlesisches Oberpräsidium 200, Acc. 54/16, 2646: 101-104, in Gąsiorowska-Grabowska, p. 359; for 1900, OBB report, WAP Wroclaw, Schlesisches Oberpräsidium 200, Acc. 54/16, 2648: 216-200, in Gąsiorowska-Grabowska, pp. 436-437. Cf. also Szerer, "Klasowe związki zawodowe," pp. 28-32, 38-47.
    [49] Figowa, pp. 12, 43-48.
    [50] ZBHS 62 (1914): B-402-404.
    [51] *Ibid.*
    [52] Employers' complaint: ZOBH 52 (1913): 275. Mine inspectors: JRGB 1913: 631.
    [53] Arthur Spiethoff, *Die wirtschaftlichen Wechsellagen* (Tübingen, 1955), summarized in Bry, pp. 474-476.

CHAPTER 10

    [1] Jonca, *Polozenie, passim.*
    [2] Formulation by Charles Kindleberger, "Technical Education and the French Entrepreneur," in *Enterprise and Entrepreneurs in Nineteenth and Twentieth Century France*, eds. E. C. Carter II, R. Forster, and J. N. Moody (Baltimore, forthcoming).
    [3] Radicals: Marglin, esp. pp. 31-73. Technological change: Samuel Hollander, *The Sources of Increased Efficiency: A Study of DuPont Rayon Plants* (Cambridge, Mass., 1965), summary statement on pp. 189-207.
    [4] David S. Landes, *The Unbound Prometheus* (Cambridge, England, 1969), p. 81.
    [5] Medieval and early modern mining: John U. Nef, "Mining and Metallurgy in Medieval Civilization," *The Cambridge Economic History of Europe*, vol. 2 (Cambridge, England, 1952), pp. 474-478. Legal status in Upper Silesia: Büchsel, pp. 106-137. Legal status in neighboring Poland: Kaczyńska and Kowalska, *passim*. Rus-

sian gold mining: John P. McKay, *Pioneers for Profit. Foreign Entrepreneurship and Russian Industrialization, 1885-1913* (Chicago, 1970), pp. 154, 266-267.

[6] Forms of mining organization: Nef, pp. 473-479. Hierarchy: It is significant that Marglin's historical examples are drawn from small industries in the sixteenth and seventeenth centuries, from agriculture, from light industry, and in a curious way from mining; no examples come from modern heavy industry.

Index